The Art of Writing

♥

LOVE SONGS

PAMELA PHILLIPS OLAND

ALLWORTH PRESS
NEW YORK

07   06   05   04   03   5   4   3   2   1

Published by Allworth Press
An imprint of Allworth Communications, Inc.
10 East 23rd Street, New York, NY 10010

Cover and Interior page design by Annemarie Redmond, Stroudsburg, PA

Page composition/typography by Integra Software Services Pvt Ltd, Pondicherry,
India

Library of Congress Cataloging-in-Publication Data

Oland, Pamela Phillips,
The art of writing love songs/Pamela Phillips Oland.
p. cm.
Includes index.
ISBN 1-58115-271-X
1. Lyric writing (Popular music) 2. Love songs—History and criticism. I. Title.

MT67.O41 2003
782.42164'0268—dc21
2003002613

Printed in Canada

This book is dedicated to Karl R. Wolfe, who has helped me in so many ways to understand the nature of Happiness as a choice, Personal Empowerment as a decision, and Love as a gift we give ourselves.

♥

Many thanks to my editor Kate Lothman, for her superb insights, and to my publisher Tad Crawford for his irresistible suggestion that I develop a book about writing Love Songs!

♥

Thank you, Bobby, for putting up with the long hours of writing and rewriting on this book—tiptoeing around so that I could think clearly, and for giving me your endless love and support. You're my inspiration.

—P

We like someone *because,* we love someone *although.*

—HENRI DE MONTHERLANT

Contents

Preface

Music is Love in search of a word.
—AUTHOR UNKNOWN

Have you ever felt frustrated at the thought that love is so difficult to understand? If you've ever wanted to make better sense of that enigma we call "love," read on.

As a by-product of writing love songs for twenty-five years, the degree of enlightenment I've achieved about love is stunning! You see, in order to write great, inspired love songs, you first have to pump up by a hundredfold your awareness of what love is. Well, doesn't that make perfect sense? The more you know about how love works, the better your love songs will become. The unique discovery that I have made, however, is that by a sort of reverse emotional symbiosis, the better your love songs get, the better you will be at "love"!

Who we love, how we love, why we love, are all subjects that contribute mightily to the way we experience life, and yet, surprisingly, most of us understand very little about what love is. So it is trying to understand the process of falling in love, loving, falling out of love, finding new love, and repeating the cycle that dominates our lives, right alongside work concerns, education, friendships, and recreational activities.

By drawing you into *The Art of Writing Love Songs*, I will help you not only to discover your inner muse, learn to write brilliantly, and expand your creative thinking abilities, but also—as this remarkable by-product of learning to write songs about love—to become enlightened as to the dynamics of love in general, and the way it shapes your own life in particular.

Writing love songs will bring out in you the observer, the voyeur, and the lover, and in discovering how to express yourself in your songwriting, you'll be reintroduced to your passionate core. I am quite certain you will learn to express yourself better in all of your love relationships once you have acquired the skill of writing love songs.

Romantic love, the kind we usually choose to write songs about, is something we all have dreamed about having from the time we were kids. We've read fairy tales recounting handsome princes and beautiful princesses falling in love forever, and we want that for ourselves. The reality is not always as easy for most of us!

Most of us are so "reactive" that we forget to be thoughtful. Our own point of view—our longing to be heard and understood—dominates our ability to be objective and sympathetic to our partner's perspective. Thus, misunderstandings are one of the greatest causes of strife in love. By learning to write songs looking through the eyes of your partner, you will gain a much greater insight on how to understand, think, and react from the other person's point of view in love relationships.

It's actually pretty simple. Once we nurture communication by considering our partner's perspectives on love issues, we'll develop better tools with which to plumb our inner depths of thought on love—tools usually within the domain of students of psychology and psychotherapy. Unless we're studying to be psychologists or therapists, few of us have developed the skills for detailed analysis of our thoughts on love. So is it any wonder that when we first attempt to write love songs, they come out shallow and superficial, or dark and depressed? We skirt the ideas furtively, not wanting to dig too deep for fear of unearthing some home truths. Or we pour out our angst on paper—the pain, the tragedy of love unreturned or love in shambles. But in either event, our results are all questions and few answers. This book is designed to engage you in the rewarding quest to make writing about love—whether love found or love lost—a truly uplifting, gratifying, and releasing experience.

Love is not a matter of trends; it is timeless—an integral part of our consciousness. Each of us in our own way experiences good and bad, happy and sad feelings about love every single day. Our needs for loving and being loved transcend many of our other basic life needs, so our love antenna is up at all times, subliminally running in the background like a watchdog computer program. We work and wonder about love; we eat and worry about love; we visit with friends and ruminate on love. And those of us who write love songs don't let all those important thoughts and emotions go to waste!

Is there one among us who could not benefit from a clearer understanding of how we act and react in love situations, and why? Come along on this journey with me, and as you learn to tap into your powers of intuition, creativity, observation, and insight, along the way you'll learn to write incredibly thoughtful, illuminating songs about love. And don't be surprised if, in the process, that lightbulb of comprehension pops and pops and pops in your head, as you get a grip on "love"—that sorely misunderstood subject that so dominates and contributes to the success, or failure, of our lives.

THE ART OF WRITING LOVE SONGS

So, first, I'll help you find your inspiration and enlighten you as to how a songwriter opens up to new ideas. We'll take a journey together, reflecting on how to express your ideas in a song, then learning to trust your "Inner Songwriter," and discovering how to examine a love relationship in surprising detail, enabling you to write about it. We'll examine songwriting essentials—how to identify with your genre, structure a lyric, and be equipped to revise your thoughts once they're drafted on paper. You'll have great fun discovering how to hone your skills both as a listener and an observer. And, of great importance to each of you, you'll learn how to turn your emotions and experiences into amazingly good songs!

If you are interested in delving further into songwriting fundamentals, I hope you'll read my first book, *The Art of Writing Great Lyrics,* also published by Allworth Press.

Getting Started

Why do fools fall in love?
—Frankie Lymon and The Teenagers
(Morris Levy/Frankie Lymon)

Every single day of our lives, we experience hundreds of fleeting emotions that run through our minds, invade our hearts, and create in us sensations such as well-being, sadness, euphoria, anger, chagrin, aloneness, comfort, loss, infatuation, longing, regret, sexual arousal, passion, wistfulness, fear, and sometimes a tickling unease.

And what do we do with all of these fleeting emotions? Well, there are several ways we deal with them.

- We address them head-on with the person who caused them.
- We address them in a roundabout way with the person who caused them.
- We don't address them to the person who caused them, but discuss them with a friend, co-worker, or therapist.
- We suppress them for later consideration.
- We suppress them, and never return to them directly.
- If we know how to write them as songs, we release them and feel a lot better!

LEARNING TO WRITE IT IN A LOVE SONG

The best way to become adept at writing love songs is to delve into your own mind and develop an understanding of how you personally connect to love. Some of this book will deal with exposing you to yourself—and believe me, it will be a surprising and wild ride. You'll get in touch with your opinions, hostilities, grievances, vulnerabilities, predilections, and prejudices gained through past love relationships, and you will discover both your emotional breadth and your limits with regard to love. Why is it important to know all of this about yourself before writing love songs? Because you approach everything you write by starting with your own points of view, and although you think you know what they are, the truth is you are only aware of your biases in limited ways.

EXPRESSING "SELF"

You are a unique individual, built of your own life experiences, totally separate, uniquely poised to write from a fresh perspective unlike any others. But you have to know your "self" to express yourself in writing.

Peeling the Onion

Throughout your life, your psyche has been a private sanctuary that you keep so well guarded, you yourself are barely allowed in for a peek. Especially when it comes to love, you want nobody to really know what's going on in there, in case they can somehow use it against you. Your self-protection instinct is like an onion that has grown in tight layers around you. Each successive experience of love's pain, disappointment, or disenchantment has formed another stratification of onion, and your free spirit within is suffocating in there under all those layers of cocoon-like self-preservation.

So, guess what: It's time to peel the onion! You're ready to find out what makes you tick. I know you believe you already have a handle on all of that, but you will be amazed when you discover, through the process of writing love songs, the rich complexity of the person who lives inside your skin.

Who Am I?

When you ask yourself the question "Who am I?," what comes up for you? Do you identify yourself by your ethnicity, religion, the country of your birth, the country of your ancestors, your sex, your age, your financial status, your job title, your education level, your marital status? We all tend to define ourselves within the confines of these general parameters. But none of these are spiritual or emotional. They are physical—not in fact definitions of the real inner you.

As you travel through your life, you are regularly identified by all of these designations I've named. People look at you and make a quick judgment based upon what they observe with their eyes. Astute observers such as writers will see a little more, if they bother to read facial expressions. But, by and large, you will be judged by all and sundry more for your physical appearance and your intellect than for your inner self. Only to those who know you well—life partners, parents, siblings, kids, and great friends—do you ever grant insights into your depths.

Perhaps that is why betrayals from lovers and friends, to whom you entrust vulnerable parts of yourself, sting and hurt so much. You feel so exposed. It is a difficult thing to expose oneself emotionally, but it can also be one of the most freeing experiences life offers.

Psychologists and their ilk have long encouraged clients to talk about "what they feel inside." In this "safe" environment, people pour out their experiences in volumes. Every detail is told; nothing is held back or spared. Stories of emotional upheaval and the scars they have left behind are blurted out amid tears and hand wringing. Therapists absorb the information and give their knowledgeable advice as to how to conduct life thenceforth.

What psychology doesn't offer is a means to take all this inner fire and smoke and put it to amazingly wonderful use. When you've learned how to express yourself in love songs, a whole new world of emotional catharsis will open up for you.

It isn't enough just to know the form that writing love songs takes. While form and style are extremely important, and songs cannot stand without them, it is quite clearly the heart that is imbued into a love song that makes it work. It is not enough to say words that sound loving, unless those words ring true to a listener. And in order to ring true for a listener, they must first ring true for the author.

Trying Too Hard

Finding your "voice" as a songwriter is a big part of this process. You don't need or want to learn to write like me, or like any other songwriter. The only person whose lyrical point of view you need to establish is your own. You are a unique entity, a person with your own voice, and hidden within you are as many points of view as the best writer in the world. Like all songwriters, your life and times are a goldmine of experiences and observations. The difference between you and the professionals is that we who write are regularly working that mine of experience, and you are not.

Having said that, don't lose heart worrying about trying too hard to make the songs you attempt to write "sound professional." Every time you put artificial limitations on your creativity, the results will be a squelched flow of ideas, and your songs will reflect that awkwardness. Catering to some vague notion of what is and is not "professional-sounding" is hugely restraining to your natural thoughts and impulses. Also, perhaps most importantly, that defeats the purpose of doing it for pure pleasure. If you're going to write, do it for the love of it—because isn't that the best reason to do almost anything in life?

Words That Communicate

When you cannot say or put across to others what you feel, you know full well how frustrated you get. You're not alone in this; failure to communicate feelings is so prevalent that it may come as no surprise to you that the English language doesn't even contain a word that describes the act of communicating, communing, relating, and touching in order to express feelings to others!

I've always found it interesting to note that the languages of some cultures have failed to create appropriate words to describe certain interpersonal experiences that other cultures take for granted. I've been told, for instance, that there is not a single-word equivalent to "privacy" in the Chinese language. Several words must be used to create an approximation of the concept. While English is a vast and descriptive language, it is somehow repressive about communication; and as the great author Pearl S. Buck once said, "Self-expression must pass into communication for its fulfillment."

Most of us can express ourselves in areas in which we feel confident, such as business knowledge, political debates, or facts we have studied and committed to memory. We have plenty of language skills to describe everyday, nonemotional matters. Expressing complex interpersonal feelings is a whole 'nother matter. We get tongue-tied, and in trying so hard to say the right thing, end up saying the wrong thing. There are many reasons for this communication shortcoming.

In this busy world, we live beyond our time allotments, and many of us never catch up with ourselves. As we rush through our lives, we experience feelings we do not make time to acknowledge, until ironically, when we're ready to do so, we can no longer recall them accurately.

I'm here to tell you that it is incredibly important to make time to express feelings—and more to the point, feelings about love—on paper. Whatever the aspect of love is that you are trying to access, capture, and share, you will understand it better once you have expressed it in writing. If verbally communicating feelings has taken a backseat to the rest of your life, commit yourself

> We have plenty of language skills to describe everyday, nonemotional matters. Expressing complex interpersonal feelings is a whole 'nother matter. We get tongue-tied, and in trying so hard to say the right thing, end up saying the wrong thing.

THE ART OF WRITING LOVE SONGS

to releasing whatever's pent up inside you by setting it out in love songs.

It is not important whether the current object of your feelings knows anything about what you feel at this point. What is important is that you define and make sense of all your jumbled emotions, thoughts, and feelings, plus associated guilt and remorse, with complete and utter clarity. Doing so cleanses your heart and soul with the kind of rush you'd get standing under a waterfall

When we talk to each other these days, don't we just express what we need to say, and not bother to consider what the other person needs to hear?

and letting the water dash away your troubles. It is vital to do this if you are to gain any objectivity in your approach to writing love songs.

The Sad Fact of Shorthand Communication

Whatever happened to sharing feelings? Where did the time go that allowed us to express ourselves to each other regularly and in depth? Or has there never been such a time in our modern, post–Industrial Revolution world?

Once upon a time in America, the home was the center of all things, most people rarely traveled beyond their town limits, what was felt was said, and communication was alive and well. But with the encroachment of "civilization" in the form of high-speed transportation, all-consuming computers, business travel, and sophisticated media pounding on our heads, we get all our communication spoon-fed through movies, magazines, and, yes, songs.

Our civilization has devolved into a society marked by shorthand communication. We approach each other in such a casual and offhand manner that it is hard for us to find meaning in conversation any more. People encapsulate their thoughts into the fewest words they can muster to get their points across. They do not soothe and massage their issues and rarely consider how to make sure they are palatable to those who will be on the receiving end of them.

We barely have any time for love anymore. We take perhaps an hour for lunch, during which we discuss business and more business. How often do we meet our loved one for lunch and hold hands and murmur words of love and encouragement? It is as if our day is "hermetically sealed" as belonging to our business life. Our loved one has no part in that day; it is quite clearly demarcated as off limits. If our partner does happen to meet us for lunch now and again, it is given "special event" status, and not repeated for quite some time.

The Sad Fact of Shorthand Communication (Continued)

Televisions in our bedrooms have been the death knell of bedtime pillow talk. How do you squeeze in an expression of love to your significant other while a comic on *The Tonight Show* is bombarding your senses with jokes? Do you simply mute during commercials and share a moment of intimacy? It's so catastrophic that it's actually funny!

Family dinnertime, long the last bastion of communing, has almost ceased to exist for many families, because everyone in the family is scattered about. Dad's working late, Mom's exercising after work at her Pilates class, Junior is out at baseball practice, and Sis is staying overnight at her friend's house. Each of them is orbiting off in their own private world, a world that is becoming less and less inclusive of the rest of the family. This is just so sad, because it means that less is known of each other's heart.

None of us intentionally draw away from people we love. We all think we're keeping up. After all, don't we write short e-mail notes, and send on e-mail jokes every day? Well, at least we start out writing to each other every day, and then when the novelty wears off, we're writing about once a fortnight, if that. We jot down cute little thoughts. But we don't speak our hearts, and we don't share our lives in the same way we once took for granted.

Even when a family dinner does occur, obviously conversation is about what happened at school today, what the boss said at work, or how there's too much month at the end of the money. The phone will ring, and someone will leave the table for an extended conversation, and then the plates are empty, and everyone disperses either to sit down for a long interlude at the computer terminal, to sit glued to the TV for a few hours, or to head out with friends. What happens to feelings that family members wanted to share? Well, they just get bottled up again, shoved to the back of the line, the bottom of the pile.

When a parent looks at a child's schoolwork, does the parent approach it from the point of view of that assignment only, or the whole child, and the child's connection to the subject matter? When we discuss an issue with our partner, do we cover only the subject at hand, or do we also make some warm personal comments at the same time? When we talk to each other these days, don't we just express what we need to say, and not bother to consider what the other person needs to hear?

Even when we write someone a note or an e-mail, isn't it all about what is going on with ourselves, and not much about the other person? Again, we're a self-absorbed group of loners, all attempting to live with one another using our dwindling communication skills. So what's up with love? And how can we have relationships that mean anything if we never give them priority in our lives? How can we ever get around to identifying our feelings, let alone expressing them?

I believe that writing love songs is one powerful antidote to the lost art of being loving and romantic, a way to get to know our romantic center—perhaps as a refresher course, and for many of us, perhaps for the first time. Why?

The Sad Fact of Shorthand Communication (Continued)

Because not only do we have a new tool for fleshing out our layers of feelings, but we also find out how our lack of skills in expressing ourselves is hurting our important relationships. We remember that love needs constant expression, and we can't expect others to know what we feel if we can't find the words to tell them. We discover that it's way too easy to say the wrong thing and be irreversibly misunderstood. We learn that the words for truly expressing feelings relating to love are all there within each one of us, waiting to be unearthed.

While it is indescribably important to "show" love through positive gestures, what differentiates us from other creatures is our ability to be *verbal*.

Tongue-Tied and Torn Up

Getting sidetracked is an irritating but real part of life. Many are the times you have started to express a feeling to the one you love and the dog starts barking to be walked, or the phone rings, or a deliveryman knocks. It's frustrating, as the conversation takes forever to get back on track, and if it ever does, it's no longer the precise conversation you had in mind in the beginning.

On those rare occasions when you have a perfectly willing listener, you often cannot come up with the exact words you wish to express because you suddenly realize with dismay that now that the moment's here, the approach you've planned seems flawed. So you lose the precious moment to internally questioning what you were going to say, and how you were going to say it, and then something comes out of your mouth that sounds all wrong, as if uttered by a Martian, and you know you missed it even as you speak.

Ah . . . but say it in a song! It is all there. Everything. Every bit of it, just the way you want to say it.

Face it, even if we have rehearsed our words in the car while driving, or gone over them in the half-awake state of dawn, even if we have dissected and discussed what we want to express with a friend or co-worker, when the moment comes, we usually blow it.

Shyness and embarrassment may prevent us from speaking our minds, yet it's far more likely that when we finally are ready to communicate, the object

...tions is not in the headspace to listen to what we have to say! So ... say it after all. That irony is admirably expressed by Stephen ... n in "Send in the Clowns," his powerful lyric from A *Little Night* ... using the poignant circus metaphor to draw attention to a tragic moment with an amusing distraction.

And so we end up speaking of other things, forced into unrelated conversations, waiting for the right moment to broach our subject matter—and then when we do express what we were planning, it comes out differently than we planned. It is truncated, altered, lacking in many of the carefully thought out phrases. That is, of course, because *conversation goes two ways.* We rarely deliver an expression of feelings in an uninterrupted monologue! And compounding the problem, frequently the person on the receiving end of our words responds to what we've said completely out of context. And in order to answer what they've sidetracked to, we get involved in discussions that are about completely unrelated issues, lose our way completely, and have to improvise.

Ah . . . but say it in a song! It is all there. Everything. Every bit of it, just the way you want to say it. Every phrase is carefully arranged, every effect carefully planned for, each word and thought is present and spoken just as you would have the listener hear it. Only the exact words you mean to say are there; everything extraneous has been omitted. And when they do listen, they are a captive audience, caught up in your words and the spell you've spun.

Beyond that, when written as lyrics, your words are entertaining, rhythmic, lilting, rhyming, expressive, emotional, and just plain the real deal. What a release! What a joy! What a concept!

THE WONDER OF PUTTING YOUR PEN TO PAPER

There are few joys more superbly satisfying than the sound you hear applying the nib of a fountain pen to a fresh, crisp sheet of blank paper. But whether you write with an eyebrow pencil or a laundry marker, the experience of writing a love song is astonishingly fulfilling. Think of the power you have in your grasp! You are creating something where nothing existed before. You are giving birth to an idea that has never been said in quite the same way. You are putting your own personal spin and unduplicated perspective on love. Your work bears your signature, your fingerprint. It carries your irony, your wit, your outlook. Though the paper it is written on may not survive forever, your thought, once created, will exist till the end of time, a part of your legacy to the universe!

Creating Private Moments to Write

I have observed that we are all so busy all of the time that we can never find time to do anything. If you've ever heard me speak, you know I believe that since we cannot ever *find* time, we need to *make* time.

Time is finite. There are and will always be only twenty-four hours in a day—not a minute more, not a minute less. We have our responsibilities to jobs, studies, and our families. We have further responsibilities we've imposed upon ourselves, such as exercise regimens, music lessons, hobbies, sports endeavors. We feel that if we take on one more thing, we will collapse under the weight of our obligations.

But what about uplifting our souls? What about soothing our minds? When do we make time for love?

We all know making love should not be a hurried affair squeezed into an anxious moment before rushing to a meeting or running off to work. Even if those are our true time constraints, love should be fun. Woe unto those of us who are making love and making dinner in our heads, or making love and making plans for the closing of a business deal. If I were a therapist, I'd make this rule: *Compartmentalize your mind! Shut off everything not relevant to the love you are making!* But since I'm a songwriter and not a therapist, I'll simply say the same rule goes for the time you allot to writing love songs. Compartmentalize your mind! Shut off everything not relevant to the song you are writing!

Here's my adage: *Open a window of time, and you let in an opportunity.* Suddenly, thoughts and ideas, creativity you never dreamed of, has room to exist within your life, your soul, your reality. Fail to create the window through which you can let in a new light, and all you will have are the old solid walls, preventing the enlightenment from ever breaking through.

Truly, you don't know what you don't know. But will you miss what you don't know you're missing? I think so. I believe there will ultimately be within you a sense of sadness, a nameless unease, perhaps. Many of us are so afraid to break the rhythm of routine, that we never permit ourselves to discover our inner muse. Our never-identified ideas are gifts from the universe, intellectual and emotional progeny that will die a'bornin'. How sad never to permit ourselves to encounter our most precious gifts of creativity and expression, because we're dancing attendance to mere duty and schedule.

Location! Location! Location!

When I write, I want the radio off, I want the room quiet, and I want a comfortable place to sit. I want the light to be comforting, and I want a cup of strong hot English tea with milk, no sugar, on the table beside me. I want a place to put my feet up, and I want to be in comfortable clothes. My writing arena is my own little world, and I'll darn well set it up any way I want to. And so must you.

The location in which you write is only important in that you have to make it work for you. If it has to be a noisy place such as a restaurant, or an uncomfortable place such as a bus seat, prepare yourself with a moment of quiet meditation. Allow your mind to slip into something more comfortable—a creative space. Shut out the noise, the discomfort, anything that imposes itself. And if there are interruptions—a waiter bringing food, a family member needing an answer—don't become irritated or lose your place, simply deal with the interruption mildly, then return to your creative space effortlessly. It can be done. With a little practice, you can become an expert at pulling moments from your life to write your love song lyrics.

However large or small the creative window you are able to carve out, consider your songwriting time an oasis from life. Consider it very much in the way you would view a week on Kauai lying out under a palm tree sucking on a piña colada. It may be a short amount of time, such as a ten-minute coffee break from work or a half-hour train commute to the office. Or it may be a long luxurious evening where there is nothing else you have to do and you can shut off the ringer on the phone. The amount of time you have is simply the amount of time you have. More is better, but if you have less to work with, make the most of it.

EXERCISE 1:

Letting Go

Here's an exercise to do when you have very little time and need to get in the mood to write in a matter of moments.

Sit quietly, drop your head forward and shut your eyes, hanging your arms comfortably down at your sides. Take a deep breath, slowly letting it out. Take two more breaths the same way. Allow your head to clear of cluttering thoughts by snapping your fingers on both hands and spreading your hands out right where they hang, to simulate letting the thoughts go.

The Art of Writing Love Songs

Great. Now allow the first line that pops into your head to be the first line of your song. Whatever it is. Even if it's *I've still got a pile of work to do.* Even that line can form an idea:

> I've still got a pile of work to do
> Before I can head on home to you
> I'll spend the afternoon counting each minute
> Knowing my world is fine because you're in it.

I'm not telling you to do something I wouldn't do myself. I wrote the above four lines in the time it took to put them on the page. I want you to do the same thing. The lines don't have to make a lot of sense, and they don't have to be brilliant; they just have to represent your freedom to write whatever comes into your head.

Since optimally I want you to have the most fun you possibly can with this, I encourage you to find a comfortable place to write where you will be undisturbed. If you're at home, tell your family or your roommates to buzz off for a while, as you are going to go and "create." If they laugh at you or make snide remarks about your wanting to be creative, don't get all hurt and anxious and defensive; just say, "I'm going to create something about *you!*" The minute it becomes about them, they will suddenly be incredibly interested in what you are doing and hopeful that it will be something stupendously wonderful that will reflect well on them. They will happily leave you alone to "create," and may even offer to bring you a cup of coffee!

The Liberation of Expressing Honest Thoughts

It is not always easy to express honest thoughts when others are around—especially when the others happen to be the ones you are having the thoughts about. From the gunfighters of the Old West, we got the expression "shooting from the hip" to describe speaking one's mind. But in our modern, "cool" society, speaking one's mind can be "the hip shooting themselves in the foot!" In any event, it's much easier to say something honest and truthful when nobody is around to hear you say it.

Your thoughts on love will flow onto the paper if you absolutely know that nobody is ever going to read them. So write each song with the intent of simply expressing yourself, not worrying about whether it will later be heard. By the time you have completed your song, who knows, maybe you'll be so proud of what you've said, and how well you've said it, that you will be happy for the person who inspired it to see it. But that's not the point of the exercise, and fear of "what will they think?" will only stultify and stifle your creativity.

Don't Worry about What Others May Think

All of us—writers, painters, poets, designers, dancers, musicians—who follow artistic pursuits are dogged by critics. Some are professional critics, and some are amateurs, but they have something in common: they are in a position to make you feel worthless. Remember, the great impressionist painter Vincent van Gogh wasn't a critical success until after he died.

Since it's almost impossible to avoid critical opinions of your work, there's no point in being thin-skinned, easily hurt, or deterred by evaluations of your songwriting. Just keep writing and stay true to your vision.

Any outside emotion that you let interfere with your freedom to be creative—such as the scorn or jealousy of whomever you live with—will make it harder to get started with your creative process. And who needs to spend the first ten minutes of precious creative time stewing over someone else's bad attitude? So the minute you close the door and sit down with your pad and pen, leave the rest of the world outside your space. If you have to go out and sit in the car, or go to a coffee house nearby, do so. But whatever you do, give yourself permission to enjoy this hard-won time you have carved out of your life to create something.

Opinions Are Like Noses—Everybody Has One

You will definitely come across a lot of "doubting Thomases" as you pursue your new hobby of writing love songs. You won't have to look far, either. The harbingers of failure, the deliverers of ridicule and teasing will live in your house, work at your office, and be the people you think of as close acquaintances.

Notice that I didn't include "close friends" in this category. You can usually differentiate between friends and acquaintances by whether they are supportive and encouraging about issues you hold close to the chest. There will be those who will congratulate you on your desire to find creative expression in writing love songs. And there will be those who will scoff at you and call you anything from silly to ridiculous. All are entitled to their opinions. Give their ungracious comments no importance, and allow them no power over you. Let the skeptics go and mumble in a corner about what they think. As for you, you have wonderful things to express.

I truly believe that millions of people never experience their artistic talents in this life because they forget to incorporate them in their schedules! They've simply never given themselves permission to discover and explore their creative potential. Just take a leaf out of my book and start to imagine love songs every day. Sometimes write just a title, sometimes a few lines, sometimes a whole song. Whatever it is, it feels like an accomplishment. As a result, you will never have to look back and ask, How did so much joyful inspiration pass me by?

So, if there are people you know who think the talents your Creator gave to you don't merit your pursuing an amazing new passion in the form of writing love songs, all I can say is, blow them a raspberry and get to work doing what you want to do. Let nobody step on your creative toes; let no one tell you that you can't do it because you

- ❤ Don't have talent
- ❤ Are too old to start now
- ❤ Have better things to do with your time
- ❤ Can't put two words together to make a sentence
- ❤ Are out of your league
- ❤ Can't even write a greeting card
- ❤ Have nothing to say that anyone would want to hear

It is time to be fearless, not to let anybody's point of view but your own influence your decision to get involved in this new pursuit of writing love songs. Whether you ever get a love song recorded or not is beside the point. You will be so much richer for the experience of knowing how to express your feelings and plumb the depths of your emotions on paper.

CHAPTER 2

The Universe of Ideas

My heart has a mind of its own.
—CONNIE FRANCIS
(Howard Greenfield/Jack Keller)

It is such a spectacular feeling to get a great idea, like a rush of warmth that flows through your body all the way to your fingertips and toes. Savor and enjoy it! Allow yourself to bask in the incredible pleasure of it. This is personal bliss at its best. No compliment from another person can compete. You can feel it in the breathless pull around your heart and the flush in your head. Yes, it is a physical sensation of euphoria. You did not expect to feel anything remotely like this, but here it is, self-satisfaction in living color.

FREE ASSOCIATION OF IDEAS

Think of your life as a treasure trove of ideas, thoughts, experiences, and emotions just waiting to be mined. You have lived through thousands of days and nights, heard and spoken millions of words of endearment, anger, conciliation, joy, and sorrow. And there they are, all stored away, catalogued and filed in a sort of mental computerized Dewey Decimal System. All you have to do is think a particular thought, and your mind will "click on" the time, the place, the moment, the feeling.

If you start writing love songs today and keep going for the rest of your life, you should technically never run out of ideas. The universe will trigger ideas in you constantly. For instance, you may be looking out of your car window, and see a couple walking down the street with their arms linked, and it will call to mind such a moment in your own life. Or perhaps it will call to mind a moment in two friends' lives, indelibly etched in your mind for some reason or another, and this will set off a song idea.

Perhaps the couple you are remembering were so very much in love that it was breathtaking to observe. Perhaps the last time you saw them together was the last day before he was shipped off overseas to fight in a war. Perhaps he never came home. So, theoretically, you could look at this couple walking down the street with their arms around each other today, this minute, and sit down and write a song called "If I'd Known I'd Never See You Again." And the song might be written from the point of view of your friend, the woman who was left behind.

This example suggests how important it is to be open-minded to ideas. Let your thoughts wander, free-associate, go wherever they want to. Don't limit yourself by what you originally "thought this song ought to be about." Sometimes your song will start out to be about one thing and end up evolving into something completely different. In fact, you might like where your ideas have led you so much that you will want to keep the last part and rewrite the beginning section—replacing the concept you started out with!

Writing about Imaginary Characters

When I write love songs, I use my own love experiences as a foundation for my ideas. Of course I do. But to write only about myself would be eliminating those other amazing characters I could be writing about—the rest of the people in the world!

Transferring your own experiences onto the lives of song characters you create as composites of yourself and others you've known or can imagine, and turning those ideas into love songs about those characters, will totally unlock your creativity.

Say you have had a disastrous breakup with someone you have loved, someone who has left you eating dirt. You feel very close to the information and don't really want to make yourself vulnerable by actually writing about it. So you think about a couple you know who are still together, and you decide to make your song a "what if" about them breaking up, instead. It's simple transference.

You decide to write the song about their relationship as if they have had a huge rift and are splitting up. Then you are free to write anything you'd like about your situation, because it is now about them. In adding some details from your own life, you have made them "composite" characters.

You can slant your song from either point of view, but for the sake of this example, let's say you are writing it from the woman's viewpoint.

You think back and realize that you have observed behavior from this woman's man that you found annoying or objectionable. So you decide to work that into your song. Perhaps you start with *Sometimes you've treated me unkind / Sometimes you've messed with my mind.* And then you think about your own relationship and how you hung in there, so you add, *But I've loved you through it all.*

You envision the heroine of the song and decide to enhance her natural qualities, as she is a bit boring in real life. So you choose to make her strong, and make her the one who is doing the leaving! That is the opposite of what happened in your own relationship, but you are making this up to fit your storytelling choices, so you write, *I never thought I wouldn't grieve / And that I'd be the one to leave.* This is a very rewarding approach, as you have now turned the whole concept around, and you feel really good about what the heroine is doing.

To end the verse, you need to sum up your concept, so you would now need not only to rhyme the word "all" (from the *But I've loved you through it all* line), but also provide the listener with an explanation of what happened; for instance, *We reached so high, we had to fall.*

Thus, your plaint, which started out to be about your own breakup, has now been transferred onto the shoulders of this other couple, leaving you out of the picture personally and allowing you the freedom to imagine the events that transpired in a vastly different way than what actually occurred.

Perhaps you think about how your heroine has gotten out of a bad relationship (like you did, though you were forced out of it); has taken control (like you wanted to); has begun to move on with her life (as you know you must); and has strength even when looking back (the archetype that will hopefully be you, given time). So you think about what you want to accomplish in the song that you didn't in real life, and you decide it's about her telling the guy that he really lost out big time. You want some irony in the title so that the girl singing the story looks good, so the title you come up with for this song could be "That's Why They Call It Breaking Up." You decide to make the feel of the song "blues." The title suggests a song that needs a so-called laundry list of "that's why"s. Perhaps, staying with the theme of "breaking up," the lines could be, *You shattered all my dreams / After you broke down my resistance.* Then you get the idea that he was a cheat, and that gives you the line, *I busted you for seeing her,* and you set yourself up for a word that rhymes with "resistance," so how about, *Now love me from a distance.* Since this song is an ultimatum, and the woman is declaring her strength, she's telling him like it is. You have her say, *You can't have it both ways,* and then you have a difficult word to rhyme, because you've set up the words "breaking up." So now is the time to be original. You want to say something about the fact that he can't have you and the other girl too, so you write, *You can't drink from both sides of the cup.* The final line has to set up the concept inherent in the title, so what can you say that's actually going to lead up into the last line and make it pay off? How about, *Too late for picking up the pieces / That's why they call it breaking up.* Now that I've walked you through the process of writing this song that was originally meant to get a breakup out of your system, let's look at the song through the end of the first chorus, all assembled together. The verse and chorus lyrics in order are:

THAT'S WHY THEY CALL IT BREAKING UP

VERSE 1:	Sometimes you've treated me unkind
	Sometimes you've messed with my mind
	But I've loved you through it all
VERSE 2:	I never thought I wouldn't grieve
	And that I'd be the one to leave
	We reached so high, we had to fall
"B" SECTION:	You shattered all my dreams
	After you broke down my resistance
	I busted you for seeing her
	Now love me from a distance
CHORUS:	**You can't have it both ways**
	You can't drink from both sides of the cup
	Too late for picking up the pieces
	That's why they call it breaking up

© Lyrics/Pamela Phillips Oland

All the words in this song are conversational words you have used a million times in everyday communication with friends, family, teachers, and just generally as you travel about your life. There are no stupendous or advanced concepts in here. There is just a statement of facts, a palatable, simple story being told. The lines individually are simplistic, yet when they are put together, they make a powerful statement of a woman's strength. In the end, for you the song is about what you would have preferred to have had happen, rather than what really did happen.

If you use this technique of transference, every time you put pen to paper, you are capable of transforming any personal incident into a song—and in the process expounding on some aspect of love that you never even realized you knew so much about!

Is What I'm Saying What You're Hearing?

It is true that the hardest part of a relationship is making the other partner understand not only *how* we see things but *why* we see things as we do. We go into detailed explanations that sound very clear to us as we say them. They often fall on uncomprehending ears. This only exacerbates our frustration, and frequently causes fights. Songs are very often expressions of this communication gap. They are our attempts to be heard, put to music.

Miscommunication is a wonderful topic for songs. It's often a product of two people looking at the same idea differently. A silence in a room, for instance, can be looked at by one of the parties as peace and quiet where nothing need be said. The other party may look at it as a fearful development, signifying that there is a communication breakdown. Words, gestures, and looks are all subject to interpretation. And interpretation has a lot to do with mood, attitude, and comparative past experiences. Love songs can address a subject with a particular slant rather than a "generalist" approach.

In this lyric about communication breakdown, I used an "alone in a crowded room" slant. It was written for a musicalized version of *The Sterile Cuckoo*. Pookie, the kooky young heroine, is sitting across the room from her boyfriend Jerry, wishing she could connect with him, and fearing that he no longer "gets" her at all. The idea I came up with, encapsulated in the the title as "If You Could Hear What I'm Thinking," visually expresses her aloneness:

IF YOU COULD HEAR WHAT I'M THINKING[1]

VERSE:
We sit together in silence
Except for the rumble of rain on the way
I want to speak but the words I can't say
Are the loudest I've ever heard

The moment's framed like a picture
Together alone in two worlds of our own
You in your easy chair
And I in my quiet despair . . . feeling absurd
But . . .

CHORUS:
If you could hear what I'm thinking
If you could listen to what my eyes say
Maybe we'd find a way
To bridge the river of our regrets

---

[1] The rule in a show song, unlike a pop song, is that successive choruses must move the idea along lyrically. In pop, the identical chorus is repeated.

At night in dreams the words come easy
But with the dawn they slip away . . .
In rehearsal it works like a charm
And I know you'd be here in my arms
You'd get it clear . . . you'd get it clear
If you could only hear . . .what I'm thinking

BRIDGE: *Inside I can see me laughing and happy*
The way you once liked me to be
When did I lose the magic for you?
Oh I wish you were in here with me
'Cause . . .

CHORUS: **If you could hear what I'm thinking**
If you could listen to what my eyes say
We'd find a place to meet
Between forever and what's behind us

TAG: You look my way, why don't you see me?
This wall of doubt would simply fall away
And disappear
If you could only hear . . . what I'm thinking

© Lyrics/Pamela Phillips Oland; Music/Peter Matz for *The Sterile Cuckoo*

In this lyric, I was writing about a situation I visualized, not my personal experience. I have been in situations amounting to this one, but not this one. I wrote it by getting into the mind of the character and working out what she felt and what she needed to say.

A song doesn't have time to give all of the background and all of the nuances of a situation; a writer only has a few lines to work with in a song. Thus, you have to offer your most compelling arguments right from line one. I want you to realize right at the start of this study that no listener will stay focused on your song if it takes too long to get to the point. Usually, less is more. Hone your ideas down to their essence, like a member of a debate team: At the end of a debate, the winner is the one whose argument was most succinct and clearly expressed. The same holds true in the world of songwriting.

TRUSTING INTUITION

The private moments you allot to writing your love songs will be some of the most freeing and satisfying moments you will ever experience if you let your *intuition* lead the way rather than trying to be totally in control. Trust me, I know that for a fact. I have written a couple of thousand love songs in my lifetime, and I know how wonderful it feels to let my subconscious mind fill the blank page in front of me.

The very best ideas come *through* you, not to you. They appear on the page before you've had time to wrack your brains. Your intuition is your greatest friend and ally. Trust it! Don't try to intellectualize it or reason where this intuition came from. Your mind contains a wealth of sensational ideas, if you will only allow them to reveal themselves.

Great ideas are instantly appealing, much in the same way that other pleasant things are immediately appealing in life. Aromas either hit your olfactory nerves with delight, or you screw up your nose and sneeze. Food is presented on a plate and either makes you go "yum, yum" or "I'm not really hungry." A person walks into the room and your mind registers him or her with a sense of pleasure, or with a sense of distaste. Basic intuitive, instinctual responses occur, immediately and precisely, the minute you are presented with a stimulus.

A writer of love songs must come into a relationship with ideas, must open up to trusting the combinations of words and images as they come to mind. Don't worry about whether the words you're committing to paper constitute a hit record—at this stage, that is neither here nor there. Concentrate on expressing yourself. Concentrate on releasing your stream of consciousness.

DEFINING THE APPROACH TO AN IDEA

When you first come up with an idea for a song, it is useful to consider how many ways there are to tell that particular story. Each way will still tell a variation on the same story, but deciding on the perspective of the singer will be critical to how you write it. Even a personal story from your own life can be altered dramatically by changing the spin you put on it. Say, for instance, that you have repressed an idea that came to you some years ago when you watched despairingly as your parents were fighting. Say that the idea that went through your mind was, "If this goes on, they're going to say goodbye and break up."

If you were to discuss this in a therapy session, you'd be going right back to square one, in the pain of that moment. If you're a songwriter, you turn it into a love song!

So, now you're going to use this experience and write a song about a couple who are fighting. If they're not careful, they're going to end it all and walk

Saving a Great Idea for Later?

Make sure that whichever song you are writing at the moment is the best one you've ever written. Don't ever save a great line or idea for "later," as the tomorrow you are envisioning never comes; when it is tomorrow, a different set of needs and circumstances exists. Today is all we have; we must invest our best efforts and talents in the work at hand. Don't write anything as a "throwaway" effort—invest the same love in a birthday song for a friend as you would in a love theme for a multimillion-dollar movie!

away from each other. But it doesn't have to be about your parents; it is a commonly experienced story, and can be expressed about two imaginary people.

There are several ways to approach this storyline, depending on which inversion of the song idea you might want to write at that particular moment. Here are some story choices:

- A song in which the woman is saying, "If you don't treat me the way I want to be treated, I'm out of here."
- A song in which the man is saying, "If you'd only try to understand me better, we'd be able to make this work."
- A song sung by a neighbor saying, "That couple next door are just driving me to drink with their fighting."
- A song in which a friend is saying, "They're going to do what I did, and I've got to stop them before it's too late."
- A song in which their grown-up child is saying, "If I'd only understood then what I understand now, I'd have stopped that dam from busting and the river from breaking on through."
- A song in which her lover is saying, "When the fighting is all over, she is coming to be with me."
- A song where the lovers sing to each other in a duet, "We've got to have it out, say what must be said, and risk it ending, or make it stronger."
- The original story could be told, just as it happened, from the child's point of view, singing, "Mom and Dad, don't say those hurtful things, because words like that only lead to goodbye."

These are all powerful approaches to telling this story. Any one of them could make a wonderful song. Perhaps at different times you would want to write all of them, until you have explored your hidden repressed story from many different angles.

CHAPTER 3

Thinking as a Songwriter

I've felt passion, I've felt happiness
I've felt moved by music . . .
But nothing feels like love.
—DENISE STEWART
© Lyrics/Pamela Phillips Oland; Music/Larry Prentiss

From now on, as you begin to get in touch with ideas that occur to you, I want you to become acutely aware of the people and events around you. The more you hone your senses as an observer, the more insightful your song lyrics will be.

BECOMING AWARE

Begin to observe things you've never noticed before—I mean all sorts of things all around you, including aspects of your own love relationships and those of friends and acquaintances. But more than just noticing what people are saying and doing, which is a lot of fun and marvelously voyeuristic, you will make the kind of profound observations that will give style and originality to your writing.

You may look at a couple who are standing and talking to each other, and after you have noted their clothing, their stance, their hair, and so forth, you might also get a sudden flash of intuition that says, "These people are cheating! They belong to others, and what I am witnessing is a furtive meeting!" It is a great rush to notice a thing like this, and there is no way to explain where that idea came from, because it just came to you from the universe. The reason you normally miss many such insights is that you've been taught to mind your own business. If songwriters mind their own business, they're *out* of business! Without being rude or intrusive, permit yourself to speculate about people you see throughout your day. Boil down these speculations as future song ideas and entries in your song title notebook. Trusting these flashes of insight will lead you to trusting the creative notions that occur to you when you are writing love songs.

Defining the Perfect Love

As a songwriter, in order to be able to see love through the eyes of others, first you must define love through your own eyes.

EXERCISE 2

Defining Your Perfect Love

- Make a list of all the desirable components and attributes that would make up your own perfect love.
  - ♡ Leave nothing out; make this a complete and wonderful wish list. Let this be a revelation of the true way you see a perfect love.
  - ♡ Make sure you do this in writing, as you will look back on it later.
- Next (and this is a revelation), put yourself in the mindset of someone you know. It can be a best friend or a co-worker, as long as it's someone you know well and have had conversations with about love. Choose who that person is, and then "become" that person within your mind.
- Now write the same sort of list as in the first step in this exercise, defining the perfect love, but this time writing it from the point of view of this other person whom you have "become." You will be amazed at how different this new list will be, when love is defined through somebody else's eyes.

EXERCISE 3

Seeing Love in Others

- When you are out and about in a public place, observe a couple who are out together.
- Without trying to lip-read, imagine what they are saying to each other, judging by the look in their eyes, their body language, the way they hold their heads, their closeness, their distance.

- Create a scenario about these strangers in your mind.
- Try to imagine why they love or have fallen out of love with each other.

Over a period of time, start to look at love not just through the myopic view of your own two eyes, but in the way others may see it. You will write far better love songs once you have a broader view of what love means to a myriad of different people, and you will know yourself and your own views and attitudes about love a lot better.

The Freedom of Looking beyond Self

I found out, while engaging in the hundreds of lyric evaluations I have done at songwriter seminars around the country, that nobody wants to be critiqued. Most people would rather see hell freeze over than have someone examine their creative output and comment unfavorably upon it. None of us wish to acknowledge that our views are in any way flawed. (What— imperfect? *Moi?*)

But the truth is that when we begin to write love songs, the first few hundred are invariably 100 percent about ourselves. Even the characteristics we attribute to characters we create in our songs belong to us. That often makes our work one-dimensional.

Screenwriters, playwrights, and novelists often fall prey to this problem also. The characters in their work spout the writers' philosophies like little puppets. The writers can't seem to find a way to get past themselves.

I recently saw a reading of a theatrical musical written by an eminent psychotherapist in which all of the characters espoused points of view to which the therapist avidly subscribed. Even though they came out of different mouths, none of the song lyrics provided contrast as to the individual points of the view of the characters, because they all were locked into the writer's personal biases.

Your knowledge and experience in the realm of love is your greatest asset and also, as a writer, your greatest detriment. Unless you become aware of the fact that you are simply telling and retelling the story of your own life and experiences, thinly disguised as coming from different characters, you will spend your future writing one song over and over again.

You and the Blank Page

Writing songs is an extremely personal experience, a relationship between you and the written word. There is nothing on earth that should insert itself

The Blank Page

There is nothing more revealing than a blank page.

It contains a universe of ideas—all the good ones and all the stinkers.

It is the outline and vessel for every love, every hatred, every envy, every longing you have ever known or imagined.

It is the cesspool of your basest thoughts, and it is the exaltation of your finest moments.

Ah! The Blank Page! Was there ever so enviable a measure of a man's worth? Was there ever so sultry a repose for a woman's best lies?

The blank page is already filled. All you have to do is discern the lines of invisible ink, the pen strokes across the white surface, to plumb its depths. All you need is the inner eye to read between the lines already written by some great cosmic hand. Yours is the pen that will suss out the meaning already divulged by the very existence of that smooth surface.

It is blank to the eyes only, for the heart has already filled with the wonder of it.

The blank page is sexy, filled with promise and wanton pleasure. It is seedy, shadowy, soporific.

It is a tale of love lost, love found, great tragedy, and great pain.

It is a saga of endings and beginnings, of tender dreams and sweet sorrow.

Ah, yes, its message is engraved in stone, yet the stone turns to clay, and the clay runs to water and spills away. For it is mobile and ever changing. It is insubstantial yet full of substance.

They all began there, Shakespeare's sonnets, Schiller's "Ode to Joy," the wisdoms of the Ancients, the maps of the world.

Ah, no, there is nothing more replete with life, light, sound, and fury; no, nothing more filled with stories than the blank page.

---

between you and your idea. Not another person, and not a distraction, a fear, a concern about ability, should intrude. You—together with your conscious and unconscious mind—are about to create an entirely new entity.

The process of approaching a blank page is somewhat frightening. There is something about the crisp cleanness of the paper, and the empty lines on it waiting to be filled, that is a bit intimidating. It happens to each and every one of us when we begin a new song. It is inevitable. Yet it is taking the pristine emptiness of a blank space and giving it life that is so truly awesome.

Your mind will be crowded with all the ideas of love that you have been thinking about prior to starting, and you will not want to write anything down until just the right thought comes into your mind. Yet, what is the right thought? Is there such a thing? Is there a way to judge whether to write your thought down or not?

Once again, you must trust your Inner Songwriter, the person within you who is taking charge of this effort. Just simply let the first line pour out of you and find its way onto the page. Then look at it and be fascinated by what you've written there.

As you put your words to paper, you will surely have doubts. You'll ask yourself: "Am I saying this right?" "Does this sound good?" "Is this a stupid thing to say?" Be your own judge of such things, because if you start asking others' opinions, you will surely get them. And beware of opinions!

"Right," "good," and "stupid" are all subjective terms. Sure, if something sounds dumb to you, it probably is. But that's okay, because first drafts are not inscribed in stone, and because there are a lot of dumb-sounding ideas that make a lot of sense in a song!

If you wrote, "Gee Baby, you look tasty enough to eat," you might think to yourself, *that's pretty silly*. But it works in a song. If you wrote, "Come-a-here-to-Mama"—ditto. If you wrote, "My love is a one-way ticket down a dead-end street," you might ask yourself, *Is that too down, would someone really say that in a song?* And the answer is a resounding "Yes!" A country songwriter would spin it one image further and write, "My love is a one-way ticket down a two-way street." And the meaning would be a happy one—that this was leading to a perfect relationship.

The truth is that the answers to all your songwriting questions about words, thoughts, ideas, and direction are within yourself. Again, they are very intuitive. But "intuition" is all very well, and beginning a song is a practical matter. It gets easier once you have your first line, so to "get the ball rolling," try the following.

Write down a series of potential "first lines" that pop into your head. Don't stop to edit yourself, just be absurd, bizarre, deep, outrageous, whimsical, truthful, angry, or—what have you? If you're planning, for instance, to write about running into an old love again, you could consider:

- *You look like someone I used to love*
- *You're comin' in the front door, and I'm runnin' out the back door*
- *I can't believe my ever-loving eyes*
- *Only seeing you can tear me up like this*
- *I thought I never wanted to see you again*
- *Fate musta sent your footsteps through this door*
- *My old heartbreak walked back into my life tonight*
- *You walked in, and it started all over again*

Capturing Intuitions

When your Inner Songwriter—which is actually the part of your inner self that thinks up and imagines all of these creative thoughts you are putting on paper—gets an intuition about how to proceed with an idea, take it very seriously. Make sure to write it down, even if you are sitting in a class, or at your desk at work, or in an elevator, or out to lunch with a friend. Just grab a piece of paper or a digital voice recorder, and memorialize the idea that has just come through you. You will probably never think that thought in quite the same way ever again, as your set of life circumstances changes from moment to moment while you move through your days. So that fleeting perception must be caught and captured like a butterfly in a net.

The definition of "trusting intuition" is *learning not to question an insight that suddenly flashes through your mind and consciousness so that you feel compelled to write it down.* Your intuition is ultimately your most powerful tool to separate you from all other writers. It is how you get your best ideas.

Striking Just the Right Tone

The tone you use to write your love song will have a large impact on how it is received by the listener. Is it to be angry or conciliatory? Is it to be respectful or does it disrespect? Does it cajole or plead? Does it seduce or reject?

To give your song maximum impact, once you have decided on the tone you want to use in your lyric, stay with it. Don't bounce all over the place, flip-flopping from yin to yang (passive to active) and back, as the lack of consistency will prove confusing to a listener trying to make heads or tails of the message.

Sometimes, the tone will be something you plan in advance, something you go into the writing process knowing. Other times, a first line will appear on the page, written from your subconscious creative core, and it will immediately set a clear and recognizable tone for you to follow. That's another reason to pay extra attention to your first line. Not only does it set up the story, but it also sets the tone in motion.

DIGGING FOR EMOTIONS

Your perspectives on love will not all be right there on the surface of your mind. Much of what you think or feel has been buried away under the flotsam and jetsam of your life experiences.

Unlocking Hidden or Repressed Ideas

Your reactions to things that have happened to you along the way have been pushed down, repressed in your subconscious mind, and you have never taken them out to look at them again.

You could go through hypnosis in order to recall things that have happened in your past, situations and events that have inflamed, excited, hurt, or angered you. But merely bringing these ideas to the surface is of very little use, because now all you have are more ingredients with which to pepper your stew of confusion.

> You have to know what for you is real, and where you need to write from speculation, innovation, fiction, and imagination.

But aha! Writing these repressed ideas down in a constructive way—in a song—is (to keep the food analogies going) a whole different kettle of fish. The emotion has somewhere constructive to go. Turning an emotion into a song is incredibly satisfying. It not only releases an idea, but it also takes it to a productive and useful level.

Assessing Your Points of View

You must understand what limitations you have as to how you see things, your views framed and colored as they are by your own life experiences. The following questions are posed so you can know yourself better. Before you can write about love—yours or anyone else's—knowing where you stand on a variety of love issues helps you recognize the jumping-off point for your "suspension of disbelief." In other words, you have to know what for you is real, and where you need to write from speculation, innovation, fiction, and imagination.

Once you have a clear mental picture of your own personal responses to and prejudices, opinions, and expectations about the dynamics of love, you will have the incredibly useful revelation of just exactly how narrow your points of view are. Although it is important in some ways to write about what you know, what you know doesn't apply to every listener out in the world who will be hearing your songs. And since *when you say "I," you are speaking for the listener*, your ability to get beyond your limited frame of reference when you write your love songs will make them far more accessible.

Your Point of View on Love

Get a pad and pen and, knowing that there are no "right" or "wrong" answers, detail in at least a full sentence each of your true gut responses to the following questions:

- ❤ Who are you currently in love with? Why are you in love with him or her?
    - ♡ Is this a person you're actually with, or a lost relationship you can't let go of?
    - ♡ Do you love the person deeply or superficially?
    - ♡ Is the way you love this person typical for your relationships?
    - ♡ Is your love for this someone on the upswing or going downhill?
- ❤ Is your love returned?
    - ♡ Sincerely?
    - ♡ Hesitantly?
    - ♡ With gusto?
    - ♡ Mainly physically?
    - ♡ Mainly spiritually?
    - ♡ With words but not deeds?
    - ♡ With deeds but not words?
- ❤ What is it you love about this person (honestly)?
    - ♡ Is it superficial things about the person—that he or she is good looking, popular, a "good catch"?
    - ♡ Does this person have social status? Does that matter to you?
    - ♡ Do you love how you feel when you're around the person?
    - ♡ Is it that this person loves you that makes you love him or her?
    - ♡ Do you love this person for what he or she can do for you?
    - ♡ What do you love more, this person's intellect or passion for life?
    - ♡ Would you love this person if he or she were socially inept?
- ❤ Do you choose romantic relationships based primarily:
    - ♡ On sexual attraction and lust?
    - ♡ On settling for who is available?
    - ♡ On financial considerations?
    - ♡ On mental stimulation?
    - ♡ On a sense of well-being that your partners give you?

- How do you define a successful relationship?
- Do you imagine that love at first sight is possible?
  - What exactly is "love" at first sight?
  - What would a person who falls in love at first sight be falling in love with?
- Have you ever had a whirlwind, smash-bang, all-in-one-breathless-day relationship experience?
  - Did you expect it to continue after that day?
  - How did you deal with the disappointment when you never saw that lover again?
  - Why do you think it was such an amazing experience?
  - What was different about the attitude with which you approached it than the attitude with which you approach your normal relationships?
- Do you spend any time fantasizing about someone you can't have?
  - Is your fantasy a person you know, someone in your world?
  - Do you believe your feelings are returned by the object of your fantasy?
  - Is your fantasy a well-known personality, such as an actor or singer whom you don't know personally?
  - Do you unfavorably compare the one you're with to your fantasy love?
  - Do you ever have romantic fantasies about your real partner?
- How do you feel about other people having illicit love affairs?
- If you've ever had an illicit love affair, why did you get involved?
  - If you're no longer involved, why not?
  - If you're still involved, what do you want?
  - Do or did you feel you have as much right to that person as his or her actual partner has?
  - Would your feelings for that person lead you to write joyous love songs, sad love songs, or both, and why?
- How do you think a problem in a relationship is usually solved in your life? (Be honest; don't change the truth or you'll miss the whole point of the exercise.)
  - Great sex can always make things right again.
  - Talking it over always works.
  - Pretending it doesn't exist; it eventually dissipates.
  - If you're in the right, you have to show your partner why, so that he or she can see the light and you can both get past the hump.

- ♡ You have to blow up and get into a fight with your partner until he or she finally capitulates to your argument, accepts blame, and apologizes.
- ♡ You look within yourself for answers, solutions, share of the blame, and try to discover what you've done, even inadvertently or unknowingly, to contribute to the trouble.

- ❤ Do you think love with one person over time:
  - ♡ Gets stale and loses its magic or gets better and more fulfilling?
  - ♡ Gets gentler and more comfortable or gets lustier and sexier?
  - ♡ Gets on your nerves?
- ❤ Under what circumstances are little white lies okay between love partners?
- ❤ You have expectations of a lover to behave a certain way; describe that and whether your expectations are fulfilled in relation to:
  - ♡ The way seduction happens, the way lovemaking follows.
  - ♡ The way your lover supports you in your daily life issues.
  - ♡ The way your lover handles anger.
  - ♡ The way your lover acknowledges your accomplishments.
  - ♡ The way your lover shows you how he or she feels about you on a daily basis.
- ❤ Regarding the prior question, what would be the advantages of going into a relationship with no expectations?
  - ♡ If you had no expectations, could you eliminate heartbreak from the equation?
- ❤ What is the best way to break up?
  - ♡ Bluntly, simply admit: I'm not in love anymore; I want to move on.
  - ♡ Become distant and start staying out later and later; leave clues around that point to interest in someone else.
  - ♡ Go to therapy and spend weeks and months and a fortune in therapist bills, in order to prove to yourself and your partner that you tried to make it work.
- ❤ Do you let your lover have free reign to be whoever he or she is without limitations?
  - ♡ What would be acceptable limitations to place on a partner?
  - ♡ Is a person with boundaries a better partner than a person without limitations?
- ❤ Do you believe a woman should initiate sex?
- ❤ When it comes to love, are you shy and old fashioned, or bold and forward?

- Are you a free spirit sexually, or repressed?
- *In your dreams*, are you a free spirit sexually, or repressed?
- How important is it that everyone finds someone to love and be loved by?
- Would you say the word "love" is overrated?
- Would you say love is a four-letter word?
- Do you believe that if you love someone, you should let them go, and that if they want to be with you, they will return?
- Do you believe that two people are fated to be together, and that they simply have to find each other?
- Do you keep looking for someone else, just to make sure you're not missing something, even when you've met a great potential candidate to love?
- Are you in love with the challenge, the thrill of the chase?
- Do you believe two people who love each other can work it out in spite of the obstacles between them?
- If you were washed up on a desert island with someone you were unattracted to, do you believe you could come to love him or her?
  - ♡ In regular old real-life, could you learn to love such a person given enough time?
  - ♡ What is it that makes you know you are unattracted to a person?
- Do you believe in happy endings—finding the right partner and settling down to love and being happy for the rest of your life?
  - ♡ Why is that possible or impossible for others?
  - ♡ Why is it possible or impossible for you?
- Do TV- and movie-love scenarios make people have unrealistic expectations?
  - ♡ Does the happiness experienced by the couples acting it out on the screen encourage you to feel, *well, maybe this could happen to me?*
- Do you believe love is what you feel for someone else or what someone else makes you feel about yourself?

Now, go back over each of your answers and ask yourself:

- If this is a feeling you think most people share?
- Is this a good thing or a fault?
- Do you tend to categorize people by this?
- How much weight do you give to this concept when judging others' relationships?

Now that you have reacted to these questions, you know some of the prejudices and limitations you must overcome in your love song writing. But I'm sure it's a revelation when you understand that the way you see these things in your own life will in fact color the way you write your characters and their responses and actions in your love songs. Make an effort when you are writing to allow your characters to have points of view you don't share, and explore these points of view with them. Allow them, in fact, to be more well-rounded than you are.

CHAPTER 4

What Are You Going to Write About

Only love can break a heart.
—GENE PITNEY
(Burt Bacharach/Hal David)

Love found at last, love lost too soon, love hungered for at a distance, love driven away in anger. Love that consumes, love that gnaws at the soul, love that terrifies, taunts, entices, enfolds, crushes, suffocates, uplifts, agitates, is irrational, is illogical, is incomprehensible, is dark and seedy, is illuminating and heady, is fulfilling, is challenging, is foolish, is frantic, is zany, is undeniable, is insatiable. And those are just a few of the topics you can write a love song about!

CALLING UPON MEMORIES

We are built of our memories. They are the bricks and mortar that form us as people. We remember the looks in the eyes of our parents, the scorn of our teachers, the feeling of the first lips that ever pressed a kiss upon ours, the giddiness of hearing "I love you" for the first time.

Every memory we have is valuable; good or bad, it has helped to define us. It can be part of a song if we use it well.

Say you want to describe that first kiss in a song. There are many song scenarios that would be enhanced by that particular memory. For instance:

❤ A song that is truly about remembering the feeling of the first time you were kissed: "I remember how it was, or at least it seems to me this is how I felt: awkward and silly and longing, and scared that I'd make a fool of myself."

- A song that takes place in the moment of the kiss, that says, "Here we are, and I can feel the warmth of your breath on my face, and your lips are so close, my head is rushing, giddy with excitement, and then, mmm, here you are, pressing those lips on mine, and oh what a feeling."
- A song written as if by an observer: "There they were, two young lovers, alone in the dark, fear and excitement coursing through their bodies and driving their faces together for that perfect kiss. That first kiss."
- A song of disappointment: *Your lips on mine were everything I thought they would be, and less / You just didn't move me, I guess / So the next time around with someone new, I'll still be waiting / And anticipating my first kiss.*

In every memory lives a potential song. How you interpret that memory is your unique art. What you have to say about that moment in your memory is totally singular. Just remember, though, that although the basis for the song is your own memory, the song doesn't have to be about you!

FINDING THE THREAD BETWEEN YOUR EXPERIENCES AND EVERYONE ELSE'S

Nothing is more fascinating to a songwriter than being caught up in exploring the tangles of love relationships. If you're a voyeuristic songwriter in search of fodder for the next great lyric idea, from first glance through courtship and onward, you'll surrender to the web of intrigues.

Volatile Relationships

The more you watch people, the more you'll understand how many reasons people can drum up for not staying together. Any excuse will do. If a person is of a mind to start an argument, then there will be an argument, mark my words. It will be about the first infraction that comes up, and it will not be preventable by the partner being argued with. It might go from sizzle to fizzle in a few moments, with a hand patted, a hug, an apology. Or it may burst into flames and consume the relationship, unexpectedly, like a match thrown in a gas tank that someone forgot to cap.

Relationships are volatile, and we all know we are guilty of being capable of starting a fight at the drop of a hat. Or at the drop of a sock in the middle of the bedroom floor. Or at the drop of an unkind jibe at an unsuspecting and momentarily vulnerable partner. Escalation can be instantaneous, zero to sixty in ten seconds, like a Maserati on a coast road.

There can never be enough songs written about relationships in trouble. The best of them begin with astute observation. Much of the best inspiration comes from noticing ordinary, everyday scenarios. Normally speaking, you might look at, yet not even see, the intricate dances of fate that go on around you. You may not be aware of relationship tableaus evolving right in front of your face.

Observe and Create

You're sitting in a commuter train heading home, and a drama unfolds on the banquette across from you. You were reading the chain of ads on the perimeter of the wall above the window, but now your eyes are drawn down to the couple who are going through some soul searching. You don't have a clue as to the origin of the conflict, but they are well into it, and it's moving fast beyond bickering into unknown, perhaps irreversible territory.

She looks away from him in complete annoyance. Your own mind is saying, "Don't do that, idiot! You'll lose him!" You're seeing the expression in his face that she can't see, because she's facing away. Then you see the resolve form in his eyes, "Well, that's that, then, I've done the best I can with her, I can't do this any more." And you're thinking, "No, wait a minute, you two can fix this, I know you can—don't just roll over like that and take the easy way out!"

Uh-oh. You're becoming involved, embroiled, entangled in *les affaires de coeur* of two perfect strangers! And you couldn't be happier. You have now totally inserted yourself into their struggle. You are like an observer at a tennis match, not part of it but one with it.

And as you watch, you reminisce, take a little unexpected stroll down memory lane. A gesture or a look displayed by one of these strangers on the train will trigger a fractional memory of a moment with someone you have loved yourself. Oh yes, the words will come back to you: what you said, what they said, where it led, how it ended. Then you will begin to try to remember how that moment happened to happen, where it came from, and all of a sudden, watching this couple of total strangers in a commuter car has you remembering an amazingly indelible moment in your own life, a pivotal moment that could have changed everything, that—if not for observing these strangers—you might never have bothered to recall.

Dinner on the stove . . . the clock ticking forward . . . no call . . . pacing the floor . . . clothing becoming less fresh looking . . . makeup starting to fade . . . dinner beginning to spoil . . . temper becoming sour . . . plans for a beautiful evening ruined. And then, at last, the doorbell ringing . . . opening the door in

What Are "Universal" Songs?

I frequently use the term "universal" to describe certain songs. They are "universal" because their concepts are appealing to the world at large—accessible to many people, rather than the few who relate to your very specific situation. It's just a fact that the more "universal" an idea is, the greater its chance of being recorded.

Songs about world peace, world hunger, and loving your neighbor would all be "universal" songs. Universal *love* songs are those that deal with experiences in love relationships that most people can relate to.

anger . . . staring at a disheveled figure . . . forming the words you'll forever regret speaking . . . looking into chastened eyes. . . .

And then, hearing a perfectly plausible excuse . . . a hug . . . sweet kisses . . . words of endearment . . . and, suddenly, you're high, you're elated, you're happy, and to hell with the messed-up dinner, and it doesn't taste bad after all anyway. Were you going to throw it all away for this? And there it is—the inspiration for an amazing song.

So you write that song about holding on through the fire, and it starts, *And if sometimes I doubt you, yeah, I'm a fool, I know / 'Cause what would I do without you, if I ever let you go?* And of course it's not just about you; it's about the couple across the train car, also. It's a universal idea, because it happened to you, and it's happening to them, too.

Look at that! You have the beginning of a song about having and holding a strong and healthy relationship, all because you happened to pay attention to two strangers fighting on a train.

Songs Represent Emotions

When you are writing a love song, ask yourself *what type* of love song you're writing. What is the state of the relationship you are writing about? Who are these two people? What age are they? Are they singing about new love? Lust? Romantic love? Comfortable, longstanding love? Is your song to be sexy or chaste, or somewhere in between? You must strike just the right attitude, and have a clear idea of the kind of love you want your song to concern itself with.

Once you have determined the type of song and created a mental picture of the characters involved, it's time to hone in on the song's primary emotion. What is the underlying emotion you wish to express, and how does it relate to the people who populate your song? Ask yourself, is it:

- Fear
- Anguish
- Need
- Lust
- Forgiveness
- Contrition
- Longing
- Sadness
- Passion

- Anger
- Understanding
- Desire
- Remorse
- Regret
- Perplexity
- Ambivalence
- Wistfulness
- Shame

Once you're clear on which emotion you're going for, ask yourself what kind of a storyline that emotion would lend itself to. Decide how much humor and irony is allowed in a sad idea. Decide how plainspoken you want to be—and how outrageous, how refined, how poetic, how noble, how loose, how controlled. Your hand is at the end of your arm, your pen is in your hand, your hand responds with movement to the ideas that flow to it from your mind.

Allow the thoughts, the ideas, the pictures and images to come forth. Reach down deep for the emotions you need to communicate; don't be afraid to explore and express them. If you have the power of an arresting idea driven by a pulsing emotion, you're on your way to a sensational song.

Remembering "First Love"

No other love is quite like first love. Or so we've been led to believe by writers through the ages. But the truth is, each new love is first love all over again. Whether you're fifteen or fifty, falling in love is always falling in love for the first time.

When you are writing a love song, every first date, first kiss, first touch, first lovemaking, is a brand-new and tender experience for both people going through it. Vulnerability, sensitivity, nerves, excitement, dry mouth—all are symptoms of the endearingly repeated experience of first love.

First love is an attitude, not just a time and place. So when you're digging for the emotions of first love in order to put them into a song lyric, remember that you can pull up any one of the "first loves" along the way. The very, *very* first one has a pristine place in your heart and soul anyway—not to be messed with, tampered with, or distorted in your memory. And if you do

Knowing Your Characters

There are so many types of love relationships, from extremely possessive, to impossibly sexual, to simple fervent admiration. The subject of love is limited only by how far you can push your imagination to create characters you can write about—whether these characters turn out to be based on movie stars or the couple who live next door. Make the characters who populate your songs believable and real. Even if their characteristics are an amalgam of several people you know, plus a little imagination, make sure they come to life as clear and definable individuals. Know who they are and write them so that your listeners can identify easily with them.

The dynamic tension between the partners in a love song relationship is whatever you, the writer, say it is. Knowing all you can about your characters will help you to understand how they might spar, fear, understand and misunderstand, express passion, and generally interact with each other. Knowing who they are, you can best ask yourself: Must the singer tread on eggshells when talking to the loved one, or can that singer be open and honest about feelings? Can the truth be told or must it be sugarcoated? Is the singer afraid of offending or coming on too strong?

Approach a song about a relationship the way you would approach an actual real-life relationship—carefully or discreetly, wonderingly or longingly, with humor or with serenity. A song is a mini-relationship, an imitation of life, in two verses and a chorus.

put that first very tender love into a love song, treat it affectionately, with love and gentleness, sweetness and bittersweet. Do it justice and give it perhaps just a touch of fantasy.

Songs about Giving New Relationships a Chance

Perhaps you'll write that only foolish people would allow the hurts inflicted by past lovers to color their new relationships. If so, you might choose to incorporate the thought that clearly nobody new is going to treat you the same way as somebody from the past. Even an identical twin is going to be different from his brother. Perhaps you'd conclude that thus, each new partner must be allowed to make his or her own mistakes, to try and fail, to stumble around in the dark, and ultimately, to love and become loved in return.

I strongly addressed the subject of not letting a past hurt get in the way of a new relationship, in a song I wrote with Santana's Andy Vargas called "I'm Not Him." The angle of the lyric is that the singer is fed up with competing with a memory, on the one hand, and having to prove that he has better intentions than his predecessor, on the other.

I'M NOT HIM

VERSE: Why do I have to always wonder
What you're thinkin', why can't
You just be honest with my heart

You can't blame me for what
Somebody else has done or said
You'll move on if you're smart

Can you just let go?
Well don't you already know . . .

CHORUS: **I'm not him!**
I'm not that!
I'm here to tell you to be where you're at
You're not her! Any more
I'm gonna show you what you're put here for
'Cause I'm not him!

VERSE: You're always playin' push me-pull me
Messin' with my mind and
Here I am crazy about you

Woman, I give you what you need
But you're too blind to see
What have I got to do?

This is now, not then
I've told you over and over again

CHORUS: **I'm not him!**
I'm not that!
I'm here to tell you to be where you're at
You're not her! Any more
I'm gonna show you what you're put here for
'Cause I'm not him!

BRIDGE: *I don't do those things he did*
I don't say those things he said
Sorry he didn't give a damn . . .
But . . .

CHORUS: **I'm not him!**
            I'm not that!
            I'm here to tell you to be where you're at
            You're not her! Any more
            I'm gonna show you what you're put here for
            'Cause I'm not him!

© Lyrics/Pamela Phillips Oland; Music/Andy
Vargas-Shirlee Elliott

The point that came to me as an unexpected revelation in the process of writing this song was the line, *You're not her / Any more.* Suddenly, I realized how often people hold on to old fears and painful feelings and carry them over into new relationships. What struck me, not for the first time, was the unfairness of punishing a new relationship because the old one was bungled. It causes and leads to mutual frustration, a topic that always works in love songs.

Expressing Anger
Words of anger can be incredibly powerful when written in a love song. They can be very visual:

    I want to see you cry until the color of your eyes fades away.

They can be cool:

    Watching you walk out of my life is a good thing.

They can be mean:

    You're everything that I don't want in my life.

They can be sorrowful:

    These tears can never wash away my pain.

They can be ironic:

    You know all the best ways to break a heart.

They can be hurtful:

    I don't love you any more!

They can be impassioned:
>   You're no good! You never were! You'll never be!

They can be vengeful:
>   I'm gonna make you sorry that you ever dreamed of me!

Don't be afraid of anger in a song, but don't make it a diatribe, either. Use economy of expression—and always remember that less is often more. Allow the pure emotion of the anger to come out onto the paper and find expression in words more biting, potent, and emotionally invasive than any four-letter words and thoughts spoken could ever be.

LUST VERSUS LOVE

Nearly every love song, whether about a good love or a love gone bad, alludes to or has elements of lust in it. A song that is about pure sweet emotion might get a bit mushy, so be careful of goopy lyrics!

Can Love Be Lust? Can Lust Be Love?

Lust is simply the steamy and sometimes seamy side of intimacy. We've all heard the concepts of a woman being a virgin in the kitchen and a vixen in the bedroom. The two concepts, lust and love, are both contained within each person's being, like the two sides of the moon; one is available for anyone to see, but the other is often kept dark and shadowed. Lust and love usually inspire different types of songs.

Most songs are actually written about lust, not love, and that's a fact. Any song that indicates any of the following:

- I'm here for you, baby, come and get me.
- Forget about tomorrow, love me tonight.
- Oooh, what are you doing touching me like that!
- I know I shouldn't, but I will.
- I want your fire.
- Do that to me again.

and so forth, are all songs that are expressing lust. Young singers and bands increasingly prefer to sing songs about "doing it." That's quite reasonable, as their relationships have not really progressed beyond that stage.

The Differences between Love and Lust

Understand these differences between love and lust before you write your love songs: When the singer is consumed with lust, the lyrics are all about fulfilling sexual drive and consummating a relationship sexually. When the singer is consumed with romantic love, he's all about adoration of the one he's set his sights on because of the intense euphoria he feels around her.

"Love" is a word that implies emotional bonding, spiritual connection, and desire for a special intimacy between two individuals that is more than simply lust. Loving someone can mean that you lust after him, also. Lusting after someone does not imply in any way or sense that you love him. Perhaps that's the big difference. Love can include lust. Lust doesn't require love. Lust is it's own yearning, need, desire for fulfillment. When a person burns with lust for another, love isn't always part of the equation, even when the lusting party also loves the one after whom they lust.

Adolescent love, contrasted with adolescent lust as expressed in many pop songs, is most likely the "I want to love you forever, bay-beh, bay-beh" variety. In fact, the first time I was ever kissed on the lips by a boy at a party, the Carole King-Gerry Goffin song "Will You Still Love Me Tomorrow?" was playing, and even *that* was a profoundly adult concept for me to deal with!

The complexity of relationships hasn't hit home yet for that age group, nor should it have. The difference between young impressions of what love is and mature experiences of what love is, is the difference between the complexity of a glass of *vin rosé* and that of a dry martini. One is light and frothy, the other filled with heady, dizzying nuances.

There are those who would say that lust cannot exist without love in a song, and others would aver that a love song cannot exist without lust—that the two are inextricably intertwined.

Can you separate the two concepts and have a powerful song? Frank Sinatra is said to have commented that he liked The Beatles' song "Something" because it said "I love you," without ever using those words. It alluded to loving the woman for all of the sensual reasons imaginable, but never actually said "I love you."

The Difference Between "Sexy" and "Sexual" Lyrics

The degrees of "sexy" in lyrics are *a little bit, a little bit more, a lot,* and beyond that, the only category is *blatantly sexual.*

Shock Value

A writer has an opportunity to write a love song that can move, delight, and thrill listeners. While lust is part of the experience, too much overt sexuality can also degrade women and cause listeners to become desensitized to the true sensuality of a woman. In my view, women want to see themselves exalted in love songs. Songs that are being crass just for shock value miss the whole point of love—it's the most uplifting and joyous emotion on earth.

So if you can't decide "how far to go" in your lyric, get a clue from the Holy Modal Rounders who in 1970 entitled their classic album, *Good Taste Is Timeless*.

"A little bit" means talking about eyes meeting and lips touching. "A little bit more" means talking about the magic of our bodies skin on skin, being unable to breathe for the ecstasy we're feeling. "A lot" means, "Mama's got a squeeze box, Daddy never sleeps at night"—but that famous 1976 lyric by The Who has got humor and good-natured intent in it. It's wink-wink, nudge-nudge—bawdy without really being offensive.

Sexy lyrics can be wonderful, beautiful, adoring, sensual, filled with pleasure and pleasurable images. Sexual lyrics, however, are utterly raw and openly describe actual physical acts between two sexual partners.

While there are hip-hop and rap songs that get into heavily and unabashedly sexual lyrics, and they obviously have found their audience, I'm not sure that blatant sexual images in lyrics are a particularly clever or creative way for songwriters to direct their energies. My reason for saying that is this: They destroy the mystique of sexuality. And though outright blatancy is no big deal among many men, for women, feeling sensual is all about maintaining mystique. A woman who doesn't feel her mystique working loses her sexual magic.

There is an old saying that a woman is sexier with her clothes on than with them all off, as she allows a man to use his imagination. In the same way, I am of the opinion that songs are an imaginative medium, as they create mental pictures that allow listeners to use their imagination. Certainly, imagination can go to sexual images, but to me, there is nothing more wonderful than the allure of lyrics brimming with romantic sensuality. So if you're a man writing blatantly sexual lyrics, chances are you will embarrass rather than connect with most of your female audience. Women are all about romance, I promise you!

Writing Lusty and Effective Lyrics

A show I once saw had a beautiful woman raising her skirt from her ankle, torturously, slowly, until it was above her knee. Three cute sailors were watching, their "tongues hanging out!" in an absolute frenzy over this erotic gesture, as she watched them with a gleam in her eye. In the same way, you as a songwriter have the power to entice your listeners with tantalizing and teasing mental pictures. Give them something to imagine! Check this out:

> I saw your image on the bedroom shade
> You sent me home, made sure he stayed
> And as I watched the sexy music you two made
> You crossed the line.
> I thought those ruby lips, that satin skin,
> Those shapely hips, that love he's in . . . was mine!

© Lyrics/Pamela Phillips Oland

Mental Imagery

Perhaps it is the video explosion that has made it more difficult for people to use their own imaginations to create original mental images when listening to songs. Today, images are spoon-fed to us from the television screen. Sexy lyrics are interpreted by some video director, and that becomes our mental picture any time we listen to the song, depriving us of the ability to create our own personal mental scenario.

Remember at all times who your listeners are, and give them the gift of their own mental pictures.

As a culture, we appear to have lost sight of the fact that videos are to great songs what movies are to great novels— just one person's interpretation and vision of the characters. Personally, I'd rather read the novel first, *then* look at what the director has created with the movie of it; in the same way I'd rather muse on a song *before* I watch the video.

We each want to place ourselves inside a song lyric we're listening to. Each of us needs the freedom to create our own degree of sexuality in our mind's eye. So, remember at all times who your listeners are, and give them the gift of their own mental pictures. Be as sexy as you like in your songwriting; just develop a sense of when enough is enough, and too much is too much.

Euphemisms

In 1960 the recording duo of Skip and Flip scandalized parents everywhere by recording a song with the innocuous title of "Cherry Pie." Underground rumors ran rampant that this was a song that had overtly sexual context, disguised as a song about eating cherry pie. In another instance, in an old jazz record that appeared on the *Devil in a Blue Dress* soundtrack of the 1990s, Joe Milton sings that his baby's kisses taste like cherry pie. When these songs were written, the "cherry pie" symbolism was scandalous. Today, that would seem laughable. But cherry pie simply became a euphemism for a woman's sex.

Another pair of scandalous euphemistic songs were Prince's "Little Red Corvette" followed by Sheena Easton's "Sugar Walls." The author of that song is listed as "Alexander Nevermind" but was thought to be Prince also. Both were euphemisms for a woman's sex.

If you think I'm about to say, "That's terrible!" you're wrong. I think that inventiveness is the cornerstone of writing anything at all. Whether you're writing letters, books, screenplays, or e-mails, being inventive with your language usage will engage your reader far more than using trite, overused phrases.

In writing love songs, however, inventiveness is *everything*. I don't believe in writing lyrics that are blatantly sexual because the true artistry of a songwriter is shown by how adroitly he or she can invent clever euphemisms.

The dictionary would tell us that euphemisms are nothing more than milder ways of saying things that otherwise might cause discomfort. Calling a mortician an "artist of slumber," for instance, or calling the deaf "the hearing-impaired" are ways our society has found for adding respectfulness to our terminologies.

To a songwriter, however, a euphemism is a way of saying something about love, lust, and sexuality in a brand new way, with a spin on words that perhaps nobody ever has said before. A woman describing her internal sexuality as "sugar walls" was certainly without precedent. Was it in bad taste? Did it go too far? I'll let you make up your own mind. But you can't deny it was inventive.

Whatever the style of songs you are writing, there is never a substitute for plain old good taste. You may not want to be charming, vivacious, or gentle. But your judgment in your choice of phrases to talk about sex in songs should always take into consideration your audience and what will please them to hear. The object of writing a song is, after all, to have it sung for someone's ears to hear and heart to receive.

The pen is in *your* hand. Being the author of your own songs is a divine pursuit and carries with it a certain degree of responsibility. It also definitely offers you an opportunity to break new ground in the colorful arena of euphemisms.

ROMANTIC LOVE

Sometimes all that's needed in a love song is for it to be a "mash note." A romantic come-on from a flirt can be just the thing to get the receiver's juices flowing!

In setting up songs about romantic love, just seeing the face and touching the skin of the person who is loved is enough to set the singer off into paroxysms of joy. Compare this phenomenon with:

- **Friendship with a lover.** When you are writing a song that is about friendship with a lover, you are writing about the trust, the understanding, the shoulder to lean on, the hand to hold. You are writing about someone who will be there when you need him or her. You are offering up a paean to knowing you're not alone in the world because you have your friend-lover.
- **Respect with a lover.** When your song deals with respect in a love relationship, it's about having the freedom to be and do what you want in this world and knowing you have the support and love of your lover through it all. Or, conversely, it talks about having all the rest of the stuff—the lust and the companionship—but *lack of* respect, which makes you angry.
- **Magic with a lover.** This well-used (some might say *overused*) word "magic" connotes the indefinable sparkle that exists in an uplifting love relationship. It is marked by such concepts as "tingling," "finding it hard to breathe," "heavenly sensations," "feeling high," and "electricity." It evokes images of exultation, luxuriating in pleasure, and generally feeling good.
- **Being "turned on" by a lover.** This is harder to define, as it is sort of a mixed bag of descriptions. It is a one-size-fits-all expression that has to do a little bit with lust, a little bit with rapture, a little bit with intellectual stimulation, and a lot to do with thinking about continuing into the future with this person. When a singer sings, "Baby, you turn me on," he is saying, in effect, "this feels really right, I could keep on seeing you for the indefinite future."

Romantic love is the kind that poets have long written about in the glowing terms for which they are famous, comparing their love to a sunrise or to a red rose in bloom. There is no contempt in romantic love; typically, nothing sordid or base is part of it. It exults the sexual experience in words that are glossy and glowing. Sometimes romantic love as described in poetry is rather winsome, childlike in its delicacy. It might include references to knightly gallantry, fairy tale endings, and serenity of the highest order.

IRONY AS A SONG DEVICE

Irony is one of the best devices in the songwriter's arsenal. Country songwriters are very good at it. As a great example of irony, Garth Brooks sings in "Unanswered Prayers" that he thanks God prayers that certain things would work out in his life (such as a relationship with a certain girl), God in His wisdom chose not to grant. I think most songwriters would have approached that title by talking about how sad it is that so many prayers go unanswered. Garth and his co-writers took this unusual path that led to the conclusion that the singer (Garth, in this case) was the happiest man in the world because of the prayers that went *unanswered*.

In the brilliant "Stranger in My House," Ronnie Milsap sings about a suspected lover, someone he can't see but whom he senses as an invisible presence in his home, coming between him and his woman.

Irony can also be used to make a sad song funny. In Jerry Reed's "She Got the Goldmine and I Got the Shaft," the situation is a sad one, but it is described in such a heartwarming way that the sympathetic listener finds it uplifting rather than depressing.

If the love song idea you want to write has an irony with a country sensibility, think simplicity and authenticity. Such songs are not frivolous, but extremely heartfelt. Here is an example of such a lyric, which I remember writing one pleasant afternoon on the wide wooden verandah of Angela Kaset's house in Bell Buckle, Tennessee:

THANKS FOR NOTHIN'

VERSE:
> I told mama how I loved you
> She said, "Hon, it's just a phase
> Well that boy, he ain't got nothin'
> And that don't go far these days."

VERSE: But who is gonna stop a girl
Who's stone blind in love
When she thinks that's enough
Just knows that's enough

VERSE: Sure, there are winters we are grateful
For a quilt to keep us warm
But there's food upon our table
And a roof against a storm

VERSE: And you gave me the rainbow
When you couldn't find the gold
And I have lacked for nothing in this world

CHORUS: **You gave me nothin' but your time**
Nothin' but your heart
And nothin' short of ev'rything you are
And after all this livin'
If everything you've given me is nothin' . . .
Well darlin' . . .
Thanks for nothin'

VERSE: Last year for my birthday
You said, "It's nothin', just the park"
We watched the sun go down as the moon came up
Then we made love in the dark

VERSE: And there was nothin' like a diamond
In your dandelion ring
But I love nothing more than anything

CHORUS: **You gave me nothin' but your time**
Nothin' but your heart
And nothin' short of ev'rything you are
And after all this livin'
If everything you've given me is nothin' . . .
Well darlin' . . .
Thanks for nothin'

© Words and Music/Pamela Phillips Oland
and Angela Kaset

THE ART OF WRITING LOVE SONGS

CHAPTER 5

Expressing an Idea in Lyric Form

My eyes adored you.
—FRANKIE VALLI AND THE FOUR SEASONS
(Robert Crewe/Kenny Nolan)

Finessing an idea into a song lyric is more than just outlining what you're seeing in your mind. The listener must envision whatever the song is describing, and find a way to express it so that the picture is enticing. Think of the famous Dustin Hoffman–Anne Bancroft seduction scene in *The Graduate*, for example. If he were looking back and singing about it, you could have him say, *I was young, what did she see in me?* Or *In the arms of that woman, I became a man.*

> I wish I had a dollar for every idea I haven't written down, thinking, Oh, I'll remember *that!* Now I even get up in the middle of the night if an idea wakes me up. Yes, I get up and write it down!

PUTTING YOUR THOUGHTS INTO WORDS

Thoughts begin as mental pictures. Mental pictures can be described in words. Visualize what you are describing in your thoughts, and say out loud what you are seeing. Take notes. Find the key elements within the mental pictures, create immediate verbal descriptions of them, and they will become part of your song.

Speak lots of ideas out loud. Let them come out of your mouth as they come to you, rather than giving them deep thought and analysis. Be spontaneous and keep a cassette recorder running so that you don't forget the exact shapes of your ideas a moment after you have blurted them out. I wish I had a dollar for every idea I hadn't written down, thinking, Oh, I'll remember *that!* Now I even get up in the middle of the night if an idea wakes me up. Yes, I get up and write it down!

Visualize

It's no use merely setting words upon a page if you cannot see them spring to life in your mind's eye. The characters and events that populate your songs should appear to you visually. How on earth can you convey a scenario to your listeners if you have no clear visual yourself?

Writing a song is in fact painting a picture with words and music, and it's your job to describe a viable situation and scene. Like a Japanese watercolorist, you might convey this with a concise series of words that equal a few brief brushstrokes. Your images don't have to involve a complicated diatribe; they don't have to break down every conceivable detail behind your story—remember, less is more. But make every word count!

The words "ooh, baby, you make me feel so good" are useless, unless we the listeners see "baby" in our own minds. Furthermore—just to complicate things—to grab me as the listener, "baby" has to be my baby, not your baby. Even while I understand that this is a story being told by you, I need to be able to place myself in the song. Thus, ideally your images have to be specific, yet just universal enough for every listener to enjoy them.

When we listen to songs, our minds process the lyrics and turn them into little films that we see spin by as in a Moviola. Each of us as a listener supplies the faces and features of the characters being sung about. What our individual views have in common is that they are all entirely different from each other, as different as we are. For all of us, the human life and love experience has many commonalities, but we each relate to the stimuli of words and images according to what we've seen and where we've been.

For instance, if we hear the common word "bedroom" in a song, we immediately conjure one up in our minds based on past experiences—perhaps a composite of several bedrooms we've seen—or we may even see our own room. If we hear a less common word, such as "bayou," we will immediately picture the one we've been to or seen in a movie, whichever is the sum total of our experience of bayous. But if we've never actually seen one, our minds instantly conjure up a cinematic visual of whatever we perceive a bayou to be, which could be anything from a running stream in lush green backwoods, to a swamp.

If we hear the description "beautiful woman"—well, that's as subjective as the listener's definition. Some might conjure a tall, thin, leggy beauty with long blonde hair, and others a dark mysterious woman with secrets in her eyes. The point is, when you write *I love you* in a song, the listener will morph into the "I" or the "you"—make no mistake about it.

Though a music video is the director's view of a song's lyrical ideas, when we're driving down the street listening to the same song, we insert ourselves into the picture. The bottom line for you as a songwriter is this: Before anyone else can visualize the images in your story, first you have to do so. Thoughts are framed in your mind as pictures, more often than not. To put your

Visualize (continued)

thoughts into words, simply describe those mental pictures.

Imagine the lyric line, *The last time I kissed you.* What does that call to mind? Quick! What is the first image you get? Is it the face of someone crying and looking miserable at being left "the last time," or is it a passionate-faced, sensual lover? Ask yourself: Why was the person being kissed for the last time? Was it that you (speaking for the singer) had somehow accidentally lost touch and were frantically trying to find this person again? Was it a matter of the person being married to or somehow belonging to someone else? Was "the last time I kissed you" just this morning when you left the house (and you have since realized how much you love this person)? Or was it years and years ago? Were there autumn leaves on the ground beneath this person? Was it in a tousled bed with sheets in a tangle? Was it in the backseat of a '57 Chevy, or the back row of the Ritz when you didn't watch the movie at all? What is the story you want to tell? See it!

Was it on a Greyhound bus, a westbound train, or a silver-winged plane? Was it at Chattanooga Airport saying farewell or when you were let off at the curb of Hard Luck Road? Was it at her mama's front door, or in a creaking back porch swing? Were you saying goodbye forever, or saying hello for the first time? The scenarios, as you see, are as endless as your imagination. What you see in your mind will help you frame the story you write in your lyrics. They will provide you with the attitude, the style, the conflict, and the resolution. Look beyond your own life experiences— embroider and embellish them and have fun. This is not brain surgery—it's songwriting!

If the lyrics sometimes come hard to you, focusing on visual images of your ideas will help you so much, and elevate your songwriting to a far more rewarding experience. Remember these words: *See it,* then *write it!*

Getting Comfortable with Word Flow

Because the way you "phrase" your ideas—meaning the way you connect words together—varies according to genres, chapter 6 will include a discussion of genres of music. Writers in the country, pop, rock, and R&B genres, for instance, all arrive at their lyrical ideas via certain unique ways of phrasing.

Regardless of the genre, allow the images in your mind's eye to become pictures everyone else can see. Let the ideas flow freely without restricting them, and don't edit yourself too much till you have a full first draft on paper. You'll be surprised at how much good stuff is there right from the first attempt!

This approach is called "stream of consciousness" writing. Learning to let go and see what comes out of you spontaneously is a skill well worth developing.

Streaming Ideas

- Let your mind go completely blank.
- *Stop thinking so hard!!!*
- Now, let the first words that come into your mind stream onto the paper before you've had a chance to examine them, worry about them, or discard them without ever writing them down.
- Fine, now keep going. Let your first thoughts be the ones that make it to the paper. Don't try to second-guess yourself; you can always rewrite.
- Keep writing down your ideas until they fill the page.
- Go back and reread them. There will be a germ of something wonderful in there. See it?
- Recognize your own brilliance—it is a sensational feeling. Allow yourself to bask in anything great you have written, whether it's a single phrase or an entire verse.
- Now you can go back and make adjustments, throw out what you don't like, add a little, take a little away. Compare it to a sculptor discovering a face in a block of marble: Your block of marble is your idea, and your process is finding the nuances and subtleties of your story by chipping away at the idea until the crux of the story is revealed to you.
- Don't be afraid to throw out everything but that one terrific germ of an idea, and then build a whole new lyric around it.

Trusting Your Sixth Sense

The feeling that many of us refer to as a "sixth sense" occurs constantly in our lives. For some of us, it is more developed than for others. Discovering that you know things intuitively is one of the great mystical experiences of life. "Sixth sense" can partially be verbalized and is partially hackles rising on the back of the neck. It is the same sense that gives us trepidations about driving through wooded areas

Pay attention to those insights and intuitive "feelings" you get . . . they're probably right!

THE ART OF WRITING LOVE SONGS

or ill-lit neighborhoods at night. It is the same heightened sense that sends up red flares when you first become aware you are getting involved with the wrong love partner. It is the same sense you had in school when you were given an assignment to work on a topic that you knew was out of your comfort zone.

Sometimes you have to write a whole long paragraph to find the sentence that best says what you want to say. Keep the best, discard the rest!

So it goes with the art of writing love songs: Your sixth sense will help attune you to which lines to keep, which ones to toss, and, particularly, which poetic ideas are being expressed as poetry and not lyrics.[1] Great ideas frequently come to you when you least expect them, rather than when you try to "think them up." So, pay attention to those insights and intuitive "feelings" you get . . . they're probably right!

Brevity

Excess words are unnecessary puff. Take away the extra descriptive words, the ideas that weigh down what you are trying to get across, and you will have something clear and real and meaningful. Boil your thoughts down to their marrow; get to the point!

Writing a love song is art imitating life, and life experiences are generally very demarcated, very black and white. When you're creating a love song, keep in mind that communication is always about clarity. When you have a conversation with your neighbors across the garden fence, the minute they start blathering on about something like their TV being on the fritz or their brother-in-law's ulcer acting up, telling you all the gruesome details, your eyes begin to cross and you try to think of a plausible excuse to escape. Even when a friend starts to tell you a problem, you want to know, what's the point here? What happened? What can I help you solve? You usually don't want the exhaustive details; you want to get to the essence of the situation. Well, guess what, the same goes for writing songs.

You probably are in step with most of the world in your inability to get at the core of your life issues and problems and find simple solutions. Well, just as you need to do in life, in songwriting you must learn to break down an issue to its essence, eliminate the fear and worry and anxiety you feel about it, and just

---

[1] See chapter 11 for more on the differences between poetry and lyrics. The topic is also covered in depth in my book *The Art of Writing Great Lyrics,* from Allworth Press.

Rewriting

Rewriting is a big part of writing. So don't worry if the first words and ideas that come out of your mind and onto the page don't feel right to you. It's very easy to scrap them and write something else! Unless you inscribe it in stone, anything you write you can also rewrite.

Once you get further along in this process, you will find that the idea of rewriting will not be as annoying to you as it seems to be at first. It will, however, always be challenging. Rewriting takes twice as long as writing, as it is not a product of inspiration but rather a result of perspiration—dogged effort to try to redo and rethink what came to you so easily the first time. It is the essence of the difference between *Art* and *Craft*: Working hard to get the lesser ideas to sound as good as the best ones is the Craft, whereas writing the original great ideas that flowed out of you is the Art.

look at it for what it is. You cannot usually solve all aspects of anything in one stroke, so don't try to do so in one stroke of the pen either.

Sometimes you have to write a whole long paragraph to find the sentence that best says what you want to say. *Keep the best, discard the rest!* Put your thoughts into lyrics by making simple conversational statements. If you want to ask, "Where are you tonight?" say it. If you want to admit, "I'm afraid of dreaming," say that. Once you know what you want to say, embellish the idea simply: *I'm staring at your photo wond'ring / Where are you tonight?* or *You feel too good to be true / I'm afraid of dreaming.*

SONGS ARE MINI-MOVIES SET TO MUSIC

In order for the listener to "see" the "mini-movie" of your song that you've got in mind, your story must be translated into a format that is compatible with singing. Thus, it will be built in a traditional song structure,[2] will run three to four minutes, and all has to be revealed by the end of it.

The style of song must be chosen—what genre[3] of music it will be; then you must decide how many verses and choruses it will take to tell the story. (Remember not to have more than two verses in a row in any song!) Once you've chosen an ideal tempo (speed) for your song, at that point you're almost ready to begin writing.

[2] Basic song structure is broken down for you in chapter 7, pages 73-77.

[3] "Genre" refers to any unique style of songwriting that serves a particular population of listening audience. "Country," "Pop," "Rock," "Gospel," and "R&B" are examples. Genre is covered in depth in chapter 6.

Give some thought to whether this song's narrative will be set in the distant past, immediate past, present, or wishful future. Think about whether your story is best served as a history, an event of this moment, or a "what could be." If you move around among tenses, read your lyrics carefully when you're done writing, to make sure the tenses have not become confusing.

Linear Stories

The story might be a linear telling of a tale, meaning that it covers the stages of the story in a straight line from beginning to end. A perfect song in that style would be "El Paso," the famous Marty Robbins first-person story of a cowboy in love with a Mexican maiden named Selena. The story begins with the narrator entering the town of El Paso, seeing Selena in a cantina and falling for her deeply, realizing she belongs to another man, risking his life to be with her even briefly, and then after a confrontation, riding off with her jealous lover following in hot pursuit. The song ends literally as he dies from a bullet in his side saying goodbye to Selena. There is no finer example of a linear story song.

Using Flashbacks

Your song might also be a story told in flashback fashion. It might begin with the first verse telling the present state of affairs, the second verse talking about the incident that led up to the present situation, and the final verse might talk about prospects for the future. The chorus would perhaps lament or rejoice in what happened. The bridge, which is the part of the song that interjects an additional morsel of information that can bring an ironic twist—perhaps a "what if" to the song—could say, "I'd give anything for the original incident not to have happened, and to go back to the moment before it changed our lives," or could ask, "Is this truly happening to us?"

Clarity of Ideas

Though I cannot encourage you enough to research and develop the backgrounds of your characters for your own use, lyrics are a short form, and unlike a script or novel, you don't have time within a song to delve deeply into full character backgrounds.

Your listeners will want you to get to the point right away, and draw them into the narrative. Just as you hate a movie that you have to sit through only to ask yourself at the end, "What was that about?" or even worse, "Why did I bother to watch that whole thing?," the same will hold true for your listeners. Make sure you have a definite idea to get across. It doesn't have to be high drama; it can be the simplest of stories. Writing out the idea in narrative form first, I could make it as simple as a lyric called "Brown Suede Shoes," in which I say in the first verse, "I found your shoes underneath my bed this morning, and I wondered why it took so long to have you put them there."

And then in the second verse I might say, "You and I have wanted to be together for so long, it's amazing that the road we took was so winding to get here." And then the chorus would comment, "Brown suede shoes, just an ordinary pair, with laces and scuffs and worn down heels, but they've changed my life." And the next verse might talk about how "the floor underneath the bed was so cluttered with old memories and things I'd lost and thought I'd never find again." And then the chorus would repeat. And then the bridge might interject, "Who'd'a believed I could get such a rush looking at an old pair of shoes, but I hope you'll keep them under my bed forever." And then the chorus would repeat a final time or two as the song would end on that "they've changed my life" idea.

And you can see that the song I've conceptualized is not about any lofty issues; it doesn't solve world hunger, but it gets to the heart of the matter, is real and true and gritty and from a deep wellspring. And, of course, the shoes are symbolic of everything love means—they are a device to express what love is. The depth of love is simply stated in terms of the brown suede shoes.

THE ART OF WRITING LOVE SONGS

I think you can visualize in your mind's eye all of what you just read, as if it were a mini-movie going by. If you can do that with each one of your song lyrics, you will surely become a marvelous storyteller.

UNDERSTANDING THE SINGER'S NEEDS

A singer can only deliver what is written. If you give the singer nothing to say, he or she can sing vocal gymnastics around every note, and an emotional delivery may compensate for the lack of great words, but the song will still say what it says. If the message of a lyric is lacking, it is what it is.

When writing a song about love, put yourself in the position of the singer, for the singer is the one who must deliver the idea and get it across. Give the singer something substantial to say, use open vowel sounds where a note must be held, and don't stick in words that are difficult to sing. Remember, this is not prose you're writing, this is a song. Songs are to be sung, not read.

Give the singers the types of words and expressions that will allow them to show their full range of emotions. Give them ways to show love, hate, passion, anger, and so forth. Understand that they need words to sink their teeth into. The more you give them to express, the more they can express themselves. When you listen to songs on radio and records, get to know how singers think, how they interpret lyric ideas, how they have a laugh or tears in their voice.

I am always reminded of the show-stopping song "And I'm Telling You I'm Not Leaving," the first-act closer from the musical *Dreamgirls*. Jennifer Holliday, a brilliant young singer with a voice that came from the depths of her soul, wailed these words, and they rang so true and deep that the awed audience were riveted to their seats after the curtain came down. Likewise, when Whitney Houston reinterpreted the superb Dolly Parton song "I Will Always Love You," those simple words were so compelling that her delivery of that song was a career pinnacle for Whitney.

As you write, don't simply wonder, "What do *I* want to say here?" Write thinking of the emotions the singer will be able to work up to deliver this song lyric.

CONNECTING WITH THE LISTENER

With songwriting, the object of the exercise is to make the visual that's in your mind fly through space and leap into the mind of your listener.

Do not ever assume that the listener knows what you're talking about, or can read your mind. The listener knows for sure only what you have specifically written. True, the rest can be inferred from the context, but in order for the listener to "get it," you first need clarity in your own mind.

> Communication is not just about knowing *what you want to say,* but also realizing exactly *what your listener will hear.*

The clearer you are about the setting and details of your story, the more likely you are to be a good storyteller. If you are vague, the story comes across in a muddy way, alluding to the idea you wish to get across, but never really selling it.

If, for instance, you are writing about a relationship that started out strong and then somehow slipped through your fingertips, you need to set that up right off the bat in the first verse. You don't necessarily have to make the completely blunt statement, "You're gone, and I'm lonely," however. You can express it in a more interesting fashion. One excellent way to do that is to describe the situation of the moment, such as:

- The radio's playing our favorite song, I wish you were here to listen to it.
- I'm staring at a fading photo of you.
- There's too much room in this double bed.
- I drove past your house again today, hoping I'd get a glimpse of you.
- I can't get used to my empty ring finger.
- I can't be bothered to cook your favorite foods for just me.

The purpose of this first verse is to communicate to the listener exactly the state of mind the singer is in while singing this lyric.

Similarly, if the song is a love song about how well the relationship is going, it doesn't need to simply say, "I love you so much I'm amazed." Rather, the first verse might talk about:

- We haven't left the house for days, there's no place we'd rather be than here.
- Being with you is like a vacation on a tropic isle.
- Pizza tastes like a banquet when I share it with you.
- Every song on the radio becomes "our song" when I'm loving you.
- I don't want to hang out with my old friends, I just want to be with you.

To communicate with an audience, remember that every audience is made up of individuals, so you need to push buttons that they will not only collectively respond to, but that they will also individually resonate with. Speak of familiar things, yet keep your ideas interesting. Even though many boring and repetitive songs do become hits, usually the reasons have to do with an artist's clout or the brilliance of the arrangement or track. It's a concept humorously referred to by the Brits as "dressing up mutton as lamb!"

I know that your heart is filled with a desire to communicate. You want to talk about what you think, feel, and care about. You want to get across how you love, hurt, feel joy, feel sorrow, feel frustration, and feel passion. But if you want to become an expert communicator, here's a big tip: Communication is not just about knowing *what you want to say*, but also realizing exactly *what your listener will hear.*

How Love Songs Are Used to Communicate

From lyrics at their most humorous and tongue-in-cheek ("How Could You Believe Me When I Said I Love You When You Know I've Been a Liar All My Life," recorded by Fred Astaire and Jane Powell, from the film *Royal Wedding*) to their most despairing ("He Stopped Loving Her Today," recorded by George Jones, on the subject of a man burying his wife after a lifelong, loving marriage), love songs have been able to communicate in ways that no other art form possibly could.

Love songs offer immediacy of feelings, and are in fact feelings condensed into immediately accessible expressions. When you listen to great love songs, they always induce reactions in you as a listener. Similarly, when you write them, you will be stimulating your audience to get in touch with their own emotions.

Because a song is such a short form, notice that all a songwriter has to work with is:

* About four lines in each of the verses. That means that to tell the entire story in three verses, a songwriter only has twelve lines, total, to address the beginning, middle, and end of the situation being sung about.
* No more than four lines in a chorus or eight lines in a double chorus. (Remember that the chorus in a pop song uses the same lines each time it's repeated.)
* Between one and four lines max in the bridge, if a bridge is used at all. In order to have impact, the bridge should deliver its message in as few lines as possible.

Thus, you will notice when you are "listening as a lyricist" that the most skillful songs do not waste a word or a syllable.

You want to get your point across in the most straightforward and conversational way possible, make the most interesting use of language, and touch the heart of your listener. These are all skills you would do well to learn from listening to others who have communicated marvelously in their songs. Lyricists such as Lorenz Hart, Noel Coward, Ira Gershwin, Alan and Marilyn Bergman, Bernie Taupin, Gerry Goffin, Smokey Robinson, Sting, Harlan Howard, Fats Domino, Alan Jay Lerner, Hal David, Joni Mitchell, Sammy Cahn, Lamont Dozier, Will Jennings, Hank Williams, Yip Harburg, Chuck Berry, Cole Porter, Bob Dylan, Jerry Leiber, Sylvia Fine, Ray Davies, Willie Nelson, Jimmy Webb, Billy Joel, Rod Temperton, Cynthia Weill, Al Dubin, Dolly Parton, Carl Sigman, and Jim Steinman are among the best examples of songwriters who have valued and set the standard for lyric craft. If you have something important to say when you write, you will want to make sure the listener is on the exact same page as the singer when your song is heard.

It's pretty amazing how you can write a love song about something you've been thinking about, and it seems to address the precise situation of a perfect stranger who hears it. A couple who have had a spat, but feel they do not know how to fix it, can be sitting silently in a restaurant picking at the food on their plates, when a song comes on the PA system that says, *We belong together / I'd die if you ever leave me / We can agree to disagree / But I love you, believe me!* They will recognize that this song says something totally relevant to their own relationship, make eye contact, perhaps reach their hands across the table, and close the communication gap.

This illustrates why songs are a powerful tool for communicating and being properly understood. Unlike a conversation that requires back-and-forth banter and perhaps cleverly skirts the issues, a song allows a person to express a whole idea all in one fell swoop, yet at the same time staying in a conversational style! The listener hears and absorbs it, and sometimes it can solve a heartache or problem just by putting forth a solution nicely packaged in a palatable and easily understandable song form.

CHAPTER 6
♥

The Fundamentals of Songwriting

All you need is love.
—THE BEATLES
(John Lennon-Paul McCartney)

Now that you have been somewhat immersed in painting mental pictures, learning to observe and getting to know love from a songwriter's perspective, let's get to more technical issues to help you properly frame your song ideas.

The rhythm styles we use for writing love songs are pretty basic—slow ballad (slow tempo, usually 4/4 beat), power ballad (slow to medium tempo, most often 4/4 beat), up-tempo (a variety of beats), country waltz (usually slow to mid-tempo, 3/4 time beat), shuffle (based on a triplet beat), and various Latin rhythms.

Ballad and up-tempo styles are popular for writing love songs in every musical genre from jazz to disco, pop to R&B, rock to hip-hop. You could comfortably write in these two styles only and never run out of fresh song ideas.

KNOWING YOUR GENRE

There are more genres of music than you probably realize, and new genres are being invented every day. Check out the racks at your local record store to get a good idea of the numerous genre classifications of popular recording artists. Before you start to write a set of lyrics, consider what musical genre is influencing your words.

When you begin writing love songs, you will be well prepared if you understand the evolution of the contemporary song, where it came from, and what influenced it. When you begin working in any one of these genres and styles, or any blend thereof, it is not only helpful but essential to understand the musical roots of the genre.

Is There Such an Animal as "Specific Music for Love Songs"?

There are only twelve notes! None of them are specifically reserved for love songs! No chords or chord progressions are the "magic ones" to use in love songs. Love songs come in all melodic interpretations and styles, and melody ideas for them are limited only by the creativity and imagination of the songwriter.

The only caveat to this is that whatever melody you write to your verses, whether you are using a chorus-style song or an old-fashioned thirty-two-bar-style song, that melody should always build up to a strong musical "hook" idea. Great melodies make forever-cherished songs.

Whether you're writing adult contemporary, bebop, big band, bluegrass, blues, country, dance, disco, folk, Gospel, heavy metal, hillbilly, house, jazz, new age, pop, punk, rap, reggae, R&B, rock, rockabilly, swing, theatrical, western, or world music, or any of the lesser known musical genres that have fanned out into branches of this towering musical tree, remember that the roots run deep and are all intertwined with their historical forerunners.

If you are an artist and are writing your own love songs, you couldn't do yourself a greater favor than listening to the wonderful works that have preceded you in your genre. Always aspire to be the best at what you do. Don't let any line in your song slip by without it containing the best ideas you know how to write. There is no question that a well-written lyric about love, coupled with a dynamite melody and a great rhythmic groove, creates a song that has longevity way beyond gimmicky songs or gimmicky sounds that smack of passing musical trends.

Love and Song Styles

In a song designed for the youth market, "I love you" is usually a dating expression meaning, "Isn't what we're doing together neat, and wow, isn't the sexuality cool?" The love being sung about is all about heat! When you write a song in this genre, don't make the story too heavy or the expectation from the lyric too ponderous. Love in a light pop song is usually temporary and charming, not about commitment beyond being happy to be dating each other.

Country songs are skewing younger than they used to. Once the staple concept of country love songs was deep intense love relationships between mature people. Patsy Cline's "Crazy" (written by the great Willie Nelson) was about her obsessive love for someone who's gone. It was at once simply said

THE ART OF WRITING LOVE SONGS

and heartbreakingly powerful. Why was it so popular? Because who hasn't had an unrequited love affair? This is a truly universal idea.

Tammy Wynette's "D-I-V-O-R-C-E" was a song about a relationship that had crumbled and the effects it was going to have on the family; her "Stand by Your Man," was a call to all women to love their men in spite of all of their faults, the gist of her message being, "having a good man's love is paramount." Though I concede that not *all* women would agree on that point, it is a traditionally held feeling that a majority of female listeners will subscribe to. I'm not saying write words you don't believe, but I *am* saying understand who your audience is going to be and write something they will respond to.

Glenn Campbell's wonderful Jimmy Webb song "By the Time I Get to Phoenix" is a man singing about how he's finally left a relationship, knowing that he's left the woman behind crying. At its heart it's a song about a relationship that just doesn't work no matter how hard the two of them try. Instead of just saying, "I'm leaving you because I can't do this any more," however, he sings about her in the reminiscent third person, imagining how she's getting through her day, believing that his goodbye note isn't for real.

Today's country love songs are far more geared to the hip young dating or newlywed set. They're more "fluffy" in context, not as gritty or controversial in their ideas. Mainly, they are simple commentaries on a feeling. Faith Hill's award-winning "Breathe" is a great example of a song about a feeling. However, I do believe that there is always room for a great country story song, and country music certainly has veered back and forth from "traditional country" to "pop country" umpteen times.

Hip-hop says "I love you" with a sexual intent. Hip-hop songs, such as Destiny's Child's "Stimulate Me" and "Bootylicious"[1] are brimming with sexual attitude and street language. The singers tell their listeners "how it is." There are no punches pulled; it's very straightforward, often raunchy, and the language is way too raw to try if you are not part of the hip-hop community and comfortable with speaking and using the unique turns of phrase that hip-hop listeners would respond to.

Rock says "I love you" using power images, a lot of passion, attention to details of the relationship, and, quite often, an interesting image around which to base the song. Classic rock love songs such as KISS's ballad "Beth," The Beatles' "Michelle," and the Moody Blues' "Nights in White Satin" are extremely emotional and expressive. Though some rock groups are more about

---

[1] Check out the lyrics online at the lyrics search engine: *http://lyrics.astraweb.com.*

The Art of Writing Rock

In 1955, the charismatic James Dean starred in a film called *Rebel Without a Cause,* and within that title is a warning to rock writers: If you're going to sound like a rebel, have a cause to rebel *against.* A song from the point of view of a *rebel without a cause* is very empty—all flash and no substance.

If you are wanting to write rock 'n' roll love songs, you're looking at a wide-ranging genre, and I suggest you study the rock music that came before you to find the authenticity and depth you need. Flashy, showy, strutting lyrics fall flat if they are without substance to slam the ideas home to your listeners. Your love songs must do more than just convey images, there has to be story content to make them memorable.

Rock music comes in several delicious flavors. Get to know the artists who best represent each genre of rock so that you'll know where your music fits in, and where it got its roots. Check out the various definitions and distinctions between rock's genres at *http://musicmoz.org/Styles/Rock*

---

sex than love, male rockers are not afraid to show vulnerability toward their women in their lyrics. Consider The Rolling Stones' "Angie," which, like "By the Time I Get to Phoenix," is a song about a woman the singer (Mick Jagger) still loves, though he knows they can't make it together. The female listener hears "Angie," but substitutes her own name when she listens to Mick sing the song. Women love rock songs because they always seem to be being sung about *them.* Perhaps that's why rock 'n' roll is here to stay!

Just remember, no matter what the genre of music, a good song is a good song! If the song remains strong when stripped of the arrangement, the tracks, the pulsing rhythms, and can be simply sung a cappella in the shower, then the words and music hold up. If the song requires layers of tracks and rhythms to make it work, what you have is a *production,* not a *song,* and it is unlikely that anyone can learn it, sing it, or commit it to memory. In that event, it will never be what publishers call "a copyright," meaning a song that will continue to be recorded and earn revenue for its publishers and writers for decades to come.

WRITING WHAT YOU KNOW

When you begin to write, choose styles that feel comfortable and the most familiar to you. You'll always get the best results if you write what you know. If the genre you wish to work in is not something you are steeped in and listen to regularly, you might fail to capture the essence of it in your song. If you're working with a composer collaborator who is also out of the loop musically with the style in which you've chosen to write, the song could fall flat.

So, make sure you listen frequently to songs in the style you want to write. In fact, submerge yourself in that style if you can! Make sure that your lyrical vocabulary, the flow of words, and the slant of ideas are compatible with the style you have chosen. If you send your songs out to artists and A&R departments, here's a golden rule of thumb: If the lyrics don't feel right to you, it's a sure bet that everyone who listens to them will be able to spot their weaknesses with no trouble.

Eventually, your musical and lyrical vocabularies will grow, so that whenever people ask, "What is your favorite style of songs to write?" just like me, you'll answer, "Why . . . the one I'm writing right now!"

WORKING WITH A TEMPO

A song's "feel"—which is determined by the tempo and the time signature (4/4, 3/4, 6/8, etc.) you decide upon—is pivotal to how you will "hear" your song idea in your mind, when it is still in its embryonic stages.[2] Clarifying your mental image of your song's "feel" helps turn an idea into something that can be sung. Technically, the tempo is marked by how many beats per minute would tick by on a metronome in each bar; but for now, you don't have to worry about getting that specific. Just having the general idea of the tempo in mind when you start to write your lyric is perfectly fine. Once music is put to your lyric and you or your musicians play it, or once it is arranged for a record, a precise beats-per-minute tempo and time signature will be established to set the song off best. Finding the perfect tempo for a song is like choosing the most becoming frame to set off a painting.

> Let each thought count. Like the pennies in a kid's allowance, the fewer words you have to spend, the more valuable each of them is!

---

[2] For help in learning about how to read a musical time signature, a simple explanation is given at the Dr. Math Web site: *http://mathforum.org/library/drmath/view/58071.html*. A more detailed explanation is at PBS Mathline:
www.pbs.org/teachersource/mathline/concepts/music/activity1.shtm.

Slow Tempo

A slow love song is called a ballad.[3] A ballad generally distinguishes itself by its gentle lyrics, crooning feelings, emotional connection, and heartfelt expression.

- ♥ A ballad is the most popular form for writing love songs, and a ballad can lend itself to all genres of music. A ballad form can be used to sing songs about a variety of emotions—for instance, finding a new love, and the wonder of knowing this feeling is returned. It can be about the pain of remembering a long lost love, or the bittersweet of a love that couldn't last but stays on the mind.
- ♥ A ballad form can be used for a "universal" song about love of the world, and how we can all make it a better place. Often songs of that genre use children's choruses in the arrangement.
- ♥ A ballad can also be used to sing about sensuality and sexuality, soft purring words of love describing heavenly moments together.

Don't ever try to cram too much information or get too wordy in a slow love ballad; you'll be shortchanging yourself, and the effect will be less than you desire. Let each thought *count*. Like the pennies in a kid's allowance, the fewer words you have to spend, the more valuable each of them is! In a ballad—or with any other style of song, for that matter—don't squander words on unnecessary story digressions. A lyric in a love ballad is focused on an idea, and doesn't need a laundry list around it of all the related concepts. Pick which story to tell and tell it. Make sure that your words are so clear that the listener can step into the shoes of the singer and understand the viewpoint of the storyteller. Every vague line that makes listeners have to ask "What did he mean by that?" will hang them up, and as a result they'll miss the lines that follow.

Think "smooth" and "silky" in your choice of words and phrases. Let the story unfold gently and make each thought complete. Use words that "sing" well and allow the vocalist to open up on vowel sounds. Don't use words with sounds that are too guttural or that stop the flow of the song—avoid, for instance, sounds like the "ch" in "Bach," which closes the larynx, because they interrupt the flow of the song.

---

[3] Whether the slow tempo is 4/4, a shuffle, a waltz, or other musical form, the song may still be a ballad.

Traditional slow ballads can sound great with just a piano accompanying the vocal, or with a lovely string arrangement and perhaps a sax solo. The "feel" needs to transport the listener to a private "mental island," a place to get lost in personal reveries.

The slow ballad feel works extremely well in pop and R&B love songs and is dynamite for blues, also. Obviously, anything inherently rhythmic like hip-hop or Latin music needs to be at least mid-tempo, or it will drag too much. In the tradition of classic songs like "Unchained Melody," ballads are a superb way of lyrically expressing a deeply moving moment, either of positive love or of loss of a relationship. The many examples I could give you include recent hit ballads like Vanessa Williams's "Save the Best for Last," Britney Spears's "Don't Let Me Be the Last to Know," and Kelly Clarkson's "A Moment Like This." Doo-wop fans will recognize that almost every doo-wop song ever recorded is in the slow ballad "pocket."

Mid-Tempo

A mid-tempo song is more uplifting than a ballad, as it has a more rhythmic beat that moves along so you can tap your foot to it. It is associated with lyrics that generally are bright and mellow and make the listener smile. Mid-tempo songs lend themselves to all the genres of songwriting and music I've described.

- A mid-tempo love song can be used to sing about getting back together again, or about getting on the road again. Musically, it sounds like it has forward movement, positive messages.
- A mid-tempo song can be used to sing about trying to accomplish something, working your way toward something, the "I can do it" genre of songwriting.
- A mid-tempo song can extol how wonderful a partner is, how beautiful, how great it is to be together. It can say, "We've overcome everything in our way and here we are together making it work."
- A universal mid-tempo concept might be about gearing up for special times ahead, putting forth great efforts, joining together and making a difference in the world, enjoying the beach and the sunshine together, celebrating what a wonderful day today is, and so forth.

The band 'N Sync has had a lot of success with the mid-tempo ballad format in such songs as "It's Gonna Be Me" and "Bye Bye Bye." The "Motown Sound" of the 1970s produced such mid-tempo hits as Marvin Gaye and

Tammi Terrell's "Ain't No Mountain High Enough." A "mid-tempo ballad" sometimes describes the track bed and arrangement more than it does the song. It can be a relatively slow song if sung a cappella, but put to the music of a track, it can have quite a catchy rhythm carrying it along. I reference Toni Braxton's Diane Warren song "Unbreak My Heart," because it is a perfect example of a slow ballad on a mid-tempo track. Some songs, however, do not lend themselves to picking up the tempo. Consider a successful romantic ballad like Babyface's "Every Time I Close My Eyes," the classic Platters ballad "Smoke Gets in Your Eyes," or Elvis's "Are You Lonesome Tonight?" Make an effort to imagine any of those songs playing to a faster tempo, and you'll see how you'd lose the impact of the song. On the other hand, slow down a fast pop song and the results can be brilliant. It is extraordinary how a tempo change can affect the feeling of a song.

I can offer two wonderful examples of dramatic differences in songs due to tempo changes. Neil Sedaka had an up-tempo hit in 1962 with "Breakin' Up Is Hard to Do." In 1975 he re-released it as a slow and passionate ballad. The words and music were exactly the same, but what a difference the new version made! It went from sounding like bubble-gum pop about a high school breakup to a song about an adult, meaningful relationship. Second, the song "Happy Days Are Here Again," originally written to stir people out of their financial doldrums after the great Stock Crash of 1929, was rerecorded in 1963 by the young Barbra Streisand on her first album. In that honeyed sinuous voice that rocketed her to stardom, she sang Peter Matz's brilliant arrangement—a slow, languorous interpretation of these lyrics, and they became a song about trying to get over a love affair. Never underestimate the power of an arrangement!

Conversely, the classic "Mona Lisa" began its life as a ballad in 1949, arranged by Les Baxter and famously sung by Nat "King" Cole. But in 1959, both Conway Twitty and Carl Mann recorded Top-30 rockabilly versions of the song, which were so hot, they blistered the paint right off of your Chevy!

Mid-tempo ballads usually make sense for writing uplifting love songs. They are also frequently employed for first-person songs sung to an errant lover who has "done me wrong." The rhythmic accents are used for emphasis of the ideas. Be sure always to emphasize the proper syllable of a word on the accent note. For instance, in the line, "I can't believe you're leaving," emphasize I *can't*, *believe* you're *leaving*. Those syllables fall on the *downbeats*. There could also be a case made for emphasizing every single syllable of that line if you were using it in a hip-hop mid-tempo ballad. But clearly, songwriters who put the em-*pha*-sis on the wrong syl-*la*-ble are simply not working hard enough at their craft!

What Comes First, the Song or the Track?

It's extremely easy and especially tempting for you as a modern-day songwriter to rely on a track you've created as a basis to start a song idea percolating in your mind. By that I mean starting by laying down drums, adding some bass, getting a "feel" or a "groove" going to help to inspire you. The trouble with this approach is, your song will become limited by the very limitations of that track, especially if there is little or no chord movement on it.

Notwithstanding assignment writing, whereby a track is provided to a songwriter for lyrics to be added, the result of starting with a track is that you are writing a *record*, not a *song*! No matter how tasty the track is, it cannot compensate for the inevitable weaknesses or flaws in the songwriting that arise from making the song have to fit the track, and in fact be secondary to the track instead of the other way around.

I come from the school of songwriting that says crafting the song itself is the most important part of this endeavor. The rest is all the *arrangement* of the song. A great song is about the *melody* and the *lyrics*, how beautifully they combine, how well they tell a story, how cleverly they pay off the song title, and how they touch the listener.

Whether you are a sensational musician or your musicianship as a player is modest, you can freely imagine a great melody in your head. You can develop a soaring chorus melodically, writing words that describe and blend with it seamlessly. A great love song is not simply a melody and lyric that are an afterthought you stick on a finished track. A song has a life of its own which you need to develop first. You can then *enhance* the finished song by building a wonderful musical track around it.[4]

Starting with a lyrical idea and building music around it is still the most satisfying way to start writing a love song. It releases you from all constraints such as the chord patterns in a track. It allows you to envision the song first, leaving the arrangement to be developed later as a setting for the song. Beginning the process with the song itself even helps the arrangement a great deal, as the melody you've written will help to dictate what sort of track will best serve it. It will help you to hone in on the exact tempo, the exact rhythm, the coolest instrumentation to make this song hit its mark.

So even though you may have spent a lot of money on synthesizers and music programs such as ProTools, and these enable you to write heavenly tracks, try to resist the urge to always start with the tracks. Remember that the brilliant songwriters who came before you—you know the ones, the writers you respect and admire for their amazing timeless songs that you could sing in your sleep—started with a guitar or a piano and first wrote . . . *the song!*

---

[4] Many young writers refer to the track as the "music." Truly, the traditional view is that the music consists of the melody notes of the song, and the track is the musical arrangement—the instrumentation that sets off the song.

Up-Tempo

An up-tempo song is driving, has a lot of power in the music and the message. It has the most beats per minute, and the rhythmic patterns underlying it are a surge of adrenaline. It can have a happy message, but it can also be used as a diatribe, a way to say what's wrong and what needs to be gotten off one's chest. Musical solos are usually guitar-driven in up-tempo songs, especially rock.

- An up-tempo lyric might talk about the urgency of a love that is on the fast track or is about to be consummated. Conversely, it might be angry, with a torrent of home truths about the person being sung about or to.
- An up-tempo song will always invite listeners to tap their feet or get up and dance. It for sure won't put people to sleep.
- A *universal* up-tempo song might be Gospel, extolling the love of the Lord; or it might be secular, telling the world it's time it got its act together.
- Rock music, which is very driving in its concepts, uses up-tempo quite effectively, as does heavy metal, dance, disco, modern jazz (though frequently without lyrics), and country music, especially country-rock. Novelty songs also are frequently up-tempo, be they bluegrass style, country, or theatrical. But pure love songs are rarely written in the up-tempo vein outside of rock and country-rock.

The musical "feel" you choose to write your song to will ultimately determine how much attitude you can put into your lyrics. And as I've shown here, style, genre and tempo can also change the meaning, the sympathetic character, the potential audience, and many other essential dynamics of your song.

In time, you will also gain the ability to suss out the story and mood inherent in a piece of music, learning to intuitively hear it "speak" to you, and interpreting that into lyrics. Conversely, as you watch people having relationships and begin internalizing insights about them, lyrical and melodic expressions of your observations will occur to you. Believe me, these intuitive ideas will form the basis of some of your strongest, most satisfying songs.

♥

CHAPTER 7

Structuring and Building Your Song

I love you just the way you are.
—BILLY JOEL
(William M. Joel)

The *shape* of a song is extremely critical to making your story work. Storytelling ideas—the "setups" contained in verses—must lead smoothly into the hook of the song, which is the "payoff" of the idea.

DECIDING ON YOUR SONG STRUCTURE

Most contemporary songs have one of two structure types: "verse-chorus" and "A-A-B-A." Both of these styles, and their sections, are discussed below. Once you've taken the initial step of writing down and fleshing out your storyline, it's time to decide on what song structure will be necessary to tell it fully and convincingly.

If it isn't on the page, it isn't known. Ah, wouldn't it be nice to attach a little note to a record: WHAT THE WRITER MEANS HERE IS . . . !

"Verse-Chorus" Style Songs

♥ **Verse.** The device to tell the actual plot of a song is called the "verse." Verses are the song sections you use to set up the dynamics of the relationship you are writing a love song about. Most songs have three verses (verse-verse-chorus-verse-chorus-bridge-chorus), but some songs have two (verse-chorus-verse-chorus-bridge-chorus) and some have four (verse-verse-chorus-verse-verse-chorus).

♡ What is the *first verse* to be about? The first verse should bring the listener into the situation with some very visual information. It should set up the bottom line of what happened. Like a news story, it needs to attract the interest of the listener, drawing the listener into the story from the first line, by setting up the dynamics of the situation.

♡ Ask yourself, what is the *second verse* about? Probably it will address some history of the situation. Don't expect the listener to understand anything you don't specifically speak of. Remember that your listener knows nothing at all about the background of your story and is not privy to your thought processes. Thus, if it isn't on the page, it isn't known. Ah, wouldn't it be nice to attach a little note to a record: WHAT THE WRITER MEANS HERE IS . . . !

♡ What's the *third* (and usually final) *verse* about? It tells what the resolution of the situation is going to be. You have to tie up your idea here, and you shouldn't leave the story resolution dangling.

If the first verse is followed by a chorus, and the song contains only one additional verse, the second verse should tell the wrap-up information—it should tie up the story with a neat little bow.

A song that leaves the listener wanting to know what happened, or how the singer plans to resolve the particular issue, leaves the listener frustrated. Just think of how you feel after watching a movie that ends without a completed ending. A good case in point is *The Lord of The Rings: The Fellowship of the Ring.* You sat through three hours of exciting images, and then when you got to the end, you found that you were still in the middle, and the quest for enlightenment you embarked upon at the start had not been fulfilled. In much the same way, a song that leaves the listener wanting to know what happened, or how the singer plans to resolve the particular issue, leaves the listener frustrated.

❤ **Build.** In some songs you will want to put a "build" section leading from the verse into the chorus, in the same way that a pilot would use a runway to gain the speed to get his plane off the ground. The "build" device is musical as well as lyrical in function. It is a short (one- to four-line) section you have an option to add as a kind of ramp upwards that lifts toward and sets up the chorus.

❤ **Chorus.** The "hook" of the song is the "chorus." Usually containing the song's title, it is the repeating part that tells the listener why this song is being written, what point the writer is going for. In a murder mystery novel, the "chorus" would be the part where they discover "whodunit" and why. In a movie, it would be the moment of truth. In popular songwriting and record producing, the chorus is repeated after every verse, and repeated several times at the end, sometimes with a "fade out" of chorus repeats. Sometimes you will want to use a "double chorus," which simply consists of two chorus sections, in order to get the symmetry of the song right. (I have included a double chorus in the song example on pages 145-46.)

The rule of thumb with regard to a bridge is, *only use one if there is a compelling thought you feel driven to add to the song.*

- **Bridge.** Frequently there will be additional information to be injected into your love song that has not been covered before in the lyric; this can be achieved using a "bridge." Quite literally, it is a bridge between choruses—one more reason to lead back to and repeat the sentiment contained in the chorus. It often describes a secret feeling or longing, is used to "turn the knife" in the emotional gut of the listener, or may address some other wish or hope that adds meaning to the song. For instance, in a song that says basically, "Our relationship is over, you've left me for someone new," the bridge might offer the sentiment: "I know it's crazy to hope, but maybe one day you'll think of me and realize I am the one you love, and you'll come back to me." The rule of thumb with regard to a bridge is, *only use one if there is a compelling thought you feel driven to add to the song.* A bridge may be included in the most popular traditionally structured song form—that is, verse-verse-chorus-verse-chorus-bridge-chorus, also referred to as "A-A-B-A-B-C-B." A bridge generally comes after the second chorus and prior to a third, final chorus. In A-A-B-A songs, the "B" section is the bridge.

- **Tag.** To end a song rather than "fade" it out on repeating choruses, a "tag" is used. The tag adds a couple of extra lines to the chorus that emphasize the message of the song and tie up the story lyrically. Frequently the tag slows down at the end, and finishes with a final repeat of the "hook" line.

A-A-B-A Songs

In traditional thirty-two-bar songs, the structure is verse-verse-bridge-verse. The title or hook of the song is usually contained in the first or last line of the "A"— generally the same line in each of the A sections. Examples are Gordon Lightfoot's hit, a John Williams–Leslie Bricusse composition, "If You Could Read My Mind, Love" which has the title in the *first* line of each A; and Johnny Mathis's Stephen Sondheim–Jule Styne hit "Small World," which has the title in the *last* line of each A. The title could also be in the second line as an answer to or completion of the thought begun in the first line. Think of songs like Frank Sinatra's "It Was a Very Good Year," wherein the title in the second line of each A section is set up in the first line, by telling the age he was for each experience.

Following is a lyric in this traditional A-A-B-A style, where I used the title in the last line of the A. The song, written for the 1940s-themed detective film *Love Can Be Murder* starring Jaclyn Smith and Corbyn Bernson, is built around the "impossible love" theme. Bernson plays the ghost of a detective, searching for his killers, and Smith is a modern-day detective who helps him. The two characters fall in love, but he must go on to heaven once his quest is complete. The song had to fit two separate moments of the film: in mid-movie under a romantic dance played by a dance band in a 1940s nightclub; and then at the movie's end, when it plays under their tearful embrace as he vanishes from the earthly plane. The title I chose to fit the dramatic needs of both moments ("beginning of affair," and "goodbye") is, "How Do We Say Goodbye?" Because of the way the melody fell, I decided to rhyme the word "say" each time with the prior line. Notice that every line in the song leads directly into the hook idea.

HOW DO WE SAY GOODBYE?

A:
Now that the music is sweet as a sigh
Now that the rhythm is right
Feeling the reasons we ought to stay
How do we say goodbye?

A:
Less conversation, the hour is late
Love's all that's left of the night
And if the moonlight must have its way
How do we say goodbye?

B:
Now that all that I am has been turned all around
By the magic that's in your eyes

> I want to stay on this merry-go-round
> I don't want the sun to rise

A:
> After I've held you so terribly tight
> Feeling the rush of you near
> Why should we dream of another day?
> *How do we say goodbye?*

TAG:
> I know we've gotta go now
> But I just don't know how
> *We say goodbye.*

© Lyrics/Pamela Phillips Oland; Music/Steven Bramson

Though some writers still use it, the most popular songwriting formula changed somewhere between the 1950s and 1960s from the thirty-two-bar A-A-B-A to A-B-A-B-C-B (a verse-chorus song).

The advent of the concept of the chorus was a big change in pop songwriting. In all genres, it added an element of drama to songs, and gave the listener something memorable to walk away with and hum. You will likely find that the widest majority of all songs written today use the verse-chorus style.

DEVELOPING THE SONG

Understanding how to "think like a songwriter" includes understanding how a lyric is built from the title to the end. I want to walk you through my process here, showing you how I write down ideas and second-guess them, then why I choose to rewrite them, and what lyric choices I make and why.

Let's write a song about meeting someone you believe you're fated to meet, from the point of view of a singer. Since our song is about a destined connection, let's use the title "Kismet."[1]

The hook line that immediately comes into my mind as told by a male singer is *It was Kismet!*

I envision this "Kismet" song idea as having a verse-chorus-verse-chorus-bridge-final chorus format (form: A-B-A-B-C-B).

---

[1] "Kismet," meaning "fate," is a word rarely used in today's culture. Robert Wright and George Forrest wrote wonderful songs in 1953 for the musical *Kismet* based on Borodin's music of the Polovtsian Dances.

How Many Lines Should Be in a Song?

Though there are no hard and fast rules that apply to every song, here are some good guidelines:

- Most **verses** are four lines long. Depending on the tempo of the lyric, that comprises four or eight bars.
- **Build** sections should be between one and four lines, no more, and are usually two to four bars long.
- **Choruses** are generally four, six, or eight lines long. Each line is generally one to two bars, depending on the tempo.
- There is often a two- to four-bar **instrumental rest** between the chorus and the next verse.
- A **bridge** should rarely be longer than four lines; it can be as short as one line and even one bar.
- **"Fade" choruses** are repeats of the lyrics of prior choruses, but other lines may be interspersed into final choruses to add more dimension to the lyrics being sung.

When listening to a melody you're going to write a lyric to, count out the beats in each bar several times until you are clear as to where the bars begin and end and, thus, how much room there is for lyrics.

Writing the First Verse

The first pass at a first verse might be very simple, just getting my thoughts on paper:

If my first line were *The first time I laid eyes on you,* the question would arise, "What? What happened the first time I saw you?" Well, how about, *The stars rose in the sky?* Since I have fallen into an A-B-A-B rhyme scheme, meaning first and third lines rhyme and second and fourth lines rhyme, now I need an "oo" rhyme, which could be And *I can't say just how I knew.* Again, knew what? Well, I knew *You wouldn't pass me by.*

> The first time I laid eyes on you
> The stars rose in the sky
> And I can't say just how I knew
> You wouldn't pass me by

Later, when I've finished a first draft and take a second look at the lyric, I might reexamine those simple lines and make them more interesting. For the sake of expediency, let's do that now. The first line, *The first time I laid eyes on you,* is good—it brings the listener into what the song is about, so I will leave it alone. The second line, *The stars rose in the sky,* is okay, but it's been said so many times. What else, what wonderful thing can I say about what happened to me the first time I saw you? It has to be something that sets up a good rhyme for the word "by," which ends the verse. (Notice the rhyme is now set up backwards—rhyming line 2 with the existing line 4, instead of the reverse!)

Here's an interesting idea, with the appropriate "i" rhyme: *I heard the angels sigh . . .* Good! Now, on second reading it seems to me the third line, And *I can't say just how I knew,* feels pretty flat, and I'd like it to be more active. Why not play into the clairvoyance aspect of "Kismet," and—using the "oo" rhyme to rhyme with the setup "you"—say, *In a flash of second sight I knew.* This would lead to the last line of the verse, *You wouldn't pass me by.*

Well, now that I look at that line, it's debatable too: The question is, do I want it to be about knowing *she* wouldn't pass *him* by (which is how the line is now) or that he, the singer, wouldn't pass her by? I like the latter idea better, because I think it's more passionate if we stay in the personal first person tense and change the line to *I wouldn't pass you by . . .*

But then—wait a minute—*wouldn't* or *couldn't?* Which word is more powerful? I think that *couldn't* packs more punch, don't you? It is so much more intense. So with those alterations, now the first verse reads:

> The first time I laid eyes on you
> I heard the angels sigh
> In a flash of second sight I knew
> I couldn't pass you by

The verse is much stronger now, because every word of every line counts. I've considered (a) using more interesting language; (b) making the title more relevant in the verse lines; (c) making the idea more personal to the singer; and (d) ramping up the intensity and the stakes.

Writing the Build

If we were to jump into the chorus now, this scenario would lead from *I couldn't pass you by* to my chorus concept of *It was Kismet.* But there's a more seamless and dramatic way of transitioning from the verse to the chorus: the build. These build lines would be set up lyrically by the verse and provide a jumping-off point for the chorus words: *It was Kismet!*

My first thoughts on the build are four lines as follows:

We could hear the music playing
But I think we danced on air
If it seemed the world was ours alone
And no one else was there . . .
(Leading to: "It was Kismet")

That might work—nothing glaringly awful here. However, as with the first verse, if I were to go back and give these lines a second thought, I might come up with more story and less fluff.

Instead of stating that music was playing, which describes atmosphere but not action, I need first to set up the dynamics of the moment—what the singer experienced right then. What about playing on the "fate" idea by saying he was getting ready to go: *I was almost set for leaving.* Then I'd have to get rid of the line, *But I think we danced on air,* because that lacks the urgency this moment of the story needs.

What other "air" rhyme will not only set up a rhyme for the "there" at the end of the build, but also bring us into the emotions of the moment? How about, *But my feet froze to the stair . . . ?* Okay, next, the line, *If it seemed the world was ours alone,* definitely seems like the right idea—but is there any way to make it more conversational, less poetic? I don't have to worry about rhyming this line with anything. I believe I prefer *'Cause the world had changed to you and me.* That brings us into the singer's sense of urgency. I think I'll keep the final line, *And no one else was there,* as it says exactly what I need it to say. I'll just change the "And" to "Like," which continues the sentence and the thought better.

Now the revised build says:

I was almost set for leaving
But my feet froze to the stair
Cause the world had changed to you and me
Like no one else was there . . .

The build scenario has now completely altered from jumping right into the relationship to being about the feeling of Kismet at first sight. The song would be bursting to explode into the chorus now.

Writing the Chorus

I want to start the chorus with my "hook" idea, *It was Kismet!* And then for the rest of the chorus, I have to explain *why* it was Kismet. Here is my first draft of the chorus:

> It was Kismet . . . we were destined for each other
> It was Kismet . . . what love was meant to be
> And everything we've ever done—led us to that day
> When Kismet . . . brought your love to me

I think the first line, *We were destined for each other*, works very well; it explains what "Kismet" means. I would tweak the second line from *What love was meant to be* to a more interpersonal line about this particular pair, *A love that's meant to be*. Doesn't that small change make a big difference? The third line is exactly the sentiment I want to express: *And everything we've ever done had led us to that day.* Perhaps, though, it could be slightly finessed as *And all we'd ever been and done—led us to that day.* Finally, the last line of the chorus says, *When Kismet brought your love to me.* I have to decide, can that be said better as *When Kismet laid your love on me* or *When Kismet gave your love to me* or *When Kismet turned to you and me.* You can decide which line you like best; I'm going to choose the last idea, as I think it's got the most interesting turn of phrase. Thus, my new chorus reads:

> It was Kismet . . . We were destined for each other
> It was Kismet . . . A love that's meant to be
> And all we'd ever been and done—led us to that day
> When Kismet turned to you and me.

The second line now better describes the meaning of the word "Kismet." The third line follows in that sweet fatalism. The fourth line is arguably more interesting; "turned to" is much more active than "brought your" in the context of a verb describing what "Kismet" did, and so the line is more exciting.

Writing the Second Verse and Build

What is the second (and in this case final) verse and build about? It tells what the resolution of the situation is going to be. You have to tie up your idea here, and you shouldn't leave the story resolution dangling.

Here's how I'll approach the second verse: *The scent, the touch, the sight of you / Still amaze me every day*—which indicates that they're still together. *From a tiny seed, the love we grew / Will never slip away*—which is an attempt at imagery, and states that it's a "forever" love.

> The scent, the touch, the sight of you
> Still amaze me every day
> From a tiny seed, the love we grew
> Will never slip away

If I were going to rewrite any of the second verse, it wouldn't be the first two lines. Those strike me as very strong, for the very reason that they leave the audience knowing where the relationship went. The second set of lines bothers me, though.

The idea of "From a tiny seed, the love we grew" has lost its appeal to me, quickly. In this song, I would much rather have a line that is real, and not dependant on a metaphor. I prefer *And I can't believe the fate that drew / Me close to you this way.*

Does Your Image Have an Antecedent?

Note that "slip away" doesn't refer back to the "seed" image, and any image works better if an antecedent has set it up. For instance, "dreams" slip away; "seeds" don't. So if the prior line had said, "The dreams we dreamed that lovely night," it would naturally set up "Will never slip away."

The build for verse 2 has to ramp up, again, to the chorus. In this case, leading to *It was Kismet . . .* I'll write:

> And I guess we never doubted
> When we met that crazy night
> That the time had come to find our hearts
> You know it when it's right . . .

In giving myself a chance to have another pass at this build, I think I would make some slight lyrical adjustments, even though the story is sound in content. I would make the first line more emphatic: *And we never even doubted* is stronger. I like the image of "that crazy night," so the second line would change to *What we felt that crazy night*. I'm happy with the last line, *You know it when it's right*. But I feel that the third line—the one leading up to the last line—could be more passionate. I like *You can think and plan and hope and dream / (But)[2] you know it when it's right.*

So, the new second verse and build sections would now read:

VERSE: The scent, the touch, the sight of you
                      Still amaze me every day
                      And I can't believe the fate that drew
                      Me close to you this way

BUILD: And we never even doubted
                      What we felt that crazy night
                      You can think and plan and hope and dream
                      (But) You know it when it's right

This verse-and-build is now way more passionate than in the first draft. The energy is high, and most of all, now you can *believe* the singer. So, while the first draft offered a similar sentiment, it lacked fire.

A short *bridge* might be used to interject information that would tell the listener the difference between a "Kismet" relationship and other, less brilliant ones—something like this:

> *So many times I'd hoped and prayed*
> *To feel that wild sensation*
> *When your destiny is in your arms*
> *You need no explanation . . .*

But oh! I can't use "hope" again, as I just used it in the revised build. It's not a good idea to reuse words more than once in the same song (except in chorus repeats). So I have to rethink this. Also, I believe that the last two lines need to be more about the singer's point of view rather than a general commentary on destiny. Since no melody to this song exists yet, I'm not locked

---

[2] The "But" in parentheses is a "pickup" word. Sometimes an extra one-syllable pickup is inserted at the beginning of a line. A lyricist shows the composer that this is a pickup by using parentheses to set it off from the rest of the line. Pickup words are often conjunctions, such as "and," "but," "if," and so forth.

into the beats per measure I originally started working with! I think I'll even slightly change the shape of this lyric bridge.

> *So many times I'd imagined falling*
> *And feeling that wild sensation*
> *My destiny was in my arms—*
> *I needed no explanation*

Now this bridge has become active, personal, and dynamic.

Writing the Ending

As with A-A-B-A songs, there are two ways to end a verse-chorus song. You can "fade out" on the chorus, or use a "tag." A tag ending, should you decide to use one, comes at the very last lines of a song. As described earlier, with a tag the song simply retards (slows down) and, after one or two repeats of the final chorus, ties up the story with a tag line or tag section.

For the "Kismet" idea, here's a lyrical tie-up idea for a tag, if we were to choose to end with one:

CHORUS: **It was Kismet . . . We were destined for each other**
It was Kismet . . . A love that's meant to be
'Cause all we'd ever been and done—led us to that day
When Kismet turned to you and me.

TAG: **And I knew right then I wouldn't want it any other way . . .**
When Kismet turned to you and me.

In a "fade" ending, the song literally fades out with repeats of the chorus getting softer and softer till they become inaudible.

When you outline your story, concern yourself with how it will unfold within the confines of the song's sections, as expressed above.

Here's a final version of our "Kismet" song:

KISMET

VERSE: The first time I laid eyes on you
I heard the angels sigh
In a flash of second sight I knew
I couldn't pass you by

BUILD:	I was almost set for leaving But my feet froze to the stair 'Cause the world had changed to you and me Like no one else was there . . .
CHORUS:	**It was Kismet . . . We were destined for each other** **It was Kismet . . . A love that's meant to be** **'Cause all we'd ever been and done—led us to that day** **When Kismet turned to you and me.**
VERSE:	The scent, the touch, the sight of you Still amaze me every day And I can't believe the fate that drew Me close to you this way
BUILD:	And we never even doubted What we felt that crazy night You can think and plan and hope and dream But you know it when it's right
CHORUS:	**It was Kismet . . . We were destined for each other** **It was Kismet . . . A love that's meant to be** **'Cause all we'd ever been and done—led us to that day** **When Kismet turned to you and me.**
BRIDGE:	*So many times I'd imagined falling* *And feeling that wild sensation* *My destiny was in my arms—* *I needed no explanation*
CHORUS:	**It was Kismet . . . We were destined for each other** **It was Kismet . . . A love that's meant to be** **'Cause all we'd ever been and done—led us to that day** **When Kismet turned to you and me.**
TAG	**And I knew right then I wouldn't want it any other** **way . . .** **When Kismet turned to you and me.**

© Lyrics/Pamela Phillips Oland (Pam-O-Land Music/ASCAP)

CHAPTER 8

Telling a Love Story

What's love got to do with it?
—TINA TURNER
(Terry Britten-Graham Lyle)

I was once asked, "What is the difference between love songs and all other songs?" Perhaps the answer is: *most songs are love songs in their way.*

The Mediterraneans—the French, Italian, and Spanish—are extremely romantic souls when it comes to song-writing. I remember a lyric that Alberto Testa once translated for me from his native Italian, and it was a love song to a car. It spoke to the car as "you" and was about a car that had served its owner well and was now old and falling

> A song is in fact a vessel that contains words conveying some form of love.

apart. It was time to part company with it. And the love with which his lyric told the story of this farewell to an old friend was as touching as any love song you've ever heard between a man and a woman.

What is a school fight song or a national anthem but a love song to an ideal? What is a song about universal peace and harmony but a love song to the highest purpose of mankind? A song about going out drinking with the boys is a love song to the rowdy life. A song about someone who has died is a love song to that person's memory. A love song to one's God is the purest love song one can write.

Folk songs that recount great battles; that recall encounters with goblins or ghosts; that praise a river, a mountain, a house; or that sing of ancient days and ancient myths are all love songs in some form or other. They are paeans to something held up as grand or ideal, beautiful or touchingly sad. A song is in fact a vessel that contains words conveying some form of love.

Even a song about anger, hurt, and betrayal is a song about a love that has been ill-used. The lyrics might be irredeemably depressing, but the best songs are the ones in which there is a turnaround. Truly, most songs are not angry. Even the song "I Will Survive"—the disco version of which Gloria Gaynor rode to No. 1 in 1979, and which has been covered umpteen times, most recently in 2001 by the hit alternative band Cake—is a positive song. Although its lyrics talk about being mistreated, this song is about someone taking her life back into her own hands, rising above the abuse, and becoming strong and powerful as an individual. So, like Whitney Houston's anthem "The Greatest Love of All," it is a love song to *self*.

One thing that is unequivocal is that a song lyric must be grounded in a story. Recently a student showed me a lyric that was about moods and how they altered all day long. It queried, were the moods influenced by the weather? the surroundings? news headlines?

The song never stated any solid premise, nor joined the queries up in order to reach some sort of conclusion with them; it just asked this series of vague questions. Though the writer clearly believed this was a lyric, the truth was that it was obviously a poem.[1] A lyric would say what action the moods caused; or tell us that the moods hearkened back to some other time and place, and then say what that was.

A rule of thumb would be this: Typically, meandering on a thought, without its anchoring to any concrete conversational storyline, and without its relating to a beloved something or someone, is practically always a poem.

Though love songs can of course be about countries and cars and rivers and bars, it's no surprise that mostly they're about *people!*

DECIDING ON A STORY TO TELL

Songwriting is all about storytelling. It is very much dependent upon starting with either (a) a well-thought-out idea in search of a title, or (b) a good title in search of an idea.

I might begin my song by finding a title that fits an entirely visualized concept, such as the scenario that emerged from watching the couple on the train (see page 37). If no such concept is driving me, I must develop one before I begin to write. Since choosing a title sets off a variety of mental pictures,

---

[1] For more on this, see Telling Poetry and Lyrics Apart in chapter 11.

which offer me several options as to what song I could write, I almost always begin with a title.

The first thing I like to do is find a title that I feel I can develop into a good song concept. I might be caught by a clever phrase in a magazine article or something in a descriptive passage of a novel I'm reading. It might be the memorable slogan for an advertising campaign, or a catchy phrase I heard a character say on television last night and jotted down on a notepad. It might be something someone said in passing to me that I couldn't forget, or something that tickled my ears in a conversation overheard or on a radio talk show. And sometimes it might be something I've said myself that has rung a bell in my head—*blam!*

Ideas are precious, and we who write songs must save them and keep them for when we are ready to write. So when you are ready and in "writing mode," you can look through your title ideas and choose the one you feel like working with today.

If you are in a blue mood, don't bother trying to write a "You Make Me Feel Like Dancing." If you are in a happy mood, it could be a stretch to try an "I'm So Lonesome I Could Die."

If you are starting without music to write to, let the title suggest the musical genre and tempo that might best fit your song.

If you are a lyricist only, here's a great tip: Use a famous song as a template. Just write to the melody of something you love, but turn your ears off to the existing title, lyrics, and concept.

You could invest in some karaoke[2] tracks to successful songs and write to those. If you do that knowing that final music is to be added later by a composer, the song will be much stronger, as it will be based on a song that already "works."

Defining the Idea

When you have settled on a title for your love song, you have to decide what that title means. You see, it's all very well to start at the first line that comes into your head and hope that it leads you into a whole song, but the chances are you'll run out of steam if you don't have a direction mapped out in your head. So ask yourself:

- ❤ What style[3] am I writing in?
- ❤ What shape do I want to use (that is, verse-chorus or A-A-B-A style)?
- ❤ What tempo does this belong in?

[2] See The Joys of Karaoke Tracks in chapter 19.

[3] See the discussion of song styles in chapter 6, pages 64-66.

It's a Little Like Baking a Cake

Much like baking a cake from scratch, writing a memorable love song is a step-by-step process. First, you must assemble your thoughts, as you would first assemble ingredients. As with a recipe, if your thoughts are written in a list, you see them clearly and can refer back to them frequently. That way you can always make sure you haven't forgotten something.

When you bake a cake, you have to add ingredients in a prescribed order. You can't just throw all your ingredients into a bowl, turn on the mixer, and hope it tastes good. Similarly, when you write a love song, you have to add ideas in a prescribed order, or it will come out, well, a half-baked idea!

❤ What points are essential to be made in telling this love story in song?
❤ What portion of the love story will I use each verse to tell?
❤ In a chorus-style song, does this title belong in my opening or ending line of the "hook"? Or in an A-A-B-A song, does the title belong in the first or last line of the "A" section?
❤ Who is my audience for this love song, and how can I reach them in the simplest, most direct way?

Since the first thing you want to do is to figure out what you're going to write about, let's walk through the process so you'll get this concept clearly in your head. Say, for example, that today you feel unappreciated in your love relationship. So you want to write a song to say, "Why don't you get it that what we've got is really wonderful? What do I have to do to reach you with that idea? Why are you so unable to make a commitment to what we've got?"

Once you've settled on that as your idea, you consider the "feel." You get it in your mind that you want the song to have a driving feel to it, something impassioned. You first consider a ballad, but you are convinced that it's too intense to be a ballad. But you're sure it's not an up-tempo either. So you decide it's more like a mid-tempo with *drive.*

You come up with an inspired list of possible titles that would feel good for your concept, or you browse through the list of titles you've saved up in your title notebook. The ones that strike your fancy as being about the chosen subject are, "I Could Be the Best Thing in Your Life," "Starting Now," "When Ya Gonna Feel It?" and "Open Up Your Eyes." To your mind, all four deal approximately with the idea you were wanting to write about. Nevertheless, they each approach it slightly differently. So you ask yourself, How would they each lend themselves to best expressing my idea?

"I Could Be the Best Thing in Your Life," you realize, has an immediate problem going for it, in that it ends on the word "life," which is really hard to rhyme. There are only five perfect rhymes for "life," and they are "strife," "knife," "fife," "rife," and "wife." So you are sort of stuck with a chorus that has lines that end with "you'll be plunging in the knife," "why do we have such trouble and strife?," "I want to be your wife," "if you play me the fife," or "the implications are rife." Obviously, none of these lend themselves to a contemporary song lyric that anyone would take seriously—unfortunately, not even the wife line! Nevertheless, keep it in mind that there would be sound-alike rhymes you could use, like "-ite" or "-ice" rhymes, if push came to shove and you decided on this title.

In any event, the concept itself is an impassioned plea to realize that this is a relationship worth saving. "Starting Now" might be a statement that things are going to go better. It could say that *I'm* going to do better, or *you're* going to do better, or that *we* can do better if we just pool our resources *starting now.*

"When Ya Gonna Feel It?" is a question, so that means the song could be filled with questions that lead to the main question. *Doesn't my kiss move you?* It could also list things that exist in the relationship that should point to the lover feeling "it." *You said the sun rose in my eyes.* It could express that enough time has been invested, and it's time to go to the next level. *No more talking; time to move or move over.* Which is sort of the feeling you have right now in your own life, so this title's sounding pretty good to you.

"Open Up Your Eyes" is kind of nice because it starts with an imperative verb, "open," and so it's a challenge to the lover to see what's right in front of him or her. It also says a lot that's between the lines. In saying "Open up your eyes," you are obviously implying that the person's eyes are closed figuratively, not literally, and are not seeing what's really going on, how this relationship has grown to be something important. Hey, wasn't that what you wanted to get across in the first place? Yes, you were fed up because your partner wasn't getting it that it's become something more while he or she wasn't watching and paying attention! It's grown, developed, gone from being a dating situation to a true connection.

So, you make a decision on which title you feel best exemplifies what you want to write a song about, and the one you feel strongest about at this moment is "Open Up Your Eyes!" You're in the mood to get a strong point across, and you want to say it—not *ask* it.

Now you put the other song titles aside, because you may want to consider them again some other time. And who knows, when you look at them next time, they might suggest an entirely different idea to you. For instance, "Starting Now," on the next pass through these titles, might suggest to you a story about moving on with your life without the fool who didn't appreciate you. It would be *Starting now . . . I'm going to get on with my life, without you in it,* which perhaps by then would be an admirable decision!

Getting to the Core of the Idea

So now you've decided to write a driving mid-tempo song called "Open Up Your Eyes!" about a relationship in which the person being sung to is not "getting" how far along the couple has come, and thus still isn't ready to commit to anything deeper. The singer, on the other hand, *does* "get" it, and is totally frustrated at the partner's lack of insight.

Now you want to look at what the story steps and concepts are that might define this song.

- You might want to talk about how great it was at the beginning of the relationship, when it was all so new and sparks flew.
- You might want to mention that the person being sung to talked about "forever" and being together early on, but never wants to make a move toward that goal.
- You might want to say that you (the singer) feel hurt by the lack of appreciation of who you are and what you mean to your partner.
- It may seem reasonable to rant a bit about how only fools let a good thing slip out of their grasp.
- Perhaps you'll want to give an ultimatum of sorts—an "If you don't shape up pretty soon, I'm out of here" type of idea.
- Perhaps you'll want to get across, "Hey, I can't do all the work here, it takes two to make love happen."
- You may want to incorporate a soft and gentle thought about how beautiful it is when you're together, and how good it feels to be close.

A song that is a recitation of every conceivable aspect of a relationship is doomed to failure. You definitely have to pick one central theme and stay with it. If you get sidetracked with too much information, you'll lose your listener.

- ❤ It might be wise to get something in there that says, "You're going to miss me if you let me go, fool!"
- ❤ And you may have a need to simply state, "Look, I've held back my feelings a long time—I have never wanted to force you, I know love takes time—but really, you are pushing my patience to the limits."

The truth is that only you know what ideas you want to get across, and after all, this is *your* song. So you can put whatever spin on it you wish to.

Knowing What to Leave Out

You can see how it helps your focus to consider all the possibilities for what you might say in your song. By doing this, you have a means to consider which ideas to keep and which ones to reject.

A song that is a recitation of every conceivable aspect of a relationship is doomed to failure. You definitely have to pick one central theme and stay with it. If you get sidetracked with too much information, you'll lose your listener.

In the section above, Getting to the Core of the Idea, I've listed a whole potpourri of sentiments to include in a song on this subject. But as I've said, a song is only three minutes long, give or take, so there just isn't room to cram all of these sentiments into it. They must be narrowed down. You have to leave out the ones that are not as potent as the others. Stay with the most powerful thoughts and images that will best tell your story.

Don't lose your way in a love song by trying to address in one song every misdemeanor that has occurred along the way of the relationship (your sister bugs me, you gamble the housekeeping money, you drink with the boys, you cheated in 1982 with a girl from Laramie, you stayed out all night in 1993 after we had a fight, you got a mysterious phone call from a strange woman last year, your ex-girlfriend's still got eyes for you . . . and so on!). Pick one thing. Your song will have the maximum impact if you get your point across clearly and with a powerful thrust. Don't get sidetracked with all the minuscule details, no matter how important you believe they all are!

EXERCISE 6

Making Sense of a Love Relationship

In order to make heads or tails of what's going on in the relationship you want to write about, first you have to get the situation clearly defined on paper. You will be amazed to find the nuances and ins and outs of it that come to light when you start to examine the details.

- **Write It as a Letter.** Sometimes the best way to write an initial concept down is in letter form. You can write it as a letter to yourself, a letter to the person with whom you have issues, or even a letter to God. The letter would be a heartfelt outpouring of feelings, facts, issues, pain, emotions, all of it. Such as:

Dear Chris,

Whatever happened to the loving in our love? Lately we're both so cold to each other, maybe it's kind of tit-for-tat, you hurt me so I hurt you back! When we make love—and that's so rare—you just feel so half-hearted, like it's hardly worth the trouble. It's driving me crazy, I can't get on with my work, I'm short with everyone I talk to, I even yelled at my boss yesterday! I don't wanna even think about divorce, but I . . . keep thinking about it, 'cause I feel so empty in this relation-ship. This is nuts, Chris, when are we gonna get off this merry-go-round and get back to the feelings that got us together in the first place?
  Love,
  Me

Letter writing is a lost art in our world. This type of letter is the kind that you write but likely don't send, as it is too much, too over-whelming, too overloaded with feelings and sentiment, so much so that the reader might not recover from it. But as a template for a love song, it is magical.

- **Write It as an Essay.** Another way to write it down is in an essay:

Once upon a time there was a very happy woman who lived in a sweet little house with a fragrant garden in a small town in Maine. She thought her life was perfect until one day her world came crashing down . . .

You are writing about yourself and your situation just as if it were a fictional story you were telling. Describing it as a narrative is very freeing; you'll be amazed at how many nuances and descriptive phrases you will employ!

- **Write It as a List.** Yet another way to get your thoughts on paper is in a list. It is incredibly helpful to make a list of every slight, every grievance, every stone wall your character has come up against. Write all the points on paper so that you can eyeball them again and again when you're writing your song. You will want to have all of them before you, so that you can decide what messages will drive your lyric. Such a list might be something like this:

- ♡ He was rude to Mother when she stayed at Thanksgiving. Even though he apologized, what was he thinking of, talking like that?
- ♡ He refused to go with me to my high school reunion. I mean, he knows how much it meant to me to not to have to go alone.
- ♡ I am so crushed—the louse actually forgot my birthday!
- ♡ He made me miss an important meeting (important to me, anyway) to pick Jeff up from baseball practice, 'cause he said his own meeting was "more important." I feel like a second-class citizen!
- ♡ I wanted to go for a night out with the girls instead of being with him Friday, and he got mad at me. Can't I have a life?

Understand that these events will not likely be in the lyrics. Whether or not any of these ideas make it into the song, they are the clues through which you discover that the lyric must be about "being there for me and understanding what I need, not always looking at what you need at every moment."

- ❤ **Write It as a News Story.** One other way to write down your character's blues would be in a short comprehensive news story style, which would just give the facts the way you see them. Using the traditional format, wherein the first paragraph tells "who, what, when, where, and how," you would employ the subsequent paragraphs to unravel details of this "news story."

The most important and riveting story details would come first, and as the story continued, the less relevant information would be included. The traditional news writing style is to write so that the length of an article can be cut from the bottom if newspaper space demands it.

The news story idea would be useful in helping you to see afterward what was truly important to the situation, and what other issues are contributing to it, in descending order of importance. For instance, if your news story's opening paragraph said:

JONES MARRIAGE ON THE SKIDS

Josh Jones today announced to his wife Marie that he would be leaving her on Friday, during a surprise visit to the couple's home over the lunch hour. Black coffee was served.

Jones announced that he had been having an affair with one Sharon Johnson, a twenty-three-year-old secretary at his office, for a period exceeding three months. He gave his reasons for the breakup with Marie as "lack of emotions that stir me like they used to."

Marie, claiming she was wholly unprepared for this announcement, broke down into tears and berated Jones as a "no-good-so-and-so."

Jones refused to comment further on the status of the couple's home and its contents, saying only, "You'll hear from my lawyer." Upon his departure, Marie threw a wedding photo at the door.

Details in the final paragraph might say:

As a result, Josh left behind a wedding photo with a cracked glass frame.

Or perhaps,

Marie claims she washed his favorite coffee cup, started to put it back in the cupboard, then on second thought, tossed it in the trash.

Both of these added details of the story would be of dramatic interest to a song. The drama of the announcement is obviously the point of the story. The small details give color to the events—they are evocative of the idea, without actually saying that she was devastated and cried and called him names. Your images don't have to be "right on the money," but can be allusions to or paraphrases of what you want to say. Songwriting is an art that invites you to tell the story in a way that stirs and rouses the listener's imagination.

If we were to actually take that story idea and write a song about Josh and Marie, we would need to start with a title or "hook" idea that best describes the point of view we wish to take on the story. Since the story is being told from the point of view of an observer, in the "third person" tense, a very appropriate title that comes to mind might be, "She's Single Again." Using that title, the chorus could say, for instance:

She's Single Again
She threw his coffee cup away tonight
She watched his car till it was out of sight
And then she went to bed alone

She's Single Again
All she's got left is just a picture in a cracked glass frame
She had to blow out that old flame,
And when the room was dark, she went to sleep on her own
Just like way back when . . . 'Cause She's Single Again

WHOSE LOVE STORY IS THIS?

If you were writing a love song just as a catharsis, without worrying about its "hit" potential, I'd say get it all out on paper, and feel better after you have expressed what you've held bottled up inside. If, however, you are writing a love story that you would like other people to relate and respond to, you need to angle it for the listener, and decide through whose eyes you wish us to see it.

First, Second, or Third Person?

First of all, ask yourself what "person" this song is in.

- Is this in the *first* person—singular "I" or "me," or plural "we" or "us"? Does it express *my* point of view, what *I* want to know, how *I* see you?
- Is this in the *second* person—"you" and "your"? Does it refer to the singer's audience, the person or persons being addressed?
- Is this in the *third* person—singular "she," "he," "it," "him," or "her"; or plural "they" or "them"?

Many people like to write songs that observe others' behavior. They're called "third-person songs" because they do not involve the singer in their narrative in any way. The singer, using the pronouns "he," "she," or "they," is simply narrating a story. A good example of this style is found in narrative folk songs such as "Big John," "Little Boxes," "Puff the Magic Dragon," and "Davey Crockett." They rarely dealt with love, being more concerned with the human condition or heroes.

Third-person pop songs have included "Snoopy and the Red Baron," "Mr. Bojangles," "Three Bells," and "Eleanor Rigby." Again, these songs tell stories, and love may be only incidental to the stories. Country is an effective mode to write from the third person in a love song. Memorable third-person country songs have included George Jones's "She Stopped Loving Him Today," and Tricia Yearwood's "She's in Love with the Boy."

Titles of famous second-person love songs to the person being addressed—the "you"—include "You Go to My Head," "All the Things You Are," and "Close to You."

Which brings us to first-person songs, written from the point of view of the singer, the "I," which are by far the most popular. It is whether you use the "I" with "him/her" or with "you" that I want to talk to you about. Think about it when you're writing a song that says "I don't love *him* any more." How much more powerful would it be to say, "I don't love *you* any more"?

Always make sure in every song you write that the person you use—first, second, or third—is appropriate to this particular song, in order to best get your ideas across.

Bringing the Characters to Life

The next consideration is to define in your mind the person singing and the person being sung to.

- What do they look like—physical characteristics, clothing, age?
- What is the relationship between the singer and the person being sung to?
- What baggage or issues have been brought to the relationship by each of the parties?
- Are you designing both of the characters to be likeable?
- Are they in a high-context (familiar) or low-context (casual) relationship?
- What is the situation these people are facing?
  - Who wants what from whom, and how are they planning on getting it?
  - What are the very specific particulars of the issue, problem, or conflict (or state of euphoria!) being addressed in this song?
  - Whose point of view is being presented in this song—the singer or the person being sung to or about? (In a duet, both sides must be fully fleshed out.)
  - Who is responsible for what has happened in this relationship?
  - Which of them is willing to acknowledge responsibility for what has happened?
  - What are the stakes involved in resolving the situation? What could be gained or lost?

THE ART OF WRITING LOVE SONGS

♡ Is there a way to resolve it? What are the possible solutions? Who would have to give up what to have it?

♡ Who has the most to lose or win here?

♡ Is there any way for anyone to win here?

♡ Who is the listener rooting for in this relationship—one or the other of the parties, or both of them?

♡ How long will their problems take to fix?

♡ What obstacles do these people have to get over to get where they want to be?

♡ What do they need to do, say, or bring to each other, in order to make progress?

♡ Do either of them have any special skills or gifts to bring to the other person?

♡ If everything is perfect between them, what is the conflict they both have come through and survived to get to the perfect place? Is it something they have individually dealt with, like a prior broken heart? Or is it some crisis they've weathered together that has brought them close?

Clarity on these ideas makes writing your love song so much more focused and your rewrites so much easier.

Point of View

In a love song, after you've developed your story and fleshed out your characters, you must decide from whose point of view you are writing. If the song is written about a woman whose husband is cheating with another woman, for instance, consider:

❤ The point of view of the wife—feeling hurt, bewildered, abandoned, angry.

❤ The point of view of the husband—feeling that his wife doesn't pay enough attention to him and has caused him to stray.

❤ The point of view of the girlfriend—for whom the man has become the center of her universe, and who wants him right or wrong.

❤ The point of view of an observer, such as the man's best friend—saying, perhaps, "I've been where you are, this is going to ruin your life, don't do it!"

All of these are ways to tell the same story, but the point of view on the story differs radically according to who is telling it.

Telling a Sad Story

Any sad story works better when you tell it with a twist. Though it's more than okay to be straightforward on your first pass at an idea, letting all your emotions out onto the paper, the question is, should you simply stop at your original idea, or should you grow it, let it become something more than a description of emotions?

Let's set up a sad and melancholy situation and discover how a country song might evolve from it. The premise:

- ❤ I am a man who has been unfaithful and the truth has been found out.
- ❤ I feel great remorse, realizing how unimportant the dalliance was and how much I've hurt my loved one.
- ❤ I want to go about regaining the relationship I've ruined.

Since the country way of telling that story is generally to admit "I was a fool to break your heart," you'd write a list of titles that mean just that—for instance, "What Was I Thinkin' Of?" "I Love You More Than Ever," and "Take Me Back, I'm Sorry!" Perhaps you'd end up with the title, "Ain't That the Truth of It." So you'd plot it out based on that title.

- ❤ Your first verse might set up the following idea: "How beautiful you look to me as I watch you go about your day, making our home a place to be proud of, taking care of the kids, blowing a stray wisp of hair off your face as you pull a loaf of fresh-baked bread from the oven."
- ❤ In your second verse he might talk about how "I never intended to get involved with the other woman, it was just that I was working late, and somehow the two of us went for a harmless drink, that turned into something more complicated."
- ❤ Your chorus could then lead him to say something like:

> **Ain't that the truth of it**
> **I had everything and I almost let it go**
> **Ain't that the truth of it**
> **I was weak and I said yes instead of no**

And my lies are out in the open now
And they make you want to quit
But I love you more than ever
Ain't that the truth of it.

❤ Your third verse might go into a possible cause for the dalliance, such as, *I got myself too caught up in work, and I put some distance between us.* Or it might say, *You have every right not to take me back, but we have so much history together, so many reasons to make it right, please let me show you I'm sincere.*

❤ After the repeated chorus, the song intuitively feels like it needs a bridge. Perhaps he'd say in this bridge, *I can see the tears welling in your eyes, and I know you're on the edge between staying and leaving, but I hope and pray you'll stay,* which leads back into the hook, *Ain't that the truth of it.*

The line *Ain't that the truth of it* thereby modifies the story that's now come out about the dalliance. It also turns around to be about how much he loves the woman he's cheated on. Thus, as is popular in country songwriting, the line serves two different points being made in the song.

Universal Love Stories

Tell your lyrical story in such a way that it relates to as many people as possible. There are many general aspects of love that are common to most of us, such as:

❤ Love at first sight
❤ Waiting for someone to call
❤ Wondering whether the other person feels what I feel
❤ Disillusionment, feeling that the one you love is not who you believed him or her to be
❤ The perfect night together
❤ Asking to be treated the way you feel you deserve

Ask yourself when you start to write your love song: Why must *this* idea be immortalized in a song?

Such universal concepts should be eagerly received by any listener's ears, as we can all easily put ourselves in the shoes of the singer.

One of the most extraordinary feelings of release you will get from writing love songs is to pour out your story on paper, to hone it into the shape of a song, and then to realize that the situation you are describing is one common to millions of others. You are not alone; you are alive and well and part of the living breathing family of humanity.

If it is a personal story that you are describing, it helps to know that your tale is as old as time. Your own version of it, your own personal drama that has inspired it, will give you a unique perspective and point of view on the subject that will make your song unique. Actually writing this song and getting it out of your mind, heart, and locked vault of emotions will be extremely cathartic, as you will feel an oddly comforting sense of community with the rest of the men and women in the world who share common experiences.

WHY IS *THIS* STORY IMPORTANT TO TELL?

What urgent angle do you have in mind to approach your storytelling for this song? Why *must* this story be told? What particular issue makes *this* a compelling idea?

The standard for whether an idea is important enough to become a song derives directly from musicals. The superb songwriter Steven Schwartz tells us that in writing for musical theater, the characters talk and talk until they absolutely cannot say what they have to in conversation any more and are compelled to sing. The song becomes an urgent release of an idea that simply has to be sung. We should take note of that standard in deciding whether to go forward with *any* song.

So, ask yourself when you start to write your love song: Why must *this* idea be immortalized in a song?

WHO IS YOUR POTENTIAL AUDIENCE?

It doesn't hurt to reiterate that when you say "I," you are speaking for the listener. That is a fundamental tenet of my teachings as a songwriter. You're not writing introspectively, as with poetry, for your own narcissism; you're

Listen! Listen! Listen! Know your genre. If you're not comfortable with the style you're writing in, the savvy listeners will know it.

not even writing for the singer, though the singer must relate strongly to the content of your lyrics. Songwriting is ultimately an art form directed toward those who listen. While a love story might be about yourself, when it is written as a lyric it must transcend simply your own importance in your mind and must commend itself to the listener's ears.

When you write a love song, your potential audience is unlimited, depending upon the genre in which you write. For instance, if your songwriting slants toward R&B, your urban audience wants language with lots of attitude! Compared to pop, R&B must sound conversationally more "street," more earthy, more "in your face." Musically it needs a "groove"[4] that is rhythmic and bass heavy. You'll want to appeal to an urban audience, and they are very picky about whether a song is rhythmically "in the pocket."[5]

On the other hand, if your song slants toward country music, then you are writing for people who enjoy a more rural mindset. Even though people all over the world love country music, the roots of country are very Southern, folksy, and authentic. If you are taking country songwriting seriously, I highly recommend that you take the occasional writing trip to Nashville, to collaborate with true, passionate country songwriters. Country—more than just a turn of phrase, a way of inverting chords—is a way of looking at the world that needs to be understood from a very organic place in order to do it right.

Every time you write a new song, think about who might potentially be the audience for what you're writing, and slant your ideas so that your listeners will relate to them.

Listen! Listen! Listen! Know your genre. If you're not comfortable with the style you're writing in, the savvy listeners will know it. If it's a type of music you don't really want to listen to, why bother to write in that style anyway? Find something you like better and feel more at home with. The writing will come to you much easier if you're working in a familiar genre. And after all, this whole undertaking is all about pleasing yourself by getting your ideas out of your heart and onto the page. Why detract from that in any way?

Whether you are a music industry pro, or whether you write love songs as a hobby, your first and best critic and fan of your work must be yourself. If you feel that what you've written is lacking in some way, you are probably right. Intuition is your most wonderful gift, and you would always do well to trust it.

---

[4] Although "groove" used in this sense hasn't yet made its way into the dictionary, it is the common term for a rhythm track that underlies a record, particularly in R&B and hip-hop.

[5] Musicians speak of a rhythm track that feels exactly right for the song as being "in the pocket."

Making Your Story Interesting

Obviously, love songs have told and retold the idea of love in a million ways. And yet, songwriters continue to find new and innovative things to be said about love, and fresh settings in which to frame them.

The truth is, there is only one story in the world, and that is all contained in the concept of "the quest." In the world of books and movies, a mystery is a quest to find "whodunit," a romance is a quest for love, a thriller is a quest for righteousness or for the solution to a problem that would end the world. In television, each episode is a quest for the characters to have a better understanding of themselves and each other, as well as a quest to solve various problems that crop up in the subplots. In love-song writing, each song is a quest for love to work out.

They say that in the movies there are only seven plots: girl meets boy, girl loses boy, girl finds boy again, the lovers' triangle, the seeking of revenge, a mission to find something, and an adventure or caper. But you see, it should not limit a writer to know there are only a few plots; it is the original thing you do with those plots that makes them unique.

Think about just the word "love" alone and how many thousands of things there are to say about it, how many angles there are on it. Compare two wedding movies, such as *Monsoon Wedding* (about an Indian woman wrestling with the prospect of an arranged marriage and suddenly discovering love) and *My Big Fat Greek Wedding* (about an ugly duckling who ends up as the swan and wins the guy of her dreams). Both movies are about how a romance develops and a family prepares for a wedding, but they couldn't be more different!

Don't be afraid to dare to be different. Reach out and be innovative; find analogies and descriptive ideas that might be out of the ordinary. Let yourself go; have fun with this. Don't stifle your creativity by worrying that this song you're writing isn't like what you've heard on the radio lately. Those songs *have already been written!* Originality is its own reward, so don't limit yourself before you even get the words on paper. Write *what's next!* When you come up with something inventive, you will be so proud of yourself, I guarantee that you'll smile from ear to ear!

What do I mean by innovative? Well, here's a great example. In the song, "Where Have All the Cowboys Gone?" the singer, Paula Cole, laments the lack of romance in relationships and looks back to the heroic, romantic figures John Wayne portrayed in his larger-than-life film roles. But at its heart, it's not a song about movie cowboys. The gist of the song is the simple unspoken question, Why isn't love as exciting as I thought it would be? The answer, given as this innovative yearning for the dashing fantasy movie cowboy, is brilliant. It is a metaphor that resonates within the hearts of most women, who have lamented that their men are (*sigh*) all too human.

Out-of-the-Ordinary Images

Language can be plain or image-laden, depending on the type of song you're writing. Country songs in particular are strongest when the writers go for clever turnarounds and quirky concepts. A popular gimmick in writing country songs is to link diametrically opposed words. To illustrate that for you, I wrote the following lyric, "Married to the Single Life." Obviously it trades on the ideas of "married" and "single," which are absolutely contrasting concepts. The hero singing the song is very conflicted about his point of view, and his ambivalence makes him endearing to the listener. In this song, if he came across as a "hard nose," he wouldn't be as likeable. The fact that he has a vulnerable core makes us want him to renounce his singlehood. I left the last line of the bridge as a "cliff-hanger," to let the listener decide!

MARRIED TO THE SINGLE LIFE

VERSE:
I feel her watch me from across the room
Through her dreamy blue eyes
She's waiting for a sign . . . that says I've changed my mind
But I've said my goodbyes

She's not the first to try to turn a moment into love
She gave so much, and what she got from me was not enough . . .
But . . .

CHORUS:
I'm married to the single life
Though a girl like her makes me wanna think twice
She's an angel who's deserves a little paradise
But I'm married to the single life

VERSE:
I've got it easy, I can come and go
Where I want, when I choose
My rooms can be a mess, that works for me I guess
Though she's hard to refuse

She's giving me some feelings I don't wanna understand
The fire in my kiss tonight was never what I planned
'Cause

CHORUS: **I'm married to the single life**
            Though a girl like her makes me wanna think twice
            She's an angel who's deserves a little paradise
            But I'm married to the single life

BRIDGE: *I hear her whisper Baby, I can fix a broken heart*
            And for a moment, my feet are frozen to the floor
            Don't wanna want her, I'd leave now if I were smart
            I need to make a move . . . Lord, I'm so near to the door . . .
            And

CHORUS: **I'm married to the single life**
            Though a girl like her makes me wanna think twice
            She's an angel who's deserves a little paradise
            But I'm married to the single life

Metaphors, Similes, and Other Figures of Speech

Particularly in romantic love songs, songwriters can use a variety of "figures of speech" to heighten the impact of their writing. Using a "figure of speech," we can say something that is not literally true or valid, so as to create an interesting effect. Here are some common figures of speech worth knowing about.

Metaphors say that something *is* something else, such as "your hair is spun gold," or "your eyes are two stars," or "the moon is a ball of gouda cheese." *Similes* say that something is *like* something else, such as "your hair is *like* spun gold," "your eyes shine *like* two stars," or "the moon is yellow *as* a ball of gouda cheese." A *conceit* is a fanciful farfetched metaphor such as "our love is an electrical storm," or "the world is a rotten egg."

Onomatopoeia is using a word that is evocative of a sound, such as "babbling brook," or "jingling bell." *Euphemisms*, as we discussed in chapter 4, are socially acceptable words substituted in place of something others find offensive. When you use "heck" instead of "hell" or "jerk" instead of "asshole," you are using polite euphemisms. One of my favorites is the creative "preowned vehicle" for a "used car." We've all seen movies where the villain uses "liquidate" instead of "murder"—now *that's* a euphemism. A *personification* is a figure of speech in which inanimate objects or abstract ideas are endowed with human qualities. If you said "death *walks* among us," or "the sky *is crying*," or "the walls *have ears*," you would be using personification. A *paradox* is a statement that appears self-contradictory but actually has a basis in truth, such as "your words are clear as *mud*," or "he's crazy like a *fox*."

Metaphors, Similes, and Other Figures
of Speech (continued)

An *antitheses* describes a diametrical or direct opposite, such as "right" is the antithesis of "wrong," "North Pole" is the antitheses of "South Pole," "frantic" is the antithesis of "mellow." An *antonym* is a word whose meaning is opposite to another word: "sad," for example, is a word that's an antonym to "happy"; "bright" is a word that's an antonym to "dim."

A *synonym* is a word that means the same or a similar thing as another. For instance, "near" and "close" are synonyms. A *metonymy* refers to a figure of speech in which a quality or attribute of something may be substituted for the thing that it suggests. "Jingle in my jeans" means "money in my pocket." We might say "I sweated over that test" to mean "I *worked hard* at that test." Another example is "The *White House* says . . . ," which is frequent news-speak for "The *President* says . . ." Further, if you were to want to describe a class or group of things by using a singular word, such as "put bread on the table" for "put food on the table," or the reverse of that, such as "the *law* will be here soon" (the class or group) to mean "*a policeman* will be here soon," (the individual), then you are using a *synecdoche*.

A *hyperbole* is a figure of speech in which exaggeration is deliberately used for emphasis rather than *deception*, such as "The man is a *giant* among men," or "I feel *ten feet tall*." The complete opposite of hyperbole is *litotes*—a form of writing that emphasizes by understating. Litotes utilize a negative to express a positive! An example would be using the negative "not many" when you mean the positive "a few." If you asked a woman, "Are you ready to go?" and she answered, "Not quite ready," that would be the litotes of "almost ready."

A *homily* is a little burst of homespun wisdom such as "speak of the devil and he appears," or "more haste, less speed," and is usually intended to inspire. Many homilies are *clichés*, which are trite, stereotyped, or overused expressions such as "sadder but wiser," "it ain't over till the fat lady sings," or "too many cooks spoil the broth."

Knowledge is power (a metaphor!), and if you want to be a more powerful writer, knowing about these various figures of speech and how they work will encourage you to use them and will help you to understand which of them you need to devise to make your song-writing more interesting, entertaining, and original.

Sometimes a concept that would be used for something other than a song, such as a title for a movie or a novel, will lend itself to an out-of-the ordinary lyric idea. Take for instance the title "Killer on the Loose." What images does that bring up? Well, probably the 6:00 news, a murderer on a spree. But does it have to be that? Can it work in a love song? Why not? If you're inventive, you can write figures of speech that make language work for you in the most creative of ways. So here's an example of what I did with that unlikely phrase as a title, to make it work in a love song as a lyrical metaphor for a fiery, sexy woman:

KILLER ON THE LOOSE

VERSE:

Her lips were a streak of scarlet
That slashed across her face
Her eyes were as hard as diamonds
As they quickly swept the place
She was cool as Kilimanjaro
As she caught me in my lie
She was silent swift and deadly
Like a spider with a fly

(Now) I've seen her in throes of passion
And drowned in pools of tears
Her face when she's spending money
And with wake-up makeup smears
And I liked but never could love her
Living like an automat
Thought I knew her like her mirror
But I never saw her like *that*

CHORUS:

She was a killer on the loose
Her weapons were her eyes
Her daggers crossed the room
And she cut me down to size
And that mousy little girl
I was seein' on the sly
Looked like a pretty poor excuse
Beside my killer on the loose

VERSE:

She covered the space between us
Aroused and breathing fire
The room stood in frozen motion
As it came down to the wire
I was dazzled and enchanted
By her Jekyll and her Hyde

In a flash I knew I loved her
As I followed her outside

(repeat chorus)

BRIDGE: *All that woman power, it was somethin' to see*
            I could not believe it was all about me . . .

(repeat chorus)

© Lyrics/Pamela Phillips Oland (Pam-O-Land Music/ASCAP)

The only way to make your work stand out from that of the rest of the hoi polloi is to discover and nurture your originality. Reach, stretch, invent, and be adventurous with language. Saying what's been said and said and said before is inevitably going to be boring to the listener. Why not infuse your work with your own spirit, your own viewpoint, your own fresh turn of phrase? Let the listener be stimulated and treated to something to think about.

CHAPTER 9
♥

Developing the Dynamic of a Love Relationship

Love is just a four-letter word.
—JOAN BAEZ
(Bob Dylan)

The dynamics of a couple trying to be in love are enormously and endlessly fascinating. Almost all love relationships have certain qualities in common, in that both parties are quite capable of provoking happiness, tears, euphoria, and disillusionment.

One of my main reasons for writing this book is to equip us as songwriters with tools and devices for examining loving and not-so-loving situations that arise in relationships, in order to better portray them convincingly in our songs. If you only have a vague understanding of the aspect of love your characters are experiencing, it follows that your lyrics will be vague also.

Becoming able to observe, soak up, and sort through the layers of interpersonal dynamics will give you the kind of insights on how love works that should make your love songs a whole lot more insightful.

WHO WANTS WHAT FROM WHOM?

To write a believable love song, we must get inside the mindsets of each of our characters: we must understand the issues and the stakes from the point of view of the singer as well as the one being sung to or about. What do they want? And how can they get their views and needs across? We'll know more about that once we understand their hopes, fears, worries, wonders, infatuations, dreams, and desires.

At the start of a new love relationship, each of us is vulnerable. We put our feelings out there tentatively, like a turtle poking his head out from under his shell, to gauge what reactions they will engender. And then we unfailingly encumber the new relationship with certain expectations. We nurture those expectations and try to wheedle and work them into being fulfilled. We ignore that inner voice that says, "As soon as you have expectations, you're setting yourself up for a fall, because then everything that new love does is subject to inspection, and you'll be judging whether he or she lives up to those expectations." And of course nobody ever does live up to them, any more than we live up to their expectations of us! If you write about someone who has expectations, follow the idea in your mind to the heartbreak and disillusionment that is the logical consequence.

THE BACK-STORY

For every action there is a reaction; that's a basic tenet at play in any relationship. Words get responses. Deeds get responses. Even looks get responses. People's responses are very much based upon a number of determining factors, and those factors become the "back-story" for each character. The back-story could definitely influence what your characters say and do, and might explain the attitude behind their actions. Thus it is important to create (even if only mentally) a pretty thorough back-story for each character, albeit a brief one. Trying to write an authentic song about characters and situations you cannot see clearly in your mind's eye is like trying to write a cookbook without first having tasted your recipes yourself.

Whenever you are describing an interaction, ask yourself some questions about the back-story of the characters you write about, including:

- ❤ How has their day gone?
- ❤ How are their finances sitting?
- ❤ Do they feel vulnerable for any reason? What could that reason be?
- ❤ Do they feel attractive at the moment you're writing about them?
- ❤ What is their history with their partner?
- ❤ Do they suffer pangs of secret guilt?
- ❤ Are their reactions colored by suspicions of any kind?
- ❤ Is there anger simmering under the surface of their relationship?
- ❤ Are they pushing themselves right out of the relationship?
- ❤ What exactly do they want out of the relationship?
- ❤ What would they do to have that relationship?

These are only some of the factors that are going to have an influence on how your characters handle a given situation. Ask yourself, What do I need to know about these people and their situation to make it the most interesting and accessible lyric I can write? Having a back-story in your mind will give your song lyrics much more depth. Let's examine these considerations in more detail.

GETTING INSIDE A CHARACTER'S MIND

In the interest of keeping your song characters separate from yourself—and making them jump out as flesh-and-blood characters, not merely superficial, paper-thin characters—make sure you know them inside out. Whatever they think, feel, or eat for breakfast; whatever they wear, however they talk, and whether they're cool or hot temperaments; whether they're sultry, shadowy, sly, or mournful—they must be real for you!

How Has the Day Gone?

Essential to having a good angle on your story is this: consider each character's total life, not just his or her life at the moment of confrontation with love with which your song concerns itself. You will want to know:

- Have the characters worked all day, and are they perhaps feeling tired, overwrought, overworked—in a word, "toasted"? *If so, their reactions to an overture of love might be to push it away, emotionally and literally. In this state, people may close their ears to romantic entreaties and not even respond to initial hugs or kisses.*

- Have they been so caught up in the mundane quality of a workday that they are not yet emotionally prepared to switch gears and be right there in the "love" mentality? *If so, they need to be cajoled without pressure, gently caressed, brought back to the world of love in which they actually prefer to be.*

- Have they had a wonderful experience today, such as a bonus, a raise, praise, an award, something that makes them feel on top of their game? *If so, they need to be listened to, congratulated, caressed, made much of. Their needs have to come first, even if there is sadness and there are problems that must be brought to their attention as the evening goes on.*

- Have they believably spent most of the day preparing for this loving tryst? *If so, their efforts must be appreciated, remarked on, complimented. They must be made to feel wonderful, special, and worthwhile as a reward for their investment of effort.*

- Have they been dealing with a sick relative or a broken-down car or something else that's drained them? *If so, they just need some peace and quiet, some gentle words, perhaps a neck rub, a hot bath, maybe a seduction, something to bring them back into sorts.*

Just as in an actual relationship of your own, the participants in your song story should be real and vulnerable to you. Writing a love song is very much art imitating life. You don't have to personally participate in a situation to make it feel truthful in a song; you must simply imagine in some detail the realities of the two people involved in it.

In a song lyric, we aren't going to go into all of these minute details to get to the point—obviously, we would never get to the crux of the song if we did! But as songwriters, we are building for ourselves a back-story for each of the two primary characters (the person singing and the one being sung to or about) who star in this song. Without a description of where they are emotionally at the point of singing this song, without understanding where they each are coming from and why, how can we make their reactions described in the song believable?

How Are the Character's Finances?

Money is the cause of so much that challenges people's otherwise happy relationships. In a song, money problems need to be handled in one of two ways:

- With a "we can make it" attitude, so that the person being sung to can be uplifted, be told, "It doesn't matter, as long as we're together we'll get by." This concept is exemplified by all sorts of songs, from the self-explanatory Dorothy Fields–Jimmy McHugh song "I Can't Give You Anything but Love," to Sonny and Cher's "I've Got You, Babe," a duet that talks about a young couple who have nothing except each other.
- Or there's the, "I'm not interested in you unless you've got money" angle. To paraphrase some of the best examples of this attitude: There's a wonderful Peggy Lee classic song with Benny Goodman from the Swing era, for instance, called "Why Don't You Do Right?" In this song, the singer admonishes her no-good boyfriend to *Get lost—and get her some money*, while he's at it. (You can play the song online if you go to *www.tuxjunction.net/whydontyoudorightBG.htm.*) In Bob Dylan's song "You're No Good," he accuses a woman of *taking all his money* and *giving it to some other man.* Abba's "Money, Money, Money" basically

says *It's a world ruled by the rich, and I'd be on easy street if I found a man with money.* In Bobby Darin's "If I Were a Carpenter" he asks the question, *If I were a simple man with nothing, would you marry me all the same?* In the Gordy-Bradford song "Money," made famous by Barrett Strong and later a hit for The Beatles, the singer offers, *Love is good, but money is better!*

When you use the "short on cash" concept in a song, first figure out whether the people involved in this situation see it as a problem or as just a hiccup they can overcome. When you are putting words in their mouths, make these words seem authentic. Consider the attitudes of both the teller of the tale and the person being sung to. Is the news about "no money" being received with understanding or with hostility? As with any other subject, the feedback the singer is getting in words, gestures, or looks will influence the way he or she delivers the message.

Do the Characters Feel Vulnerable?

Vulnerability is a quality that's endearing to some and taken advantage of by others. If you are investing the singer with vulnerability, it can take the form of:

- The singer loving a great deal and not knowing truly whether the love is returned, thus being at a disadvantage.
- The singer being ready to dive headlong into an affair, knowing this could break his or her heart in the process, but doing it anyway.
- Conversely, knowing that the person being sung to is vulnerable and could be hurt by you (the singer).
- Belonging to another while acting on feelings for, or coveting, someone else.

In a song, vulnerability can be a gorgeous attribute. In the classic Fox-Gimbel song "Killing Me Softly," for instance, Roberta Flack (and, in a later hip-hop version, Lauryn Hill), is the vulnerable woman watching the singer "sing her life" and "strum her pain," thinking he is singing the song to her personally. In the brilliant Boyd-Murray song "Guess Who I Saw Today," the vulnerable singer is talking to her husband about a wonderful day she has spent shopping, and how she stopped in to have lunch at a small café, and then asks, *guess who I saw today?* She sweetly describes a couple who were having the most wonderful time, and were so in love . . . and then in the last line, after saying for the final time, "Guess who I saw," she says she saw *him.* 'Nuff said. The first time you hear that song, it'll break your heart.

Do the Characters Feel Attractive When You're Writing about Them?

A love song has everything to do with how a person feels at the given moment it's being sung. If your characters are having a bad hair day, or just feel unattractive for some reason, they are not going to respond by immediately understanding why they are loved. That will have to be coaxed along. Conversely, if they feel beautiful (as did Maria in Steven Sondheim's *West Side Story* lyric "I Feel Pretty"), they will feel as if they can dance over the moon, and they will have tremendous confidence. Certainly, confidence is evident in certain songs, and tentativeness is evident in others. Make sure that the song you are writing reflects the exact amount of confidence or diffidence that you wish the character singing to express.

Are You Consulting a Dictionary?

Question: You just read "confidence or diffidence." Did you fully understand what "diffidence" meant? Did you bother to take a moment and look that word up to really understand its nuances? I haven't curbed my language in this book to simplify all expressions in anticipation that some of my readers won't know the precise definitions of certain words I've used. Why not? Because I expect you to have a dictionary right by your side as you read and write! Not just for going through this book, but getting into the habit of referring to it, whatever you may read.

Furthermore, I expect you to begin growing your vocabulary. A writer writes, and a writer needs to understand the scope of the language he or she is writing in.

Starting now, I want your dictionary to be your constant companion, always there to consult as to nuances of meaning. Nothing is worse than using words incorrectly, so I hope you'll immediately break yourself of the habit of assuming you know what words mean, and start looking them up, either in a hardcover dictionary, or online at *www.dictionary.com*.

What Is the Characters' History?

Before you write a love song, think about how far along these two people are in terms of their love relationship:

❤ Do they share a history of a long and close relationship, whether continuous or off-and-on? *If so, they have what is known as a "high-context" relationship, meaning there is a high level of intimacy and knowledge of each other that sets the style for a personal shorthand in the way they talk to each other.*[1]

- 💜 Have they been together long enough to be comfortable in each other's company and say things that are frank and basic? *If so, they can converse in simple language and be honest with one another.*

- 💜 Are these people who have feuded and fought, recently come out on the other side of their troubles, and fallen back in love? *If so, they are going to avoid saying things that will offend and hurt; they are going to choose their words carefully, and they are going to want to keep the peace with compliments and warm words.*

- 💜 Has this couple only met a short time ago, and thus are they still under the glow of first impressions—a glow unmarred by the heavy hand of reality slapping them around? *If so, they'll probably talk about this love being the greatest thing since sliced bread that either of them has ever come across, about wanting this feeling to last forever. For their love is, in fact, a feeling at this point, not backed up by anything more substantial.*

Are the Characters Suffering Any Guilt?

A member of a couple who is thinking of leaving, is having fantasies about someone else, or is having a secret love affair is going to approach a love song differently from someone who is totally committed to the person being sung to and feels sure of that love. That person's song will contain a slyness, perhaps even an overstatement of how loved the person being sung to is.

There might be an element of "I don't want to talk right now" in the song, or an "I used to love the way you touched me" element. The song is likely being sung to the person "in absentia," meaning that it is clear to the listener that the singer is singing to someone who isn't there, but is imagining a conversation. For instance, let me write a stream-of-consciousness song on this topic, using "I Don't Wanna Say Goodbye Tonight" as a title, to bring you into the writing process of growing a song idea.

In the opening verse, I want to set up the idea that it's really difficult and touchy to get into this conversation because we've shared a meaningful, intimate, high-context relationship.

---

[1] The opposite of a "high-context" relationship is a "low-context" relationship, in which the parties do not have an established intimacy or foreknowledge of each other. Whereas in a "high-context" relationship, she might say to him, "Massage my knot!" and he would know exactly where to put his hands; in a "low-context" relationship, she would have to explain in detail to him, "I need you to massage the knot right below my left shoulder blade."

VERSE 1:   I've been trying to figure out a way to show you
                  That your touch doesn't make me tremble like before
                  And it may be a sign of just how well I know you
                  That I can't bring myself to knock on your door.

The "build" is saying something conciliatory, really throwing a bone of kindness; giving and taking away at the same time:

                  And I realize you've given me so much for so long
                  So it's painful to discover what was right feels so wrong . . .

The chorus really is saying, "I just can't deal with going through with this, knowing how it's going to hurt you, because deep down, I respect the fact that you have loved me":

CHORUS: **I don't wanna say goodbye tonight**
                  I don't wanna make you cry tonight
                  I'm putting off for one more day the words I know
                     I'll have to say
                  And I know I'll weaken when you come in sight
                  So I don't wanna say goodbye tonight

The second verse is being pretty down to earth by confessing that "I really can't go on with you, and I need to say this plainly so you get it":

VERSE 2:   I don't know exactly when it happened
                  All I know is something changed my heart
                  'Cause there once was a time when your love really mattered
                  But the days only drive us further apart

The second "build" is admitting my own failings, in effect saying I'm going to feel like two cents when you finally look at me as I say this:

                  And I really just can't bring myself to look in your eyes
                  'Cause I know that if I see you, you'll see right through my lies

CHORUS: **I don't wanna say goodbye tonight**
                  I don't wanna make you cry tonight
                  I'm putting off for one more day the words I know
                     I'll have to say
                  And I know I'll weaken when you come in sight
                  So I don't wanna say goodbye tonight

THE ART OF WRITING LOVE SONGS

The "bridge" in this song is being used to admit that my reasons for not seeing you are a fraud; what's really happening here is that I've fallen in love with someone else, but I feel like a heel doing this to you:

BRIDGE: *So I'm making excuses, why we can't meet*
            And I'm dreaming of somebody new
            'Cause I'm gonna be ending what once was so sweet
            But my inner voice will tell me when I look at you . . .

CHORUS: **I don't wanna say goodbye tonight**
            I don't wanna make you cry tonight
            I'm putting off for one more day the words I know
            **   I'll have to say**
            And I know I'll weaken when you come in sight
            So I don't wanna say goodbye tonight
            No, I don't wanna say goodbye tonight.

© Lyrics/ Pamela Phillips Oland (Pam-O-Land Music/ASCAP)

The unique point of view of this lyric is that it is quite clear that the relationship is over, yet the singer admits the connection is hard to break.

Are the Characters Suffering Any Suspicions?
Suspicion is a wonderful topic for love songs, and if there is a hint of suspicion in a lover's heart, then that will creep into the lyric. The four pertinent questions are:

1. Is he or she seeing someone else? The underlying message is, *"He or she is keeping it a secret, but I can feel something's different, feel it in my gut, and I've got to find out if I'm just imagining this or something's really going on."*
2. Is he or she making love with someone else? The underlying message is, *"He or she is making a fool out of me, is treating me bad, doing me wrong, and what if everyone knows but me? Am I a laughingstock?"*
3. Is he or she dreaming of someone else? The underlying message is, *"I've got to win him or her back from the fantasy of loving someone else. I've gotta work on this relationship, do whatever I can to make him or her see how deep my love is and how right we are for each other."*
4. Is he or she going to leave me for someone else? The underlying message is, *"I notice that he or she is going out early and staying out late, and I notice*

that there's something lacking in his or her kisses. I'm losing ground, and I'm in the dark, wondering what's going on with our relationship."

In a lyric I wrote on this subject, I built the story by setting up that premise of suspicion in the first line, this way:

SIGNS OF YOUR LEAVING

VERSE:
You wrap your arms around me, hold me tight
But the magic is gone from your touch
The smile on your lips is not in your eyes
I can't help thinkin' it's such a shame
But you tell me that it's still the same

You've started leaving early, coming in late
I pace the floor till you get home
You've changed your hair, y'got new things to wear
My heart is totally blowin' away
'Cause I guess I see what you just can't say

CHORUS:
Are these the signs of your leaving?
Are they signs of the times?
Can't help believing when you're saying "I love you"
I'm hearing "goodbye."

VERSE:
Now something's come between us, what do I do?
I'm wracking my brains for a clue
Your words are still warm, but your kisses are cold
Guess your world is no longer you and me
Well I'm not so blind that I can't see

CHORUS:
Are these the signs of your leaving?
Are they signs of the times?
Can't help believing when you're saying "I love you"
I'm hearing "goodbye."

BRIDGE:
Clinging on to the memories
Though they're fading from my sight
How do I look away this time
When you've been out all night?

THE ART OF WRITING LOVE SONGS

CHORUS   **Are these the signs of your leaving?**
            Are they signs of the times?
            Can't help believing when you're saying, "I love you"
            When you're saying "I Love You"
            I'm hearing "goodbye."

© Lyrics/Pamela Phillips Oland; Music/Dana Walden

Is There Anger in This Relationship?

The question here is whether a simmering undercurrent of resentment or anger will influence a person to react indifferently to his or her partner and to whatever the partner says or does—good or bad. Clearly, when a person feels anger toward a lover, for whatever reason—be it unfaithfulness at one end of the spectrum, or forgetting a birthday at the other—response behavior is somewhat irrational and emotionally driven. So whether the lover in the doghouse makes an apologetic gesture and brings flowers or says a few nasty words and slams the door, the angry partner may have the identical reaction.

The only thing that will be accepted by the aggrieved party is full acknowledgment of the indiscretion, sin, exhibition of bad taste, poor memory, or other blunder. And a full apology is a wonderful use for a love song—it's the ideal way for saying "I'm sorry!" No flowers, candy, or even hugs can compare with words of contrition and apology rendered in a heart-felt song lyric.

Are They Pushing Themselves Right out of the Relationship?

There is a point beyond which the words of an argument fail to hit their mark, a saturation point that, once reached, shuts the door to reconnection completely. So, if your song is about a fight, a battle, a clash, you must know how far you can take your point without ending the relationship you're writing about! In my own wedding ceremony, we said, "There is no point we could have or make that is worth invalidating our beautiful relationship."

In a song, as in life, you have to know when you've gone too far, when you've made your point and it's time to zip it. You have to recognize—in order to put these words in the mouth of the person singing—when you've pushed so hard that you've pushed him or her right out of the picture. Since there is only so much that anyone will sit there and take, only so much that any lover will put up with, your song will fall flat unless you know when to put a lid on it and become conciliatory instead.

What Do the Characters Want from the Relationship?

When you are playing chess, you know what each piece on the board is capable of doing, how to use it for offense and defense, how to guard it, how the pieces interact. Love is in many ways like a chess game. The pieces are words, actions, touches, needs, and wants.

Every person gets and stays involved in a relationship for different reasons. Some are in it for the security of knowing they belong to someone; others are in it for the financially attractive package it presents. Some people enter a relationship because they are addicted to the sex, and others because they are in awe of the other person's intellect.

If any of these sounds familiar, it's because you're experiencing it right now with someone you're with or are trying to be with. You are with that person for a reason or collection of reasons. Some reasons you may be fully aware of, such as that your partner makes you truly happy; some you have suppressed as vulgar and unmentionable, such as your partner's ability to save you from the dreaded dating scene; and some that you have never analyzed, such as your partner's dominance. Love is not only (as Perry Como once told us) a many-splendored thing; it's a multifaceted concept that we each interpret in our own way.

In order to make the characters in your song fully fleshed-out, real people, you have to have some insight into their reasoning for being together, what they each are gaining or hoping to gain from hooking up.

What Would the Characters Do for the Relationship?

People have said in countless lyrics, "I would do anything to be with you." Consider the band Garbage's song "#1 Crush" with lyrics that vow to *die, kill, or steal* for the lover. The issue in play here is urgency: *What's at stake?*

In chapter 13, and elsewhere in this book, you will find references to the stakes people have in making relationships work. In the context of back-story dynamics, I want you to always be aware, as you write, of what those stakes are both for the singer and the loved one. Ask yourself, what sacrifices are they each willing to make to have this love? Once you know that, I think you're ready to begin writing.

While you are analyzing your characters' back stories, an amazing thing will happen: fragments of images and lines will start popping into your head that will start to set your song in motion. In deciding, for instance, that *he used to like the fact that she was blonde, now he is involved with a brunette on the side . . .* you might think of the line *your golden hair was once the sunshine to my eyes.* In this way, song lines must flow naturally from larger and more general thoughts on your subject matter.

♥

Making Choices and Fine-Tuning

Cry me a river!
—JULIE LONDON
(Arthur Hamilton)

It's not enough to simply come close to the right idea in a lyric line; it's how you tweak that idea, how you fine tune it, that determines whether it is merely an adequately grammatical series of words, or a line that paints a mental picture for the listener. The art of it is all in the choices you make.

For example, if the artist is singing about wanting to leave, and you are using the phrase "walking shoes," you have to decide the most effective way to use the phrase. Ask yourself which tense is this to be in, past, present, or future:

- ♥ "I've put on my walking shoes" (past).
- ♥ "I had to put on my walking shoes" (past emphatic).
- ♥ "I'm putting on my walking shoes" (present).
- ♥ "These walkin' shoes are taking me outta here" (present emphatic).
- ♥ "I'm gonna put on my walking shoes" (future).
- ♥ "Gonna get me a brand new pair of walking shoes" (future emphatic).
- ♥ "I mean to put on my walking shoes" (future decisive).

Or perhaps you'll want to describe the shoes beyond just the fact that they're walking shoes, or use the shoes to tell more story:

- ♥ "I'm gonna put on these old walkin' shoes" ("old" or "ol'" means he's used them before).
- ♥ "Put some more miles on these ol' walkin' shoes" (same idea, different twist).
- ♥ "I'm gonna lace up these ol' walkin' shoes" (emphatic).

- "I'm dustin' off these tired ol' walkin' shoes" (sad).
- "I'm buyin' me some Goodbye Baby walkin' shoes" (personalizing the shoes).

In another example, using the phrase "treat me right," make up your mind whether you're saying:

- "If you don't treat me the way I want to be treated, then get out of here" (ultimatum).
- "I want so much to be with you, baby, won't you treat me right and appreciate me better?" (entreaty).
- "Don't go running around with others behind my back" (warning).
- "Touch me that way you do" (sexual connotation).

There are many spins on oft-used phrases; make sure you know exactly what interpretation you are going for. If you're going for a "double entendre,"[1] such as the Bellamy Brothers' amusing "If I Said You Had a Beautiful Body, Would You Hold It Against Me?" make sure you've made both interpretations work. Then let the listeners put their own spin on your words, if they choose to.

USING WORDS BRILLIANTLY

Lyricists have larger vocabularies than much of the rest of the world, as they are required to constantly refine their knowledge of the English language and all its nuances.

You must always search for the precise word to fit your meaning. That means you must always have handy the first two of your three basic tools: your *thesaurus* and your *dictionary*. First, you might look in the thesaurus for a word that interests you, then you have to look in the dictionary to decipher the word's exact meaning. Being precise about meanings is essential in song-writing. You don't have room for lengthy explanations, so every word counts. It's pretty much *What's on the page / Sets the stage.*

The dictionary will tell you if you're using the word correctly and also will show you how to spell it. Misspelled words on lyric sheets are not only unprofessional but tacky, so you must pride yourself in spelling correctly.

---

[1] An expression derived from French, referring to a word or phrase having a "double" meaning (particularly where the second meaning is risqué).

The thesaurus might turn up a word that you had a preconceived idea about, but then when you look it up in the dictionary, you might find that what you'd thought it meant all these years was completely wrong. You might even find that you've been sticking your foot right down your gullet every time you have said this word in the past.

Don't settle for obvious images when you can come up with unique ones. Is a girl "pretty," "lovely," "charming," "disarming," "adorable," or "sexy"? Is her mouth "luscious," "ripe," "glossy," "soft," or "kissable"? You get the point. Stretch out; be as inventive as you can. Describe love in interesting words. The language is at your fingertips, literally, to create wonderful word pictures in songs.

How to Use a Rhyming Dictionary

As a songwriter, your third basic tool, after your thesaurus and your dictionary, is a *rhyming dictionary*. Not all songs require perfect rhymes, though all songs in theatrical productions do. Many of your love songs will work quite well with "sound-alike" rhymes," which are simply a way to repeat a sound in a successive line, so that the ear of the listener will register completion of the sound. In popular music of all genres, there is a tendency away from perfect rhymes because so many of them would create trite images. If you rhyme "love" with "glove" or "turtle dove," you might get a paperweight thrown at you by a music publisher. But you can certainly rhyme it with "enough," which is a word you can reasonably find some meaning to lead up to.

If you can find perfect rhymes, you are doing the most professional job you can as a songwriter, for nothing works as well in the ear of the listener as a perfect rhyme. The thing is, you may have to rewrite your whole idea to get those perfect rhymes. It's a lot of work, and it's not as spontaneous. In time, you might become an expert in finding perfect rhymes, but until then, don't worry about thoughtfully using the sound-alikes.

"PSYCHO-BABBLE" DOESN'T BELONG IN SONGS!

There is a tendency among beginning songwriters, especially of the Baby Boom and "X" Generations, to write too much "psycho-babble" into their lyrics. We have perhaps been overexposed to pop-psychology-driven "psych-speak," such as the internal language of the self-empowerment group "EST," and other purveyors of such self-defining doctrines. The myriad of motivational psychologists, thought police, and enlightenment gurus have so bombarded us with their psych-speak, we have fallen into believing that they offer us the only way to communicate within relationships! We become so convinced that we need to scrutinize and dissect the psychology of our communications that we frequently *fail* to communicate! I might point out here that it has been said, "If you have to talk about whether you're having a relationship, you're not having one."

Successful love songs do not contain psychology-based self-help preaching and posturing. The truth is, love songs are not about psychology terms and concepts. They are about feelings and emotions—people getting in touch with each other through loving, trusting, and physical closeness. If your character wants to ask, "Are you psyching me out?" perhaps write instead, *Are you looking for the real me?*

THE GIST OF EVERY SONG IS CONTAINED IN THE FIRST LINE

The beginning line you write on the page as the opening of your song will most likely be a line that sums up an entire story for you. How can that be? It's all in the power of the written word. Words are so extremely powerful, they contain images far beyond what you realize could be in a short sentence. For instance, let's examine some first lines.

If your first line says, *You said you were going, but I can't believe you're gone*, it opens up a whole world of song storytelling to you about the pain of losing, the denial of a relationship being over, the length of time that was invested in the relationship, the anger, the hurt, the disbelief, and the indignation that someone would actually leave. All of those things are contained in the first line you have set to paper.

If your first line says, *Jimmy doesn't know why she loves him,* you immediately recognize that you're writing a song being told in the third person. It's a narrative idea. Most likely, it's a country song that conjures up a story of a man who is loved by someone and feels perhaps unworthy of her loving him, while at the same time feeling thrilled that she does. The first line also sets up a potential story of how he works hard all day struggling to make a living, isn't madly successful, looks at how beautiful and gentle and wonderful she is, and lives to please her. And somehow it suggests how happy they both are together.

If your first line says, *Please don't hurt me like I've been hurt before*, this is about to be a song of vulnerability. Inherent in the first line is the idea that this is a new relationship, that the singer is open and willing to have a relationship, that there have been others who have been bad news, that it is very hard to let go and trust this new lover, and that the singer desperately wants this to work out right. Yes, all of that is contained in and implied by that first line.

If your first line says, *Only in your dreams, Jack,* it's a pretty good guess that this woman singing it is very feisty and is calling Jack's bluff, that he hasn't got a snowball's chance in Hades of winning her, that she is totally in control of the situation, and that she is about to terminate the relationship and give him his walking papers. Also, it's a good bet his name isn't Jack!

It is amazing how much the inspiration flows once you commit that first line to paper. I could go on and on with examples. Just as an exercise, why not examine some of your favorite love songs, and think about how the first line the songwriters came up with set up an idea that was then the blueprint for a story's development.

Remember, *you* are in charge of this process; it is your own wonderful flow of ideas that will serve you best. Once you trust yourself enough, you will let your ideas flow from your pen. Before you know it, you will have given life to a new idea, a concept that didn't exist before in quite this way, an expression of a loving idea that could only have been written by you at this particular moment in time.

HAVING AN OPEN MIND TO REWRITING

I wrote a song with the master arranger and my great friend Jeremy Lubbock, called "Before I Stop Loving You." Jeremy had gotten very excited about the title, and I wrote a quick draft of an idea, which read like this:

BEFORE I STOP LOVING YOU (Initial Draft)

The world stood still
And I forgot to breathe
Suspended in time and lost in space
When I first saw your face

And not until
You and I were all alone
And I held you near my heart—Did the rush within me start
Of the greatest love I've ever known

CHORUS: **Before I stop loving you**
Fire will forget how to burn
The earth will forget how to turn
The sky will stop being blue

Babies will forget how to cry
Lovers will forget how to sigh
The end of time will rush on by
Before I stop loving you

I found no words
No clever things to say
How do you describe a miracle
I just loved you, that's all

It was absurd
Like I'd known you all my life
Like your soul was part of mine, like the heavenliest sign
And it came to me like lightning strikes . . .

CHORUS: **Before I stop loving you**
Fire will forget how to burn
The earth will forget how to turn
The sky will stop being blue

Babies will forget how to cry
Lovers will forget how to sigh
The end of time will rush on by
The day I . . .
Forget you

BRIDGE: *My arms are to hold you*
My eyes are to see you
My breath is to breathe you in
My cheek is to brush your skin

I'll live for your laughter, forever after
Now that I know what love is . . . I promise you this . . .

CHORUS: **Before I stop loving you**
Fire will forget how to burn
The earth will forget how to turn
The sky will stop being blue

Babies will forget how to cry
Lovers will forget how to sigh

The end of time will rush on by
Before I stop loving you

© Lyrics/Pamela Phillips Oland

Jeremy lived with this lyric for a few weeks, and then one day he came to me with a melody that had been inspired by the title alone. He asked me if I would write a new lyric with the same title, which had no references to fire, the earth, or the sky, or other "natural phenomena." He had a different twist on the idea in mind—he wanted the lyric to reflect "original personal images" instead. He said, "I don't even know if they exist, but try to find them."

Furthermore, his melody was sparser than the one I had envisioned with my first draft. A lyric written first, before there is music, isn't bound by any word limits. In this case, my collaborator felt that "less is more."

After writing songs all these years and knowing all that I know, I am always a willing participant in the process to find the best lyric for an idea, and so I was not afraid to be jogged by my collaborator into exploring for a new direction. The process reminded me that each love song we write requires pulling out all the stops in order to do the very best job we are capable of, and that collaboration is the art of working together to write something stronger than either participant can do alone.

This time I had a different sort of inspiration, and made the lyric a simple one that not only was about love of a partner, but also obliquely, a woman's song of love to her new child. This completely different lyric is what came up for me on the rewrite:

BEFORE I STOP LOVING YOU (Rewrite)

When it came to you
The difference was stunning
Nothing that I knew
Had the truth of this loving

My heart is so amazed
I can't find the right words
I love you till it hurts

CHORUS: **Before I stop loving you**
I'll breathe my final breath

There's nothing I won't go through
With no regret

And before I stop loving you
I know you'll break my heart, and yet—
I would tear my soul in two
Before I stop loving you

Something in your face
Has changed me forever
In a thousand ways
Just to love you is heaven

If loving is a song
With music unending
You've taught me how to sing

CHORUS: **Before I stop loving you**
I'll breathe my final breath
There's nothing I won't go through
With no regret

And before I stop loving you
I know you'll break my heart, and yet—
I would tear my soul in two
Before I stop loving you

BRIDGE: *Words will fly*
Oh yes, you'll make me cry
And if I doubt you
I'll be torn up about you
Then sunlight—will fill your eyes
And make me realize
I'd die without you . . .

CHORUS: **Before I stop loving you**
I'll breathe my final breath
There's nothing I won't go through
With no regret

And before I stop loving you
I know you'll break my heart, and yet—
I would tear my soul in two
Before I stop loving you

© Lyrics/Pamela Phillips Oland; Music/Jeremy Lubbock

Though my original lyric didn't click for Jeremy, I actually still like it and have given it a new title, "The Day I Forget You," which is a completely different hook idea. To see how it works, go back and read the first draft of "Before I Stop Loving You," above, inserting the new hook, "The Day I Forget You." Amazingly, the verses and choruses can stay intact and still fit this new idea, the chorus of which reads as follows:

CHORUS: The day I forget you
Fire will forget how to burn
The earth will forget how to turn
The sky will stop being blue

Babies will forget how to cry
Lovers will forget how to sigh
The end of time will rush on by
The day I . . .
Forget you

© Lyrics/Pamela Phillips Oland (Pam-O-Land Music/ASCAP)

I hope that one day the right situation will come along for a composer to add music to this lyric.

Nothing you write is ever wasted—you never know what will come of it. If it isn't right for one project, it might be right for another. Never throw anything away, keep all your unused lyrics in a file, store all your melody ideas on CD or tape, and label them accurately. If a lyric doesn't meet one composer's sensibilities, it might enchant someone else's.

The First Draft

A first draft is simply a way to get all the initial ideas on a subject out of the mind and onto the paper. While not all your songs will begin with a nagging personal anguish that's been tugging you down, if you have one, here's your chance to identify it. A first draft is the perfect device for peeling away the issues to reveal the deeper kernel of the idea.

The process of writing the first draft of your cathartic personal song lyric comprises the following elements:

- Identifying the specific buried heartache that needs to be expressed.
- Coming up with a list of various title ideas that might best describe the situation.
- Choosing among them the title that best expresses the precise idea you feel compelled to write about.
- Making an outline of the song development that would tell the story implied by your title.
- Writing your first draft of lyrics putting to use all the tools and devices described in this book.

After you're through sighing, as you release the jangled feelings that have been so long repressed and blocked, you may want to just leave your first draft alone for a while, perhaps overnight or even for a day or two. The point of that is to distance yourself from the emotions you've connected to and exposed with this release.

A first draft based on your own story is never objective, it is always emotional. Sometimes the emotional ideas are brilliant, even magical, and you will want to keep them in your final lyric as you know you can never top them; yet sometimes they are a fabulous catharsis for you personally, but "over the top" or too maudlin for a commercially viable song.[2]

There is an old adage among songwriters that "writing is rewriting." And I'd stake my house on it that the adage applies to all writers, whether they're writing songs, books, scripts, essays, news stories, or company brochures.

The Second Draft

There is an old adage among songwriters that "writing is rewriting." And I'd stake my house on it that the adage applies to all writers, whether they're writing songs, books, scripts, essays, news stories, or company brochures.

[2] I dreaded being "commercial" once upon a time, until I learned that all it means is masses of people like it!

Getting back into the song is an interesting process. The first thing you must do when you revisit the first draft lyrics is to disassociate the lyrics from yourself, your ego, your own story.

- Read your lyrics through a few times as if you were an outsider to the situation, observing them as though they were someone else's story. You can best disassociate yourself by assigning a singer in your mind—a real vocalist or an imaginary character—then imagining that voice saying or singing those words.
- Become aware of the weaknesses in the way your lyric tells this love story. Ask yourself:
    - Is this lyric too self-pitying?
    - Is the way I addressed the story too vague?
    - Is this lyric overtly mean-spirited?
    - Am I, as an observer, finding that I'm losing interest in the story? Is this song basically mundane?
    - Does it ever really get to the point, or does it meander around all the little personal details and nuances without arriving at the meat of the issue?
    - Are the concepts static or very repetitive, meaning do they say essentially the same thing in each verse, even though said in different ways?
    - In telling this story, am I impossibly expecting the listener to *already know* relevant background facts about who these people in the song are and what their story is?
    - Is the lyric, frankly, embarrassingly personal to read?

If any of the answers to these questions are "yes," well, you've got work to do if you want to take this song forward and make it a powerful and more universal representation of the story you want to tell. It's time to rethink your ideas. As you ready yourself to write the second draft of your song, be comforted in knowing you will always have this first draft; it's not going anywhere—the importance of which cannot be minimized. It was, after all, an outpouring of your deepest secret feelings and your revelations about them. You could, I suppose, stop now and say, "Well, I've gotten it out, and that was all I intended to do with this exercise," or you can think like a songwriter, and really turn it into a song. Save your first draft "as is," and make a copy of your lyric that you can use to scribble rewrite notes on. This will form the basis for your rewriting process.

I recently evaluated a student's lyric that described an encounter that was more wishful than wish fulfilled. From the point of view of a young man, it talked about seeing a lovely woman disappearing into a nightclub and being unable to follow. As the lyric went on, the singer sang of thinking about her and subsequently starting to haunt the nightclub hoping to meet her. The trouble was that when he finally met her, she gave him the brush-off, and that was that! Nothing happened between them; no drama, no stolen kisses, no cheating and lying—nothing at all! It was a strangely unsatisfying lyric to read, as the denouement[3] was devoid of passion. When the singer finally did meet this fantasy woman, in the song version anyway, sparks should have flown between them.

I wrote the following advice to this writer, and I pass it along to you.

> *I have a certainty that this song tells a story that actually happened to you, and that the song is faithful to your original story. I believe you chose not to change any details in order to remain true to what really transpired.*
>
> *You must realize that as a songwriter you have poetic license to change the truth, embellishing the facts. A songwriter's duty is to entertain the listener; if that means not accurately reciting true events, so what? Unless you're writing a historical treatise, a songwriter never needs to deal in unadulterated truth!*
>
> *Every historical novel fudges with true characters and events so that they'll sound more dynamic. Novelists often plant a suggestion of an intriguing romance for a historical figure that's a total figment of this writer's imagination. Frequently, they allude to romantic consummations of friendly relationships where there is not a shred of historical evidence, and any suggestions to the contrary represent the writer's fantasy rather than presenting a historical fact.*
>
> *A songwriter should never be afraid to mess with reality. Always go for interest and intrigue, and feel free to twist the truth so that your song's about what you would like to have had happen, regardless of the facts!*

Objectively speaking, you have to know when to let go of your song as a personal experience and imagine how to best entertain your audience. The reason for this, I reiterate once more, is that *when you say "I," you are speaking for the listener.*

So, with that in mind, what does the listener need to know about this song? Every story is different, but here are some basics.

---

[3] "Denouement" is a final revelation at the end of a story in which all is made clear.

- Who is the singer's character, and why do I care about his or her story?
- Who is the singer singing this story to?
- Is the singer talking about a longstanding or recent, committed or passing, relationship?
- What does the lyric need to accomplish to get the story across? For instance,
  - Telling the partner that it's over
  - Saying what a treasure the singer has got in the partner
  - Bringing up a painful moment in the relationship and trying to make amends
  - Describing the singer's feelings at the loss of the relationship
  - Offering to do anything to win the partner back
  - Talking about how perfect the relationship is
  - Discussing what it felt like "last night" and how everything has changed now in the singer's life
  - Letting the listener know that the relationship is solid
  - Letting the listener know what has to happen between the pair in order for them to get back on track
  - Talking to the listener as intimately as if he or she were having a secret love affair with the singer

Make sure that you've chosen your plot carefully so that it will resonate with your listeners, who will ask, *How does this lyric relate to me in my own life?* and, *Are there any clues in this lyric as to how to resolve my own love situations?* Which plot should you choose? There are endless, boundless stories you can write on the topic of love. It's the twists and turns on the subject matter that make each song unique, and such interpretations are limited only by your own wit, experience, voyeurism, imagination, and resourcefulness.

CHAPTER 11

Tapping into the Power of the Songwriter

I'll have to say "I love you" in a song.
—JIM CROCE
(James J. Croce)

We are brought up on pop music from the moment we pop out of our mothers' wombs. We are around pop music almost every waking, sensate hour of our days.

Popular music is the backdrop to every motion picture and television show we watch. It is the catchy melody we hear behind every commercial on the radio, even on classical music stations! It is playing in the elevator we ride to a meeting, and in the restaurant where we eat. It booms on the loudspeaker at the gym and it wafts through a discreet sound system while we are getting a relaxing massage. Pop music sounds as we walk through a department store or a mall. It blares at us from passing car radios. It strikes up when we turn on our computers, and it rises as we shut them down. It accompanies us on vacations, through theme parks, even onto airplanes. Popular music is so much a part of the fabric of our lives that it is breathtaking to think about its scope of influence. And where does it come from? Why, from pop songwriters, of course. We write the songs that influence the people of the Westernized world from cradle to grave.

What is it about these songs that is so appealing to the masses? (For it cannot be denied that they have universal appeal.) I believe their popularity is a result of pop songs' being colloquial forms, straight-ahead conversations between people who are relating to one another. They are not lofty flights of fancy; they are actual, relatable ideas. They are comforting, because they tell stories that we all know and have been through. We see ourselves in them, and we feel safer in our own skins knowing that others are experiencing the same ups and downs, trials and tribulations, that we also face.

In fact, why do you think they call it "pop"? Well, popular songwriting is a reflection of popular culture, popular life, popular mores, and contemporary modes of living. As we evolve, so do our songs. In every era since the beginnings of pop music in the early part of the twentieth century, songwriting styles have changed to match the times and political climes. During wartime in the 1940s, for instance, love songs helped people to express their longing to get through difficult days and back to each other. In the postwar 1950s the buoyant optimistic mood inspired light-hearted songs. The music of every era acquires a personality of its own, be it deep and brooding or happy and elated.

Love songs have always been as varied and diverse as the wonderful writers and artists who have woven them into the fabric of our lives. Don't we all recall particular moments of our lives by thinking of the popular love songs that were playing at the time?

No matter how many love songs are written and recorded, fresh ideas and approaches never stop coming to us. There is a seemingly inexhaustible supply of ways to use those twelve melodic notes, and endless combinations of words to sing on them.

As young songwriters experiment with new sounds, they take songwriting off into different directions for a time. Experimental new music always finds an enthusiastic audience among the peers of those new writers—art needs new and fresh ideas to stay alive! Yet great songwriting, like all great art, is recognizable for its quality by all who listen to it and are moved and touched by its melodic and lyrical content. Brilliant work is undeniable. Like a cello solo by Yo Yo Ma, a masterfully written song needs no busy embellishments—neither vocally, instrumentally, nor rhythmically—for its power to be recognized; it will be riveting to the listener even when performed without accompaniment. That was true a hundred years ago, and it's true now.

In striving to create your own personal best work, don't be afraid of the competition or of your lack of professional exposure, either. Just trust your gift. A great love song can be penned by anybody at any time. In 1912 Charles Gates Dawes, who was vice president of the United States and recipient of the 1925 Nobel Peace Prize, also wrote the music (and thirty-nine years later, Carl Sigman added lyrics) to one of our greatest song treasures, "It's All in the Game."

Never worry about what direction is currently on the radio, or what kind of music is playing today. Tomorrow is always a new day, and since musical tastes are fickle, there's no point in forcing yourself to write in uncomfortable or unfamiliar genres. New artists keep coming along bringing new styles and musical approaches, A&R directors at record companies play musical chairs, and tastes change like the currents in a river. Everyone's looking for "what's next"—and "what's next" may just be a revisiting of something classic.

The point is, when you write your love songs, be true to yourself and your own vision of how best to serve your own talents. If you are to invest your heart in your work, the style of song you write should be the one that comes naturally to you. Admire or despise what is on the radio, but it is irrelevant in the end, as you have to follow your own muse.

TELLING POETRY AND LYRICS APART

Most people assume that poetry and lyrics are the same thing, when they truly are two different art forms.[1] It's essential that a songwriter recognize the differences between them. If you're not sure you can tell them apart, here's some clarity: Poetry triggers the mind (you think and analyze it) and love songs trigger the heart (people respond viscerally—with tears of sadness or joy).

> You cannot write movingly and believably about love unless you allow yourself to be caught up in the thrall of love's promises, betrayals, fulfillments, and denials. Even if you are not currently in love yourself, you must elevate yourself into love's mindset before you start writing about love.

Poetry Is the Antithesis of Pop Culture

Because I've had so many songwriting students ask me to explain to them why a poem is not a lyric and a lyric is not a poem, and because the difference in their work has been dramatic once they "get" it, I believe that learning how to compare and contrast these two art forms will deeply influence any songwriter's success or failure as a lyricist. If the difference between lyrics and poetry remains a gray area to you, your writing will suffer from being "neither fish nor fowl."

Though a lyric is not a poem, it is often poetic. Many great songwriters have expressed their lyrics with a poetic train of thought. Nobody can deny, for instance, that Bob Dylan, Leonard Cohen, Laura Nyro, Judy Collins, Woody

---

[1] Chapter 1 of my first book, *The Art of Writing Great Lyrics,* goes into significant detail about how to differentiate between poetry and lyrics.

Guthrie, and so many other artists of the folk era were songwriters who wrote lyrics with poetic vision. Some, such as Donovan Leitch, frequently did write pure poetry and set it to music. Though Donovan derived great popularity as a songwriter regardless, his works—in my view—lacked the normal conversational flow of words, the story built around a repeating "hook," the contemporary speech patterns and usages that would have made them lyrics.

I respect and adore great poets, and an important part of my upbringing in England included learning and reciting poetry. Unfortunately, in today's culture, poetry—in its classic definition—is mostly an archaic and frequently incomprehensible art form that fails to find an audience among the masses. In our popular culture, a kind of poetry is found in Rap, which has its roots in other art forms, such as field hollers and talking blues. Mainly, poetry appreciation has largely devolved from great art to syrupy sentiments in greeting cards. While much of early literature is in poetic form, it probably appealed only to a rarified artsy segment of the population, even in its heyday several centuries past. Why? Because the content of poetry is so intensely personal to its author; because its language is so not conversational; and because its images are frequently so obscurely drawn. For all of these reasons, poetry is often too puzzling for the average reader to relate to.

Many of you who have already tried your hand at reading volumes of poetry have likely found your mind drifting off, getting easily distracted. You've either concluded that poetry is lightweight and insubstantial, or that poems are heavy, largely inscrutable, and difficult to decipher without investing great mental machinations. In this "McDonald's society" of fast foods and fast-moving ideas, sadly or not, poetry's complexity somehow doesn't fit our contemporary needs. But let's contrast the two art forms, poetry and lyrics, to help you gauge some of the differences, so you can spot-check your own work and see if it fits the definition of "lyrics."

- **Lyrics are usually understandable at first listen.** A poem can rarely be understood completely in one pass of reading, for poetry is all about subtleties, nuances, shades of meaning, and hidden inferences. Even the language is quaint, often relying on obscure imagery.
- **Lyrics are present day, conversational, earnest reflections of what's going on in our lives.** Relationships in poetry are exalted, are shadowy, are existential.
- **Great lyrics are about relationship issues that are easily identifiable.** Poetry takes an obscure path to identifying issues, often defining them with esoteric images.

- **Lyrics speak in contemporary usage of language**. Poetry takes license with the language.
- **Lyrics talk about real people and real situations.** Poetry makes mere mortals larger than life.

Breaking It All Down to Conversation

Up to here I've been comparing poetry and lyrics in the abstract. Now I'll offer some concrete examples:

- Poets love to utilize archaic ways of speaking—quaint language. A poet is free to say "How shall I love thee?" A lyricist is not, and might say, "What do I have to do to show you I love you?"
- A poet is free to work around the normal order of words in speech patterns—"Forever will I love you, Dearest one, I will." A lyricist would simply say, "Baby, I'm gonna love you forever."
- A poet likes to describe simple things in idyllic fashion. In his famous poem "The Daffodils,"[2] William Wordsworth wrote, "I gazed—and gazed—but little thought / What wealth the show to me had brought," whereas a songwriter viewing a field of daffodils might recount it in a lyric by saying, *I didn't know that daffodils / could give me chills / send me thrills.*

Poets don't care about their words sounding conversational. In Samuel Taylor Coleridge's poem "Kubla Khan,"[3] he sets up the location in the first line by saying, "In Xanadu did Kubla Khan / A stately pleasure-dome decree." In a popular traditional folk song, "The House of the Rising Sun," the opening line says, "There is a house in New Orleans / They call the Rising Sun."[4] Which one feels more natural to the ear? The conversational one, of course. It's a lyric, and Coleridge's line is poetry. I realize that these two lines were written centuries apart, but they offer a great opportunity to see poetic versus conversational language in action.

---

[2] To see the full text of Wordsworth's "The Daffodils" check out: *www.dovecottage.com /Wordsworth/The%20Daffodils.html.*

[3] The full text of Coleridge's "Kubla Khan" is printed out online at *http://gaming.unlv.edu/Xanadu/poem.html.*

[4] Author is unknown, but some of the verses to this traditional song can be viewed at *www.bobdylanroots.com/house.html.*

Nevertheless, a poetic mindset helps a songwriter to think "love" thoughts and to get a love song on the right track. While you need to be clear that you're writing lyrics, not poetry, writing about love is not mundane, like writing a shopping list.

Though you can probably write some semblance of love songs on the run, on a deadline, at the mixing console while chomping on a burger, or while watching the World Series, you cannot write movingly and believably about love unless you allow yourself to be seduced by the enchantment of love's promises, betrayals, fulfillments, and denials. Even if you are not currently in love yourself, you must elevate yourself into love's mindset before you start writing about love.

EXERCISE 8

Poetry in Motion

With the clear understanding that it is not lyrics, reading a little romantic poetry might inspire your songwriting. So, if you have a little spare time, kick back with a book of poetry, read awhile, then shut your eyes and conjure the pictures and images described, attempting to understand the mindset of each of the poets you've read. Then, in order to better internalize the poet's process, pick up a pen and a pad, and try expressing yourself in verse, or in free (nonrhyming) verse. (If you need guidance with form and rules regarding poetry, go online to the following Web site: *www.thewritersmentor.com/how-to-write-poetry.htm.*)

Finally, take the same idea, and write it as a song lyric, using all the forms and devices you've read about here. When both forms of expression are completed, consider them side by side, and evaluate each of them for personal impact, connection with a potential audience, clarity, and accessibility.

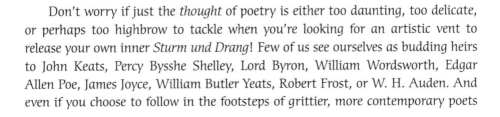

Don't worry if just the *thought* of poetry is either too daunting, too delicate, or perhaps too highbrow to tackle when you're looking for an artistic vent to release your own inner *Sturm und Drang*! Few of us see ourselves as budding heirs to John Keats, Percy Bysshe Shelley, Lord Byron, William Wordsworth, Edgar Allen Poe, James Joyce, William Butler Yeats, Robert Frost, or W. H. Auden. And even if you choose to follow in the footsteps of grittier, more contemporary poets such as Kahlil Gibran, Allen Ginsberg, Sylvia Plath, Dorothy Parker, e. e. cummings, or Langston Hughes, the truth is, we are living in pretty hard-edged times in the twenty-first century, and we have become extremely reality-oriented. Which is not to say that these great poets did not speak of reality; it's just that the way they approached it was, well, pure poetry.

Our cell-phone quick-fix civilization demands instant communication, instant understanding, get-to-the-point expression of ideas. For better or worse, this is who we are today, and so our society's most popular art forms have kept up with this. Love songs are no exception.

The state of the arts with respect to romance is of course not an idea I'm pulling out of the air like a magician's conjure trick. This is something that we all see reflected in film and television, theater and radio. It's easy to see that people want to think and talk about current events and issues. Perhaps we've lost our innocence. We are not as interested any more in flights of fancy as we are in the here and now. And the here and now is pretty gritty. You and I live in a culture of the moment. We want love, we want it our way, and we want it now.

Lyrics Get You in Touch with Yourself

Lyric writing is such a natural conversational medium that I've found it helps me to flesh out who I am, what I think and feel, and what is meaningful to me in this world. I am poised on the edge of romanticism, yet I take in a fair dose of reality every day. Perhaps for me poetry is too esoteric to invest myself in it fully. Poetry is a personal internal medium, whereas songwriting is a shared one.

A case in point is a friend of mine who wants to let his ex-girlfriend know how hurt he has been by their breakup. He wants her to understand how he perceives she led him on into believing they had something important between them, and then she let him down. Although he has a new relationship burgeoning with a wonderful woman, he feels powerless to let the connection with the old one go until he has communicated his pain to the prior girlfriend. He wants to do this by writing his pain into a song lyric.

He has attempted to write this lyric several times to get his emotions across to her and express what he feels, and yet what he writes always comes out as a poem. The reason it cannot possibly communicate effectively to her if she sees it in this form is because it is written in poetic language too intensely personal to him for her to ever "get it." It is almost embarrassingly maudlin, desperately intense, even self-annihilating. What's he doing wrong? He needs to take all of this creative energy and invest it into writing something designed not as a catharsis for *himself*, but as an eye-opener for *her!* And that would likely be in the form of a song with a conversational lyric, not a poem. The lesson here?

When you write songs, never forget that you are speaking to the listener! Write what you want them to hear, not simply what you need to get off your chest.

Lyrics Are "Straight On" an Idea, Poems Are Esoteric

You don't need to be lofty and esoteric when you're writing a lyric in a love song. Being romantic in songs is a very heartfelt affair, it gets right to the point. Spell out your idea, make it appealingly relevant, and make the idea accessible. Keep it direct.

When I wrote my first love songs many years ago, I constantly returned to themes of fairy tales—handsome princes and knights on chargers, pretty and sweet images that were almost nursery-rhyme charming. Words like "magic" and "miracle" appeared everywhere. Everything I wrote contained "wishes" and "dreams." While these words are not taboo from lyrics, they must be used judiciously.

A poem, for instance, using these four words, "magic," "miracle," "wishes," and "dreams," might say:

> *If I but had these magic pow'rs*
> *A miracle to make come true*
> *Then would my wishes to the Heavens*
> *Steal from dreams to bring me you.*

If you were to use those same four words in a song lyric, you would need to make the relevance far more conversational. You could tweak these lines and keep them quite similar, but notice how much easier they flow:

> If I could have the magic power
> To make a miracle come true
> My wish to Heaven would be heard
> No need to dream, cause I'd have you.

As you can see, when considering the difference between poetry and song lyrics, it's not *what* you say, but *how* you say it!

How Pop Music Influences Vocabulary

Perhaps because we listen to so much popular radio—whatever genre we choose—we find ourselves speaking in the peculiar shorthand that we hear in songs. So, when you write love songs, remember that you have tremendous power in your pen. You can influence how people think, how they feel, and also how they speak. Sure, use the shorthand of the times in your writing, but also make every effort to experiment with the vast and colorful English language and explore it to the fullest. If you can't *think up* a more interesting word than the one that's made it's way onto your pad, *look it up* and *find* a better one! That's what a thesaurus is for. Conversational words don't have to be limited to the few hundred words currently starring in "street" vocabulary. Good writing is timeless. You are an original, so write like one!

Creating Speech

The confines of verses and choruses, short little lines in which so much has to be said, have given rise to a sort of "new speak." The band Bread had a song some years ago called "Baby I'm-A Want You," which went to No. 3 on the pop charts. What does that phrase mean in English? Well, it's not grammatically correct, of course. Yet the songwriters imbued it with its own meaning within the context of this lyric, and so created actual vocabulary.

In a song called "In the Light" I wrote with rock guitar whiz Ben Schultz for his Ben Schultz Band on TVT Records, I created the word "realitized." When the word came to mind for the second verse, I realized that it was a nonword, but I felt compelled to use it anyway, and repeated it again in the third verse to give it validity. I've always liked writing rock, because it pushes my imagination past ordinary ideas, and nobody seems to mind! The whole song had an edgy, romantic flavor, and the concept was mystical.

IN THE LIGHT

An eternal mystery
This crazy chemistry
That bonds us heart to heart
And soul to soul
All consumed
In a perfect stranger's hold

How do I turn away from you
What's in this lover's potion
You alone can brew
Am I hypnotized or just realitized?

As I recognize you . . . my mind's expanding
I've got to do what my heart's demanding
Fate is a mistress there is no denying
Now I'm standing . . . standing

CHORUS:	**In the light of love**
	From the eyes of you
	In the light of love
	I can see what's true
	In the light of love

It can't be bought with cash or prayers
But it can hold you closer
Than the strongest snares
Am I hypnotized . . . no just realitized

I'm the architect of my . . . evolution
It's got to be you . . . no substitution
My sins of pride, girl . . . my fatal passions
Find absolution . . . resolution

(repeat chorus)

SECOND	**In the light of love**
CHORUS:	**That you shine on me**
	In the light of love
	What a man can be
	In the light of love

(repeat chorus)

© Pamela Phillips Oland and Ben Schultz

Word Origins

Nearly all contemporary "in" words have quite ordinary origins. Many of them are contractions or bastardizations of quite normal words and phrases. Vernacular is rife with derivative words. "Dis," of course, derives from "disrespect"; "Benjamins," in reference to money, obviously comes from the portrait of Benjamin Franklin on the U.S. $100 bill; and so forth.

The common descriptive words "hip," "cool," "groovy," "jazzy," "tight," "sweet," and "on the one" all started as words describing popular music. "Hip" meant cutting edge, "cool" referred to the slinky riffs that perhaps a jazz pianist might play, "groovy" meant a great rhythmic feel, "jazzy" was the musical attitude, "sweet" was a compliment given to a wonderful instrumental solo, and "on the one" meant "on the downbeat." People now use these words in conversation with the same comfort that they use the psychology words that have filtered into our conversation, such as "psych" ("don't try to psych me out"), "paranoid" ("that dude's paranoid, man"), and "schizo" ("don't go getting schizo on me!").

Being an Original

If you have heard a phrase in a love song or many love songs before, make a choice not to use it. Don't get caught up in stale, hackneyed phrases. "You make me feel so good inside," for instance, is just a deadly line, having been used about a million times!

EXERCISE 9

Finish This Thought . . .

Make lists of whatever ideas come to mind to finish the following thoughts. First write something simple, then stretch and make up something beautiful or outrageous. Teach yourself to think "outside the box" and dare to be original with the way you put words together. For example:

- "Whenever I think of you . . ."
    - ♡ I cry my eyes out
    - ♡ I go crazy
    - ♡ The stars fall from the sky
    - ♡ My heart pounds in my ears
    - ♡ I want to touch myself
    - ♡ I'm right back where I started
    - ♡ It's the end of the world all over again
    - ♡ _____?
- "There's only one thing keeping me away . . ."
    - ♡ I love you too much to break your heart
    - ♡ _____?
- "To get you back, I'd . . ."
    - ♡ Cross the burning desert on foot
    - ♡ _____?
- "The thing I love most about you is . . ."
    - ♡ The way you wriggle your toes when I'm loving you
    - ♡ _____?

- 💜 "If I ever found out you were lying to me, I'd . . ."
  - 💟 Change the locks on all the doors to my house
  - 💟 _____?

Fear of Flying

You have written down an unusual word grouping, such as:

- 💜 "Her hopes were like the cards in a poker hand, she was afraid to turn them over."
- 💜 "They stood on both sides of the razor's edge, and they could not cross."
- 💜 "She wore cherry blossoms in her hair, and black boots on her soul."
- 💜 "I wanna say I love you, but I guess I'll say goodbye."
- 💜 "You can stand on Hollywood and Vine, but that don't make you a movie star."

So, now you're staring at those words as if they're going to bite you. They look odd, out of place, not the sort of things that belong in your song. But that's where you're wrong. They are inventive, and they have taken you out of your prescribed, ordinary way of thinking.

You are still at the stage of being self-conscious about inventive ideas. But you see, it is when self-consciousness turns to self-assurance that you being to write with confidence. Think of a watercolorist who knows he cannot remove or alter a single brush stroke once it is applied to the paper. It takes exceeding confidence to do that. Surely the first many times he tries, he sweats, is overtaken with fear, and consumed with "what ifs." Yet if each subsequent brushstroke has the authority of his confidence, what a painting he will turn out!

Think of the clothes designer with the $100-a-yard fabric making that first cut with the shears. It takes swallowing hard and plowing forward, not wasting energy on whether this was the right cut to make. And as each authoritative cut continues, a fashionable garment reveals itself.

One brush stroke leads to another, one cut leads to another . . . and so it goes with songwriting. Setting forth unique lines and ideas makes the palms sweat, and causes insecurity to trickle down the forehead in beads of sweat. Ultimately, however, it is the launching of creativity and originality that separates the great writers from those who merely copy, repeat, and revisit other people's interesting ideas. Don't get left behind in the hangar for fear of flying!

What will put the stamp of originality on your work is the way you define your images. Don't be sloppy and settle for the first idea that comes into your mind. Allow the process of creativity to work through you, and be patient. The great ideas are all within your purview, waiting for you to pluck them out of the cosmos and write them down.

Learning to Listen and Observe

You're nobody 'til somebody loves you.
—DEAN MARTIN
(James Cavanaugh/Russ Morgan/Larry Stock)

If this study of writing love songs does nothing else for you, my hope is that it will ratchet up your level of awareness several-fold. I want you to truly "hear" as a songwriter hears, the nuances of music that you normally hear only on one level—as a listener. Then I want you not only to see with your eyes, but fully experience all the people and things that normally sit at the edge of your consciousness, noted, but not absorbed.

LISTENING AS A LYRICIST

A lyricist is a critical listener. Every word in a song by another writer is heard, examined, cogitated upon, and made note of. The clever lines make us smile, the truly awful lines make us chuckle, and the brilliant lines make us jealous!

But whether we smile, chuckle, or turn green, we notice what other writers have said, and how well or poorly they have expressed themselves.

Lyricists listen with grudging admiration to a wonderfully executed lyric, especially when the ideas are flawlessly integrated into a song. I feel my cheeks flush as a rush of heat goes up my neck when I hear a fantastic lyric line. I am filled with admiration for the other writer, along with regret that I didn't think of that idea! Yet of course I cannot think of every great line—each songwriter is imbued with a special gift, a way of looking at the world, a turn of phrase, a unique attitude.

When I hear something particularly well written, I feel pride at being a member of this exclusive fraternity of wordsmiths who specialize in the words to songs. When I hear something spectacularly mediocre, I cringe, and I cannot stop a dozen ideas from running through my head as to how I might have approached the idea. Sometimes I even do that with my own work, looking back at a line or turn of phrase written long enough ago for me to gain objectivity. Even some of the best ideas we have don't hold up under the scrutiny of a second look, as nothing is ever truer than the fact that hindsight is 20/20.

Though the works of other songwriters may sometimes be daunting, a hard act to follow, there's no point in being intimidated. Let these others' works be instructional, offering you a level to which you can aspire.

We all tend to become somewhat complacent about our skills if we have healthy egos. All pro baseball players had pretty good self-images in 1998 until Sammy Sosa hit sixty-two home runs! There were several women who felt they were the best ice skater in the world until sixteen-year-old Sarah Hughes skated flawlessly past them to garner her gold medal in the 2002 Winter Olympics. A little shake-up to our smugness is always useful!

When you hear great work by other writers, instead of feeling disappointed in yourself, use the opportunity to learn from their cleverness and their mistakes. The truth is, if you walk down this path toward writing great love songs, your entire perspective on songs will change. You may never be able to listen to other people's love songs in the same way again, once you really start listening as a serious writer. My father, Max Phillips, a violinist blessed (or cursed) with perfect pitch, wrinkles his nose every time he hears a classical recording where a bad note has slipped by unnoticed by most of us. Just like him, you will develop a discerning ear, your innocence lost!

In any event, sensational or soporific, heavenly or humdrum, the works of every songwriter offer you something to make you think. If you become an accomplished listener, I promise you will become a very adept lyricist.

Studying the Style of a Song
Every style of music has a different approach to lyrics. A skillful listener will start to pick up the differences in nuances and attitudes. Get to know the different shapes songwriters have traditionally used in each genre. There are different styles of ballads, for instance. The so-called Barry Manilow ballad, for instance, is a huge musical idea that keeps building and building until it explodes at the end. It is actually considered a genuine category of love songs because Manilow has been incredibly successful time after time with his formula. A blues ballad, such as the Ray Charles standard "Georgia on My Mind," is not showy like a Manilow ballad—it is more thoughtful, and the power lies in the description of feelings. A thoughtful ballad like Diane Warren's Toni Braxton hit "Unbreak My Heart," or Sting's "Every Breath You Take," must match its content with the pulsing rhythm bed in which the love lyric is carried along.

The bottom line here is, you cannot listen too much, or know too much about what else is out there. It will give you a jumping-off point by which to gauge what you are doing. Becoming a clone of other songwriters is a thankless thing to do. You need to write love songs like yourself—developing your own style and process. If you try to copy what you hear, the results will sound forced and unnatural.

I have never felt it would serve my career to be a copycat, and have always maintained my originality and my own approach to songwriting. Fads will come and go in songwriting as in all things, but a great lyric well phrased is forever memorable.

Hearing Lyrics on Two Levels

Writing songs has made me a better communicator in general. I have learned to understand motivations within relationships, to peel off the veneer of people's outward appearances to get to their intentions and inner feelings.

I suggest you develop the ability to hear lyrics on two levels:

A. Superficial
B. Subliminal

When you are listening to a song, there is the outward story, the superficial idea that tells you what's going on on the outside. There is also something called "subtext." The *American Heritage Dictionary* defines "subtext" with respect to literary texts, as well as the interpretation of a role by an actor:

> *1. The implicit meaning or theme of a literary text. 2. The underlying personality of a dramatic character as* implied or indicated *by a script or text and* interpreted *by an actor in performance [emphasis added].*

In the case of lyric writing, the "subtext" would be the underlying implied or indicated "back-story" of the song. If you have done your job skillfully, much information will be written between the lines, meaning that story points will be alluded to by what is not said but implied. For instance, if you wrote, *You didn't come home till late last night*, your subtext might be, "Therefore, I assume you had a one-night stand." If the line is altered by one word, again—that is to say, *You didn't come home till late again last night*—your subtext changes to suspecting a full-blown affair. If you add *But this time I didn't cry*, your subtext tells the listener that this has been an ongoing issue, and you (the singer) have cried enough, that you've finally come to terms with the fact that you're not going to take it anymore, and that in all likelihood, you're now prepared to break up. Every word counts, as you see. A great deal of back-story can be contained in a few words. The singer, armed with the obvious subtext, has a lot to work with when working up the emotions of the song and delivering the song's actual lyrics. Implying the back-story allows the singer to know more than the listener does about the background of the character and the history of the song's situation, in order to successfully deliver the lyrics. Don't underestimate the actor in every singer!

In an acting situation, for instance, the actor may say, "I'm fine, don't worry about me," but may be thinking, subtextually, "Momma died, and I lost my job, and life stinks." That would certainly influence the whole approach to his delivery of the words, "I'm fine, don't worry about me." Similarly, if that same line appeared in a lyric, there must be other information in the song that would help the singer to understand who this person is, who's saying "I'm fine." Say, for instance, that this is a female vocalist singing to a new love that she's ready to fall in love again, and she says the line, *I'm fine, don't worry about me.* It would be helpful, then, for her to have in a verse a line such as *I don't want you to know I still think about him.* The listener could then interpret the positive "I'm fine" line as having a darker, more intricate side to it.

Knowing How Others Have Said It

As you may have realized by now, I am a great believer in doing your homework. You are not the first person ever to have written "I love you" in a lyric, and something tells me you won't be the last. Be diligent about doing your homework. While it's okay to include familiar phrases, you don't want to write your idea in words that are ho-hum, or in phrases that have been said a million times (and probably better used). Become familiar with the work of exceptional songwriters who have come before you; study their work and determine what elements made it hit the mark. Listen to how others have used a familiar phrase, and find your own twist on the idea.

It has been said that there are no original ideas in this world that someone hasn't already thought of. That may be, but there are original ways of expressing those ideas, and that's a fact. So, whenever there are songs playing, listen, observe, cogitate, and jog your mind. Let your ability to listen well help to make you an increasingly original and interesting songwriter.

People Look to Love Songs for Answers

You'll be amazed at how often your words—in the form of song lyrics—will offer up profound wisdoms you didn't even know you knew! Many of your listeners are disenfranchised emotionally and actually turn to songs, consciously or not, for solutions to love issues. Remember, as you seize this opportunity, it's your duty to shed light on their dilemmas and offer some pretty good answers!

💙 A couple are unable to decide whether to go the distance or split up—what are their choices?

💙 A woman is trying to decide whether to tell her boyfriend her feelings are running deep, for fear he'll run away—what does she say?

💙 A man is in love with his best friend, whom he is scared won't understand his feelings—how does he express them without losing the friendship?

💙 A couple want to bring back the magic to their relationship, and don't know how—what will break the ice?

All of these scenarios, and thousands more you could write about, can bring attention to common situations and offer plausible plans of action to listeners.

BECOMING A PEOPLE-WATCHER

I know full well that your mother taught you it's impolite to stare. And believe it or not, that's true for everyone else on the planet—except for you. *You're a songwriter!*

Watching people is part of your birthright. You thrive on examining people in eensy meensy detail, from their balding heads to their scuffed cowboy boots, from their cosmetically enhanced breasts to their Louis Vuitton handbags. Come on, you know I'm right—I'm describing you, aren't I? Oh, I see, you're the surreptitious one who tries to catch a glimpse when you think you're out of range. Believe me, people have a sixth sense about that; they know when they're being watched.

As a songwriter, all of your observations are stored away in that wonderful computer in your head, waiting for later regurgitation in a lyric line. You will be searching for an image, and there it will be, some long-forgotten something that you noticed eons ago.

So go ahead, be a voyeur—knock yourself out! Just have the good grace to turn your head away when someone glares at you for staring at them. And if you are one of those who never misses an opportunity to miss an opportunity, shame on you! Remember, the guy who invented the phrase "Don't look now, but . . ." really wanted you to look, and that's the truth!

Nickel Novels

I make up stories about everyone I see, quite irrespective of the truth. My husband calls them my "nickel novels." A collaborator and I who have developed screenplays have called our company "Nickel Novel Productions." I find it impossible to ignore an opportunity to make up scenarios about perfect strangers.

Once, I was sitting with friends in a restaurant having a good old time, and I said to them, "I can tell you what anybody does for a living, just by looking at them." Well, they scoffed and scorned, and finally pointed to a man across the room and said, "All right then, what does he do?" I looked him over for a minute, and then got a very strong image about him. I told them that he was a traveling salesman who sells electronic equipment to stores. That got a hoot and a holler out of them, so they said, "Okay, go and ask him, then!"

I felt a little embarrassed, but I got up and walked over to the crowded table at which the man was sitting having fun with his friends. I tapped him on the shoulder, and he turned around and smiled as he checked me out expectantly. He said, "Hi!" and I inquired, "Excuse me, but are you a salesman who sells electronic equipment—on the road—to stores?" He beamed broadly and said, "Yes, how do I know you?" Stunning, eh! I said, "You don't! I bet my friends I could figure out what you do for a living, and that's what I guessed." The color drained out of his already pale face as he asked, "Is it that obvious?"

The answer is, Yes, it's that obvious. Either that or I'm a psychic! Here are the things I had, thinking about it in ret-

rospect, subconsciously noticed about him and dredged up to the surface when asked:

- He was pale and tired looking, which said to me that he obviously worked long hours and wasn't out in the sun much.
- His hair was in a very neat business style that I associated with a "corporate" appearance.
- He was still wearing a crumpled tie, and his suit jacket on the chair-back and white long-sleeved shirt were extremely creased, indicating to me that he had been sitting squished in his car all day.
- He had the carriage of someone who has had a college education, but I felt probably only to the bachelor's degree level, which is necessary for most baseline corporate jobs.
- His taste in apparel was lackluster and poorly cut, thus he was clearly no mover and shaker.
- He had the face of an egghead, a nerd, a dweeb.

Obviously, I was using stored up past impressions to help me "read" him. The Creator didn't just put flowers and trees and cats and dogs and skunks here for us to enjoy and be fascinated or repelled by. He put people here, too, for our endless pleasure and edification. It is up to us to observe, study, and enjoy them for all we're worth. Believe me, you know more about people than you realize you do! Use that knowledge to improve every love song you write.

Objectivity, or: Why It Is Imperative Not to Write about Yourself!

The wonders of writing a love song about your own personal experiences are eclipsed only by writing one about *someone else's!* There is nothing more agreeable than fictionalizing a story that has already become a known entity to you, right down to the sordid details. While you would never want to betray a friend's confidence, or expose a relationship issue that someone has asked you to keep secret, there are marvelous story elements in every relationship you come across, including the interactions not only of those you know, but also those whom you simply observe. String together some unbelievable but true observations, some "what if" conjectures, and some wild imaginings of your own, and I do believe you've got yourself a song!

Seeing the World through Me-Colored Glasses

Our eyes are like movie cameras photographing and storing on the "celluloid" of our brain cells everything we observe around us. But we each see the world through the lens of our own life experience. And that is limiting.

Since you are who you are, and have lived all the experiences of your life, it is only natural to begin by writing about everything from your own point of view. But it does get boring. It's like looking at the sky through a pinhole, and always having a vast dark circle around the area you're looking at; you can see one star clearly, but none of the others comes into your view.

Whether we are professional psychologists, from Dr. Freud to Dr. Laura, or whether we are award-winning cinematographers, we all begin with our own viewpoints. Being self-involved by nature, the difficult thing for us to do is to then remove ourselves from our primary views and figuratively put ourselves in the shoes of others. Which reminds me of a story about a night when I did just that.

Years ago, a very odd thing occurred to me. I went to a party where I didn't know a soul except the fellow who had brought me, who promptly disappeared into the crowd. So, I sat and entertained myself by watching people. What a floor show! Admittedly, someone passed me a funny cigarette a couple of times. But in any event, I became heavily involved in observing each person my eyes happened to glom onto at the party. For a few moments, I quite unabashedly examined them from head to toe. Nobody was paying any attention to me, as I had withdrawn into myself, and so I was a bit like a fly on the wall: there, but unobserved.

My eyes were caught by a young woman with a garishly unflattering outfit on. I studied the outfit and wondered what on earth would possess her to dress in it. I then looked at her unflattering hairdo, and wondered why she didn't try a different one that would make her attractive. Her makeup—well, I really did a number on that! I tried to imagine why *that* color lipstick, and why *that* color eye shadow. In fact, I thought as a whole she was a big mess. All I could think of was *Why???* But, of course, I was observing her through my own lens, judging her by my own standards of what I would do myself, how I would look, what makeup I would choose.

Perhaps it was a puff of the funny cigarette that caused me to all of a sudden have the sensation of being inside of her mind. But it was an amazing experience that has stayed with me till this day. I felt as if I were quite literally inside of her and looking out. As if transmogrified, I "became" her. I looked at "myself" in the mirror, and saw the shape of "my" mouth, the fall of "my" hair, the textures of "my" clothes, and in a rush I had a sense of comfort as to how "I" looked. No longer was I observing this woman as an outsider, but I had somehow briefly brushed her consciousness and been able to reason how she thought and how she saw herself. Most astonishing!

It was a profound experience, and a humbling one also. For I realized that each individual makes choices based on what they see when they look in the mirror. Perhaps many views of self are through so-called rose-colored glasses, a concept coined by the great French singer-songwriter Edith Piaf in the brilliant song "La Vie en Rose." If people's choices are unfathomable to others—their parents, friends, or the world at large—it is because, for the most part, we do not enter their mind-space containing their thought and feeling processes. We do not hold their image in our minds in the same way that they do. Our self-centered worldview keeps us from accessing the inner space of others.

What that experience taught me is that as songwriters, we need to find the magical route into others' mind-space. We must see them as they see themselves, and write from their points of view, not colored by how we personally would handle their situations and issues.

Robbie Burns, the great Scots poet, once wrote in his poem "To a Louse,"

> *O wad some Power the giftie us*
> *To see oursels as ithers see us!*
> *It wad frae monie a blunder free us*

He was perhaps referring to the fact that we would probably behave differently if we could see ourselves through the eyes of others. That if we knew what flaws they saw in us, we would correct them to be more in keeping with the way others would want us to be. Or maybe he meant that we would be able to function better in the world simply by knowing how we were perceived.

As songwriters, we must engage in a faithful commission to represent people's points of view as they are, not colored by our own. We are at fault if we assess "right" and "wrong" labels to people's viewpoints. Their truth is whatever is true for them. It is how they function and get through life, how they walk their path of existence.

I once went to a lecture by a "Yogi Rabbi" from New York, who made a large imprint on my consciousness. He spoke of his view that there are many ways to climb the mountain of truth to God, saying it doesn't matter which path you choose as long as you get to the top.

His own path had started in an Orthodox Jewish family, and over time he had become enraptured by the mystical thrall of Hinduism. He said, "You have to start somewhere," and, in his case, Judaism was where he had perforce begun. Using his own background as a basis, he explained, he had gone on to create for himself a hybrid religion that was a mix of Eastern and Western philosophies and religious tenets. The result—a quite splendid enlightenment—was because he had expanded his worldview and was now able to observe life through more than one lens.

Perhaps it was he who made me first realize that in spite of the fact that we all undergo similar life experiences, they affect us differently because of the rose- or other-colored glasses we each look through to view the world. We have to use our basic viewpoint as a starting point, but we have the power to build upon it in any way we wish.

Watching Other People Being in Love

While personal experience in love certainly has no equal as a teacher, most often we are too stubborn to change either our behavior or expectations, and so are doomed to repeat our heartbreaks and heartaches over and again! There is nothing more difficult to do than to admit we are wrong. Thus, though our own personal lessons are smack dab in front of us, as obvious as a brown suit at a black-tie dinner, we cannot see them.

Watching *other* people live their romances, however, has no such pitfalls. We have total clarity when we're not directly involved. We see what they're doing, we recognize it, and we know the behavior and where it's leading. We can give sound advice that we probably don't heed ourselves, and we knowingly watch people laugh, cry, be passionate, be jealous, cheat, make each other miserable—and scratch our heads as they sabotage their relationships.

As sad as it may be for others to go through tumultuous events in their love lives, these are the moments that give songwriters their fodder for songs. We must watch, observe, learn, and reduce these ideas to something that can be sung about. One man's divorce is another man's song.

Comparing Your Love Experience with Others'

What makes writing songs about love so wonderful is that the permutations and situations on the subject are endless. Say the word "love" itself to a room full of people, and everyone will offer a different definition.

Speak of a "perfect relationship," and some will say it's one where the couple are together all the time, can look like a wreck together, and have no pretensions. Others will say it's one where they only see each other once a week, on best behavior, dressed and scented like dreams, and go out dining and dancing feeling like Nick and Nora Charles of *The Thin Man*. But the most important question for you to ask yourself is this: *What does the character singing your song think love is?*

What, for instance, does "cheating" mean? Well, to some people it may mean anything that doesn't have to do with the two of them, which would include mental fantasizing. To some it may mean that flirting and fantasizing are okay, and the only taboo is physically going to bed with someone else.

Similarly, "commitment" to some connotes a short-term, one-on-one situation, and to others it demands a lifetime involvement. "Breaking up" means a long, drawn-out, on-again-off-again thing to some, while to others it means "See ya!" *What does the character singing your song think about cheating? Commitment? Breaking up?*

Your own love experiences are only some of the possibilities. You can gain remarkable insights as to your personal feelings about love by studying the love experiences of others, and comparing them to your own.

Truly, nobody has the perfect relationship in every respect. All couples have weak spots in the way they feel about each other. There is not a woman born who hasn't wanted to change her man in some ways. There is not a man born who didn't at some point worry about giving up his bachelorhood to his current girlfriend in case the "right" girl was the next one he'd meet.

It is not necessarily people's strengths in their relationships that are song worthy. More likely, it is their shortcomings. When the singer in the standard "My Funny Valentine" asks his girlfriend if her mouth is a little weak, it is a compliment to her vulnerability, her imperfection. In Showboat's "(Just My) Bill," the singer calls her man a plain sort of guy whom people might not even notice if they walked by him. But the point of the matter is that she loves him, and that's all that counts.

When you write a love song, imagine that the people you are writing about in the song contain elements of yourself and all the other people you have observed being vulnerable in love situations.

♥
What Is Love?

Can't help loving that man of mine.
—ELLA FITZGERALD
(Oscar Hammerstein/Jerome Kern)

No, I'm not a therapist, but I *am* your friendly local "Loveologist!" I am a unique duck, a person whose life is all about love. Anyone who knows me will tell you I live and breathe love. Well, for heaven's sake, all I've ever done for a living for the past twenty-odd years is think about love, write about love, and examine and dissect love's whys and wherefores from every imaginable angle! I daresay I know as much about the ins and outs of love as anyone on the planet!

The more love songs I write, the more I know about love; the more I know about love, the more questions I have. The more questions I have, the more answers I seek. It is an endless and endlessly thought-provoking study, which I dub "Loveology."

Thus, it is my intent in this chapter to make you acutely aware of what love is, viewed through the eyes of a songwriter: how it affects people, how it binds them and tears them apart. I want you to start contemplating, and reflecting on all the myriad aspects of love relationships, and I want you to really begin to differentiate among them, so that the love songs you write will be elevated to a new level.

I am speaking of couple-love here, as it is the subject most often written about in love songs, though of course there are the categories of parent-child love, love of God, love of friends, and love of all the rest of God's creatures, great and small.

LOVE SONG LOVE

We've been led by the media to believe that what passes for love on the movie screens is the kind of love that—if we could actually find it—would be the answer to our prayers. Songwriters have the choice of making their song content primarily light and fantasy-like, or gritty and true to life. Think about which of these goals you wish to gear toward with the song you're writing.

Movie Love versus Real People Love

The way movie directors package it, love is the goo-goo ga-ga of two people enraptured by each other, caught up in satin sheets, their perfect bodies moving sinuously together, twisting and turning like contortionists, the woman a size 0 who has no tan lines and whose makeup is still perfect, the man in oiled-to-perfection physical shape, every hair on his head still in place. Unfortunately, few of us have the genetics to look like that, and fewer still are as gymnastically gifted in the privacy of our boudoirs. But love itself is a very real connection that binds together two very real people.

If love isn't what the movies show us, what does it look like? Well, for starters, love is something you can see in the eyes of a new father who is looking at the mother of his child lying on her maternity bed, disheveled, a mess, pale and tired, and thinking she's the most beautiful woman he's ever seen.

Love is what you see in the eyes of two eighty-year-olds as they dance at their sixtieth wedding anniversary and smile at each other after a lifetime of joys, heartaches, and shared experiences.

And love is also what you observe between a smiling young couple in jeans and t-shirts strolling through a mall with their arms comfortably resting around each other's waists. They don't even have to talk, they're just glad to be in each other's company.

The giveaway is in the authenticity of the way a couple interacts. In any of these scenarios, what will strike you when you look at the loving pair is the sense that these two people belong together. Because movie actors so realistically counterfeit the truth of "belonging together," we are lulled into a false sense of what is real and possible. Since everyone wants in their hearts to belong together with someone else, "couple" love songs are the most popular form of songwriting by miles. Songs about world peace and ending hunger, songs about hot rods and trucks and the road, fill a tiny corner of the marketplace. Most songs are stories about some permutation of romantic love. But if you write your songs about the imitation love you see portrayed in movies, your songs will never be authentic enough to resonate with your audience. Song relationships, like real ones, need to be somewhat flawed in order to endear the listener.

Is This Song about First Love or True Love?

It is your job as a writer of love songs to convey the various stages and aspects of love to your listening audience, so that they can relate to, become interested in, and want to know more about the love relationship in your song. When you are writing your love songs, know intimately who these people are whom you're writing about. You need to really "get" them, and understand the stage of their relationship that they're in. Otherwise, your songs will have a hollow ring to them.

You can write a great love song once you know who the pair in your song are and how far along their relationship is. But more than that, you must understand what the stakes are for them. A couple who just met two weeks ago and are breaking up have different losses at stake than a couple with a year invested. A couple who have made love a few times have less at stake than a couple who are engaged. An engaged couple have less at stake than a married couple. The stakes are represented in songs by the degree of passion they have about what there is to lose here and how important it is to one or both of the pair.

Pop music is bursting at the seams with songs about new love, checking it out, feeling new feelings, imagining the future. Love is a whole different experience when time has gone by in a relationship than when it first starts. Truly, what is there to love when you first meet? It's largely, perhaps, the attraction of physical appearance, the spark of a kindred personality, the dancing eyes, the rocking chemistry. That's enough to get started, a reason to take a second look, a jumping-off place for a relationship. It's not love, though—not yet.

If you're writing about true love, make it wonderful, powerful, emotional. Let your listeners believe there is no moment in the world more fantastic, more glorious, than the moment of revelation when the singer truly does know what he or she feels has moved past interest and mere infatuation to the "real thing." And that doesn't happen until the song says that the singer knows, beyond a doubt, that this is "it!"

Love is part reality and also part fantasy. One without the other is not enough. Thus, every reality-oriented song ought to include some elements of lightness and fantasy; every fantasy-oriented song would do well to include elements of reality. Balance is essential in telling a love story well in a song format.

UNDERSTANDING THE CONCEPT OF LOVE

How can you successfully write love songs unless you have a clear under-standing of what "romantic love" is? I mean that for the real world, not the world of "bodice rippers" and other romantic fiction, movies, and TV, or the world of your own limited experience. Maybe you'd answer, *You can't, any more than you can describe the taste of a kumquat if you've never eaten one!* And yet literature would disagree.

Elizabeth Barrett, one of Britain's most famous and well-loved poets, was a rather sickly young woman whose tyrannical father rarely let her leave the house, let alone enjoy love relationships. Yet some of her best poetry of love was written in her imagination of what love is, before she met her great love Robert Browning when she was in her late thirties. Furthermore, *Gone with the Wind*, arguably one of the most memorable love stories ever written, was by the bedridden invalid Margaret Mitchell, who was secretly in love with Clark Gable and imaginatively molded her romantic hero Rhett Butler around him. (Which is why it's no wonder the role suited him "to a T"!)

And what do those two snippets of information tell us? Love is part real-ity and also part fantasy. One without the other is not enough. Thus, every reality-oriented song ought to include some elements of lightness and fantasy; every fantasy-oriented song would do well to include elements of reality. Balance is essential in telling a love story well in a song format.

Draw on your personal experiences in and out of love, and add to that what you've seen of others' successes and heartbreaks. Before you start writ-ing love songs, I want you to give the concept of love a chance to percolate in your mind. Answer this:

Is love:

1. A euphoric state of mind?
2. A gift given and received?
3. The way you feel about somebody else?
4. The way somebody else makes you feel about yourself?
5. A wonderful friendship interspersed with bursts of great passion?

Probably all five definitions are true at different times in a relationship.

My own definition of love is number 4—I believe it's not what I feel for someone else, but what that someone else makes me feel about myself. I believe that if someone makes you feel good about yourself, you reflect what you've received back to that person, who feels so good because of what you're showing in return, that it can be reflected back to you again, and then you reflect it back. That reflecting back and forth continues around and around in a perpetual circle of giving and taking. In my view, which I hold in my mind whenever I write, loving someone enough so that they can love themselves is truly love. Become aware of what view of love you are subconsciously holding onto as you write your love songs!

If I adore writing love songs, perhaps it's because love is a profound part of my life. I dated for a number of years before getting married, and I think I went through every heartache and fantasy imaginable. But I wouldn't trade any of those experiences for a king's ransom, even the ones that made me cry my eyes out, because they turned out to make the most wonderful fodder for love songs!

I can still recall those experiences with probably too much clarity, even though my terrific husband Bobby and I have found the happiness I thought was impossible in those difficult days. I'm glad they're long in the past, but I still find it useful to draw on those dreams, nightmares, magical interludes, hurts, insights, and slights as a jumping-off point for writing songs about love.

When you are writing love songs, keep in mind that there are two distinct ways of looking at love: (a) from the outside as an observer, and (b) from the inside as a participant. I've encouraged you to examine love from both perspectives at different points throughout this book, and each of them offers useful considerations that will make you a stronger songwriter. What is or isn't going on has a lot to do with your perception of the situation, whether you are observing or participating.

Studying Love as an Observer

You can perhaps learn more about love by watching other people going through the motions of it than you can from being in it yourself. As we've discussed, you certainly cannot see your own mistakes as easily as you can see those that others are making. Watching a couple you know well having a spat, you immediately know who is right and who is wrong, and why—even though *they* don't seem to. But you probably lack that clarity in your own relationships.

As a by-product of studying love in order to write great love songs, we become much more savvy about how to conduct our own love relationships, and that in turn is reflected in the insightful lyrics we write. It's all very circular. Become aware; learn to take inventory of what is going on in the relationships you observe around you. Start to assimilate the dynamics and consequences of such behavior as:

- ❤ One of them taking advantage of the other's good nature, and pushing too far.
- ❤ One of them being too stubborn to admit being wrong when it's obvious to anybody.
- ❤ One of them sulking and frequently being in a bad mood for no apparent reason other than general self-pity.
- ❤ One of them always trying to be the fence-mender, to fix things between them.
- ❤ One of them never accepting an apology with good grace (the "saying you're sorry doesn't make it right" syndrome).
- ❤ Neither one of them listening to the other one, as they are both too busy trying to get across their own points of view.
- ❤ Both of them saying things in anger that they can never retract, and each hammered word intended to hurt their partner in the moment, as "payback," is a nail in the coffin of their relationship.

Assess what you see as it relates to storytelling. Rather than trying to decide whether or not the observation applies to you and your own love situation, rather than judging the "wrong" or "right" of it, file it all away in your mind for later use in a song. Your objectivity as an observer will serve you more clearly than if you played an actual role in the drama.

For instance, the events in my song "Monday Morning Quarterback," which Frank Sinatra recorded, did not happen to me; yet, based on a collection of past observations of others, the entire scenario flew into my mind and rolled out on the page in a mere couple of hours.

MONDAY MORNING QUARTERBACK

I know there were a hundred ways to tell her I loved her
It's funny how they're all so clear today
And when her face was burning with sadness and yearning
I don't know why I turned my eyes away

CHORUS: **But it's so easy**
Looking at the game the morning after
Adding up the kisses and the laughter
Knowing how you'd play it
If the chance to play it over ever came
But then . . . A Monday morning quarterback
Never lost a game

The room was so alive with all her feelings and longings
I saw the spark of danger in her eyes
Well how would it have hurt me if I'd turned back and held her
A moment passes, something lovely dies

CHORUS: **But it's so easy**
Looking at the game the morning after
Adding up the kisses and the laughter
Knowing how you'd play it
If the chance to play it over ever came
But then . . . a Monday morning quarterback
Never lost a game
(Instrumental Break)

TAG: **Yes it's easier to win it**
When you know you'd never play it quite the same . . .
But then . . . this Monday morning quarterback
Never lost a game

© Lyrics/Pamela Phillips Oland; Music/Pamela Phillips Oland and Don Costa

Studying Love as a Participant
If a singer is to be singing about love from inside a relationship—i.e., in the first-person "me and you"—you need to write thoroughly intimate and

personal lyrics. Observe your own behavior as a participant in your love relationships—what you say and do, and how you react, provoke, seduce, enjoy, and respond to a lover.

Since participating in a love relationship is more about making your partner happy than it is about expectations that the partner will do something for you, it needs to come across in your lyrics. Writing the concept "What I need you to do for me . . . " is okay to a point, but nobody responds well to demands. And remember, again, you're writing for the listener!

The exceptions—such as Janet Jackson's Jimmy Jam-Terry Lewis song "What Have You Done for Me Lately?"—are usually up-tempo, tongue-in-cheek songs, especially appreciated by listeners who would ask the same question of their own partners. That song was filled with attitude and sexiness, and the singer became the enticing, proud vixen character, which always appeals to male listeners. As a love ballad, I believe the concept would not have done as well with listeners.

Can You Visualize Your Story?

Since every love song is a mini-movie, imagine yourself with a video camera in hand, following your characters around. See every motion and emotion through the lens of your video camera. Watch what these people are doing and going through, and record it on paper in the form of your lyrics.

You need to capture the essence of what your characters are feeling and experiencing with each other. Take the temperature of the interaction between them and boil it down to words. Interpret looks if nothing is being said. Interpret body language if they are together, and especially if they are standing apart.

> The truth of any relationship becomes easy to visualize and understand when you stand back dispassionately from it and view it as an observer.

Read their minds, and find the words that are unsaid. Hear what they are telling each other, and what they wish each other could "get" telepathically.

When you are embroiled in a situation in your own love life, sometimes it's hard to make heads or tails of it, which is why therapists make a lot of money—they are hired as impartial observers. (Bet you didn't know you could become your own therapist by observing yourself and writing these love songs!)

Learning the skill of impartially observing relationships is an enormous gift to give yourself as a songwriter, one that will spill over into the way you handle your own relationships. It might aid you in correcting or reinforcing your commitment to your own behavior. If so, you'll find that you're writing new love songs inspired and deepened by your new insights.

Observing relationships impartially will enable you to see and comprehend both sides of a story instead of just being caught up in your own. Since most of the love topics you'll be writing about occur in everyday life, you will have to give up your personal bias as to any of these experiences in order to deal with them objectively in your songs.

So, you see, writing a song about love is a much better deal than going through it, because the truth of any relationship becomes easier to visualize and understand when you stand back dispassionately from it and view it as an observer.

TWENTY-THREE TYPES OF LOVE RELATIONSHIPS YOU CAN WRITE ABOUT

Every love relationship is different—there are no such things as generic relationships! When you're writing a song about love, be aware of the type and stage of relationship with which your song concerns itself. I want to help you learn to focus so that your song is truly about a particular couple in a particular stage and state of alliance. Let's take a stroll through the various aspects of love, so that you can start to focus your mind on which story you are wishing to tell, rather than trying to intermingle several kinds of love into one song.

1. **Love at First Sight.** The mesmerizing glance-across-a-crowded room; the glimpse-across-a-dance-floor; the turn-around-and-see-her-face . . . These are all descriptions of love at first sight. The "gone" feeling in the pit of your stomach, the breathlessness of the first kiss . . . all are part of love at first sight. More songs are written about this than probably anything else in the pop vein. It's because this is the stuff of fantasy. This love hasn't had a chance to go bad, go sour yet. It's still all dreams and maybes and could-be's. And it's the big "what if . . ."
2. **Burgeoning Love.** This is discovery. How it feels to be together, how it feels to touch, all the new sensations of making love, finding out what you have in common, discovering you like the same kind of pizza and both love Hemingway. It's about revealing yourself to somebody, baring

your soul in small ways to see how it flies. It's about worrying whether you should hold back more or hold back less. It's all about hope.

3. **Platonic Love.** These relationships are usually very stressful, even painful for one or the other of the parties, and that's a fact. Outside of family and work-related relationships, I believe the concept of a platonic friendship between a man and a woman is balderdash. Someone is driving that relationship, and it is because of his or her unwillingness to let go of the faint hope that something may one day come of it that it continues. There is an undercurrent of sexual attraction from one or both of the parties—if neither felt it, no platonic friendship would be long lasting. A love song that someone would write who finds himself in a platonic relationship is most likely to be one of longing for what he cannot have and dare not mention for fear of breaking the fragile thread that binds him to his "platonic" love.

4. **Love from a Distance.** Unrequited love usually comes under this category. Someone loves someone who doesn't realize, or doesn't *acknowledge* the realization, that he or she has an admirer. It is actually more painful and bittersweet than real love, as there is probably never going to be a chance for the one who painfully yearns. Love of a rock star might fall into this category. Or love of a popular boy at school. Love of your best friend's brother, or secret love of your best friend's girl would also qualify.

5. **Impossible Love.** When two people find that life has a way of coming between them, interfering, spoiling, and foiling their plans. This kind of love is very fanciful, filled with drama, yearning, wishes, and usually unfulfilled dreams. The meetings are infrequent, in some cases clandestine. When they get together, they're on their best behavior. Sexually, they are over the moon, snatching moments of passion and longing. They tell each other that they find the world in each other's arms. They share long luxurious late-night phone calls, or clandestine ones from public phone booths. They spend endless hours trying to figure out how to make it work, but . . .

   ♡ **Distance Prevents It.** They don't live in the same town and cannot find a way to coordinate their lives, their jobs, their living arrangements;

   ♡ **They Belong to Another.** There is a wife, a husband, a live-in lover. This is a clandestine and secret affair that is taking over their minds and hearts, largely because it is so hard to accomplish, and so impossible to continue.

♡ **Parents Keep Them Apart.** They are fighting their parents for the right to be together, but their parents insist that they are wrong for each other for any number of parental reasons. They meet secretly behind the school, at friends' houses, after dances, at secret rendezvous. They plan to run off together as soon as they can.

♡ **Working Together Thwarts Them.** They are unable to love out in the open, because they work together, and that's against the rules. They steal away for clandestine trysts. They are heartsore and frustrated by their inability to show their love in the daylight, but their lives conspire to keep them apart.

6. **Love Denied.** A couple are fighting their feelings. They want each other with every breath in their bodies. They choose not to be together because it would break up their marriage, because their families don't approve, because they are from warring political factions, because they are of different religions, because the age gap is too large. They have a mental connection that is incredibly strong, and a physical attraction they control with difficulty.

7. **Love Longed For.** Two people have the time, the place, the motivation. They have been thinking about it, perhaps talking about it. They lust after each other. They have imagined their encounters a hundred times; they dream of each other. Each day they are getting closer to getting together. They will climb over all obstacles to be together and damn the consequences.

8. **Love That Consumes.** It's like a disease; it takes over their minds and bodies. They can't work, eat, sleep, or bother with anybody else. They are unable to function in many of the ways that count. All they want to do is be together. Some of them get together and it's pure fire. Others get together and it's desperate and emotionally draining. Many songs are about this type of love, as it is so powerful.

9. **Love That Illuminates.** A person whose life was workaday, nothing going on, just going to work, coming home, going to bed, and then repeating it the next day. Suddenly, there's that person in their lives whose face lights up the room, who cares about them and wants to be cared about. Just being together is total fulfillment. It's as if they can float on air, can sing and dance about nothing at all. It's as if a lightbulb has been turned on inside of them and they are glowing.

10. **Loving Forever One Night.** They have met in a club, on a business trip, in a restaurant, on a bus, in a taxi, on a plane, in an airport lounge, and they have time on their hands, no place else to be, just the

night to be together. They know in their hearts that they will never be together again. They think for a moment that it would be cool to see each other again. They go somewhere to be alone, make love, laugh, joke, have a blast, eat and drink (or not), explore each other's bodies with the intimacy and odd familiarity of old loves. They part on a bittersweet note making vague references to meeting again.

11. **Perfect Love.** Finally finding "the one." Being able to talk or not with comfort, without embarrassment. Wanting to listen and be involved in each other's lives. Recognizing the flaws and faults of each other and knowing they can live with those. Feeling comfortable in jammies watching TV or dressed up for a party. Not caring what friends think, but hoping friends think they're good together. Wanting to get closer and closer every day. Fighting and not wanting to go to sleep without making up. Recognizing the faults in each other that they can and will live with, and the qualities they wouldn't want to live without.

♡ **Romantic Love.** Flowers, candy, picnics in the mountains, hikes on the beach at moonlight. Dancing 'til dawn, no appetite for anything but making love. Witty banter, charming each other, surrendering into waiting arms without a fight. Thinking this is so darn good it has to go on forever, and hoping it will never change.

♡ **Newlywed Love.** The dress is perfect, lace, chiffon, crystal beads, satin; the hat is like a halo upon the beautifully coiffed hair. She looks like a princess tonight, and her eyes are as radiant as two stars plucked from the sky. He is handsome and fabulous in his tux, surrounded by faithful friends and family. They tie the knot, an exquisite moment of hopes and promises, dreams and pie-in-the sky. They are as positive about the joys of love as they will ever be, though underneath it all is a layer of vulnerability, concern, stress, agitation that will follow them around on their honeymoon and into their first weeks of marriage. Yet they offer each other endless words of optimism, and they truly are excited.

♡ **Finding Conflict in Perfect Love.** Arguing over small things, but not letting them get in the way of the relationship. Fighting for a point of view, and learning to compromise. Worrying about past peccadillos turning up and hurting them. Squabbling and not speaking for hours, then taking joy in making up. Worrying about money, friends, in-laws, job security, landlords, perspectives, thoughts they don't share. Feeling jealous of predatory friends or co-workers. Getting angry about behavior that isn't kind, warm, thoughtful, or considerate enough. Laying ground rules about the way things are.

12. **Long-Term Love.** It has withstood hills and valleys, rights and wrongs, hurts and upsets, and it never runs out of steam. The passion may or may not have cooled. The friendship remains indomitable. The two of them remain proud of who they are, and have developed as individuals within the pairing. Their companionable silences can last for hours and they don't notice. Their lives are filled with things to do, friends (both mutual friends and personal friends) and interests (mutual and personal, also). Their world still circles around each other. They draw comfort out of seeing each other's face first thing in the morning. They don't always fall asleep together, but they always sleep in the same bed.

13. **Love Forever.** Elderly couples who have been married seemingly since the beginning of time. Their love and respect for each other is stunning to watch. Seeing them arm in arm supporting each other as they walk down the street brings a tear to the eye of the most hardened watcher. They live for each other, engage in light but affectionate humor about each other's faults and foibles, and without each other they'd be—as I once wrote in my song "Until You"—*a hat without a coat.* Country music is full of songs about love that's gone the distance, and it is always, always, touching and moving stuff.

14. **Comfortable Love.** They know where they stand with each other. They read each other's minds. They laugh at the same jokes on TV. They catch each other's eyes across a party. They gossip. They wear comfy things to bed, rub each other's back, know how they each take their coffee, apologize if they've said something uncalled for. They don't worry about whether they'll be together in the future; it's not an issue. They don't like some of each other's friends, but that's okay. They go out with their cohorts, but look forward to coming home and cuddling up like an egg and a spoon.

15. **Love Past Its Peak.** They have more regrets than hopes. They remember choices they made that could have been better, or different. They don't intend to look at others, but find their eyes wandering—someone possible . . . someone potential. They are bored and dismissive with each other. They cease to be enthralled by each other's personal attractiveness. They give compliments grudgingly. They stop dressing for each other, but dress for the world outside. They make love in a perfunctory fashion; they're still friends and get on with the day-to-day business of living. They share a great deal that they're loathe to part with. They know they must put it all back together or let it go completely.

16. **Love Held Onto.** Fervently staying together, fighting all odds to be together. They are tenacious, animalistic, filled with drive, unable to let go. They are working on it, won't let it slip away. Some are holding on for the wrong reasons—fear of being alone, losing a dream, not knowing what else to do with their lives. Some are holding on for the right reasons—there is something important they have together, they are going through temporary troubles, and they will work it out and be stronger on the other side of their troubles. Some hold on for clandestine reasons—this is a love affair that helps them keep going, gives them a reason to exist; they cannot possibly leave the one they belong to, but they will hold on indefinitely to the partner on the side.

17. **Love at Cross-Purposes.** They can't seem to see eye to eye. They're always having dramatic fights. They want to be together, but they keep finding reasons to part. They are stormy, flaring up at the slightest thing. They are passionate at lovemaking, and spend hours agitating alone or agonizing with trusted friends over what their love is and what it's not. They want to change each other, know they never will; want to love each other for who they are, know they never will. They are dynamic together out in public, but forever watchful. They find their relationship exhausting and sometimes exhilarating. They love each other deeply and know in their hearts that their love is doomed to failure.

18. **Fading Love.** They have been so great with each other, they can't believe it's slipping away. They work doubly hard at it, making such an effort to make it work. They can't seem to please each other, keep saying the wrong thing; their feelings are complex and jumbled. They don't even have the energy to fight very well; it's more bickering, stumbling blocks they keep tripping over. They know something is missing, and they don't want to let go. They have loved an image of each other and never discovered who the real person is, and images change.

19. **Futile Love.** Doomed from the start, this is going nowhere for them, though they do give it a good try. They are of different backgrounds— perhaps different races or different religions. Some are married and trying to have an affair or are gay and attempting a hetero marriage. They have insurmountable differences—different needs, different wants, different desires. Their love is brief and tragic.

20. **Love That's Over but Not Forgotten.** This is a very popular topic for songs. The one that got away. The one you almost married. The one you met on vacation. The one you loved in high school or college. The one

who moved away. The one you broke up with and lived to regret it. The bittersweet, the longing and remembering, the wanting to phone but hanging up when the phone is answered. The reliving of moments in dreams, the waking in a sweat, the concealing of feelings from your new love, your spouse, your children. The running into each other unexpectedly, the feelings of loss, regret, wistfulness. The wishes for, and sometimes the opportunity for, a second chance.

21. **Love That's Over but Anger Still Simmers.** Still thinking about what the other person did wrong to you. Still churning up about how you were used, were hurt, were abused, were ignored, were destroyed emotionally. Feeling anger for lost years, anger for being a fool to believe in that person. Calling yourself a fool for trying, for hoping, for working on that relationship. Being unwilling to admit that it was love. Wanting to get even emotionally, wanting to be strong again, wanting to be a survivor and a powerful person again.

22. **Letting Go of What Used to Be Love.** Feeling regret and sadness, feeling powerlessness, loss, bittersweet. Selling the home you once lived in together and moving away. Dividing up the worldly goods. Wondering whether friends will speak to you anymore. Wondering what's next. Wondering how it all fell apart when it started so well. Wondering if you made a mistake. Wanting to be friends still, or not. Getting a stab of regret every time you pass the old hangouts, hear a tune you both loved, see an unexpected reminder of the salad days of your love.

23. **The Fine Line Between Love and Hate.** Loving them for who they are, and hating them for who they're not. Wanting what you have together, and wishing you weren't there. Feeling like you're standing on the edge of a knife and you don't know which way to fall. Angry at them for how they've hurt or betrayed you. Wishing they didn't have as much power over you. Wishing you could leave and needing to stay.

There's no question about it: Love is the most complex of human emotions. It is filled with contradictions and questions, laughter and tears. As you consider the myriad of ideas for love songs, you are like a jeweler who comes across beautiful precious stones and finds a way to set them off to their greatest advantage. It is your job as a songwriter to find a memorable setting for each of these vignettes of love that come into your purview, and to make them immortal in songs.

♥
Love Song Therapy

Love is like an itching in my heart.
—THE SUPREMES
(Eddie Holland/Lamont Dozier/Brian Holland)

Love songs can be used to express hurt and anger, and also can be used as a device for working through issues at hand. Love songs are either about a relationship that's working or one that's not—there is no in-between ground that wouldn't be boring to listen to. Believe me, I've read dozens of lyrics in evaluation sessions that detail *dysfunction* in relationships, and though those details may be scintillatingly interesting to the songwriter, frankly, no one else cares.

LETTING GO OF BLOCKED EMOTIONS

Wanna get over a broken heart? Write a song about it! Writing a love song may be just the cathartic release you need to help you get over it and move on.

Making sense of your jumbled thoughts, feelings, and emotions by sorting them out on a lyric sheet is a stress reliever like no other. And though it's a productive way to deal with your angst about love, you don't even have to stick to the original and true story. The song version of events can end up completely different from the events that actually happened.

A song lyric is a remarkable way to address the idea that a love is over, that the feelings that once existed simply do not any more. Think about it: all that pent-up anger, hurt, hostility, pathos, longing, frustration, and misery put to great use!

Though you feel that your personal angst on the issue is blindingly singular, that nobody could possibly have felt this depth of pain before, here's an earth-shattering revelation for you: It's happened to just about everybody on the planet! But aha! The point of this is that it has not happened in just the same way, with just the same pattern of unraveling emotions, the same causes, the same mistakes; it has suffered neither the same betrayals nor the identical devastating emotional cost. Your own experience is in fact like a fingerprint, totally unique to yourself.

Tangled Memories

I don't have to be Sigmund Freud to know that people continually submerge their hurts in some deep dark place within, burying them to be revisited later. The only trouble is, the hurts pile on year after year, and pretty soon trying to retrieve them is like undertaking an archeological dig!

It happens to us all. Layers are heaped on layers of sadness, rebuffed romantic overtures, misunderstandings, lonely nights, devastating breakups, passionate arguments, and foolish words that should never have been said. The idea of trying to get to the emotions squished on the bottom and squeezed in the middle of your jumbled memory heap is worse than trying to locate your high school class ring in the junkpile of your attic.

Worse, all the things that have gone wrong and have hurt, somehow become mixed up together in your mind. Instead of being separated into categories, they combine to loom large in your psyche, an overwhelming, insuperable obstacle. The result is that when something occurs in your life that in a flash makes you think of one of these events, suddenly you find that this buried memory has merged into some other painful buried memory. That stirs up something further, and before you know it, you're caught up in a mélange of remorse and regrets that are all hashed together in an emotional ragout.

Putting Feelings on Paper

As a songwriter, you are luckier than anybody else on the planet, because you have the means to tap into all this buried stuff, bring a specific emotion to the surface, address it in a song, and write it out of your heart and soul. Ah, the catharsis! Ah, the feeling of a millstone falling away from your shoulders and vanishing!

I believe that there is no greater tool for releasing blocked emotions than writing songs about them. It reduces a situation from vaguely defined anger, hurt, perhaps humiliation, self-pity, and sadness, to an orderly and methodical—you might even say businesslike—approach to revealing and expressing these emotions.

The first step—trust me on this—is not to attempt to write a hit song about it, but simply to get your first draft on paper. There is nothing as important as a first draft for defining and expressing ideas you didn't even know you had!

Examining Love's Pain through a Songwriter's Eyes

Before you attempt a song based on a personal experience, you must begin by looking at the facts through the eyes of a songwriter, which means dispassionately. Otherwise, you'll plunge headlong into solely the angst part of what happened to you, and the listener will be in the dark as to what the story's all about. So, the first thing you'll need to do is to coolly assemble and list the actual elements of the experience. Before you can create a love scenario between your singer and the lover being sung to, you must clarify on paper the details of the ill-fated love experience upon which you wish to base your story.

- Was it a long-term relationship?
    - How long were you a pair and happy together?
    - How long did you pretend that things were still okay?
    - Was the fact that it ended
        - A tremendous shock?
        - A startling surprise?
        - A foregone conclusion—in other words, was it just a matter of time?
- Was it a short, passionate encounter?
    - Did you have immediate expectations of "foreverness"?
    - Was it all based on sexual desire and wanton lust?
    - Did you think the other person was on the same page as you were right from the start?
- Were words making promises for the future exchanged?
- Was the person involved with you also married or deeply connected to another lover?
- Was there a locale associated with the relationship, such as
    - A home, filled with photos and other memorabilia?
    - A seedy setting, such as a hotel, motel, or back-alley place?
    - An exotic location, such as an island, a faraway land, the mountains, the seaside, a log cabin, a field?

- Did it start to fall apart immediately, or after some time together?
  - If immediately, did you question staying?
  - If later on, what were the clues that something was amiss?
- Was there a betrayal—an infidelity of mind or body?
  - If it was an affair—was it someone younger than you? Someone you know? Someone who was just a passing ship in the night?
  - Was the betrayal yours or your partner's?
  - If it was your partner's, what could have caused the desire to stray?
  - If it was yours, what was missing in the relationship that made you want to try someone else's love?
- What will you miss the most?
  - The person's touch?
  - The sound of laughter?
  - The emotional support?
  - The playfulness?
  - The brilliance of mind?
  - The bright light that was in your life?
- What did you bring to life and to the relationship?
  - Your whole being?
  - Your truth and honesty?
  - Your love and sex?
  - Your friendship?
  - Your very special touch?
  - Your foolishness?
- Have you wasted time?
  - Your time or your partner's time?
  - Do you feel like an idiot, a clown, a bag of dirt?
  - Are you angry, confused, furious, amazed, ready to kill, ready to fight, ready to scream, ready to get over it and move on?
- How will you go on?
  - Will you let it go and move on to something else?
  - Are you philosophical, believing that all things must end?
  - Will you hold on to the past and never let go of the feeling?
  - Will you consider this a wonderful memory, nothing more?
  - Will you compare all other loves to this one?

THE ART OF WRITING LOVE SONGS

- ♡ Will you wish your partner well with the new love?
- ♡ Will you hope your partner will be really sorry to have messed this up with you?
- ♡ Will you believe your lover will ever find anyone who can replace you?
- ♡ Will you die?

By disguising or rearranging the players and the true facts, you can revisit this story over and over again in song. And if each lyric is a different take on the same story, nobody will guess!

LET'S WRITE AN "IT'S OVER" SONG

When you're ready to write a song about a relationship that's over, begin by finding a phrase that best expresses the aspect of the breakup you want this song to describe, and that will become your title.

Plain titles could be as blunt as "It's Over" (the title of my first song ever recorded, by Lola Falana), "I Don't Love You Any More," or "I'm Leaving Today." More subtle titles might ask questions that explore the mystery of what happened—"Where Did Your Love Go?" "When Did I Stop Loving You?" "How Do I Make Sense of Goodbye?" Yet another approach would be to express that this was not the singer's fault—"You're the One Who Changed," "You Forgot How to Love Me (and Made Me Forget How to Love You)," "You Never Really Knew Me." If it's about the definitive issue of getting up the courage to leave, it could be, "Where There's a Will, There's a Why," or "All That's Left to Pack Are My Dreams," or "Leaving You Is Easier Than Staying."

> Make sure each verse has a further point of view on the overall story, not just a restatement of the situation presented in the opening verse.

Though these titles take on relatively the same issue, each provides a twist on the idea. You can see that your choice of a title makes all the difference in how a song plays out.

Almost every song about breaking off a relationship will deliver an emotional message to the person for whom it is written. Is there another medium in which we can do that as eloquently or with such clarity of purpose as a love song? I don't think so. If we consider the options, we realize:

- ❤ "Dear John" letters are vituperative and descend to just plain meanness, hostility, and a laundry list of the other person's faults.
- ❤ "Kind" goodbye letters are usually filled with explanations and whys and wherefores and descend to the maudlin.
- ❤ Poetry is too airy and mental to be as definitive.
- ❤ Conversation is blunt, and there is so much left unsaid at the end of it, as it becomes filled with pain and tears, both people speaking at once with raised voices, and neither paying attention to the other's point of view.

But ah, with a song, there is a purpose and a point, a beginning, a middle, and an end, and the whole sad tale has to be contained within a structure of a couple of verses and choruses!

So, let's choose a title and write a song. In the context of a woman singing about a love she doesn't feel any more, how about the title "I'm Over Being Under Your Spell"? The first verse—which could explore the dawning of the realization that it's over—could start by saying *I looked at you this morning in the early dawn / Before you'd even opened your eyes.* This would be a straight-forward, right-in-the-moment comment. As such, it would invite us into the mind of the singer, so that we could visualize what she is visualizing. It could be followed by *I tried to find the feeling that I knew was gone / And I searched my heart for how a feeling dies.* Again, we are in the moment with the singer, understanding and empathizing with her recognition that she doesn't feel what she used to.

Those four lines would constitute an excellent first verse, as they would set up the story properly. Now let's consider where to go next. The structure of those lines—meaning the way they read—seems to lend itself to being followed by what I've described as a "build" into the chorus.

Since the build section has to lead us into the reason we're writing the song, it has to be more urgent than the verse, a more dynamic idea. It would also have a different structure to the verse; the lines would tend to have a slightly truncated shape, such as the following: *Maybe it's just cause I once loved you so much / That I can't bear knowing I don't need your touch.* This takes what was said in the first verse and makes it have value to the overall concept. It also acts as a sort of diving board into the chorus.

Now, the chorus has to pay off the idea and leave the listener with a strong impression of the song's message. We can use our title at the beginning of the chorus or at the end—that's a choice. Let's decide, in this case, that the chorus will start right in with the title, *I'm Over Being Under Your Spell*. Thus, the second line has to say something about why the first line is what it is. A word ending in "ell" is a particularly difficult word to rhyme, as there are only a few words that rhyme with it, such as "well," "tell," "hell." So the choices for the second line might be *I think you know I once loved you well*—it's okay, but a bit forced. *My heart has a story to tell* is better, and would be totally acceptable to the premise, but it's a bit flat. *And I'm living in my personal hell*—this one is quite dramatic, but we haven't yet set up this much angst in the verse, so it doesn't match. *I wish I could say it's been swell*—this line is tempting to use, as it's exactly what I want to say, but I'm worried about the word "swell," as it is not used very much in common speech right now. (Words go in cycles, and "swell" is out of cycle.) We could also look for a more evocative, even poetic thing to say that still explains the first line. Let's consider: *I was over the moon but I fell*. I like that—it has some interest and color to it. I think I'll just change the "but" to a "when," as that gives me the extra punch of a double meaning—it could be referring to the beginning of the relationship, "when I fell," or to the moment of falling out of love.

Going back to what the title, "I'm Over Being Under Your Spell," really means to the singer, I'd say that the singer's partner once had the power to hold her to him, and that she didn't have much say on her own life. So, I would think that the next lines might start with an emphatic "But": *But my world isn't just about you / And my life will go on without you*.

By now, although we have set up the fact that she's fallen out of love, we need to start telling the "why" of it, or there'll be no back-story to her having fallen out of love! Since we have to set up one more "ell" rhyme in order for the last line of the chorus (the title) to rhyme with the word at the end of this line, we could say *You thought you knew me so well*, but that line is too much about him and not enough about the singer. I'll flip the "you"s and turn them into "I"s: *I thought I knew you so well*. That works for me.

The next job is to write the line that sets up the ending, giving us a reason to have to repeat the title. In this case, it has to talk about what being under his spell meant: *I was mesmerized by your smile / And it held me for a while*, and that would lead back to and give meaning to the title *(But) I'm Over Being Under Your Spell*.

Having now set up the first verse and chorus, we are ready to move to the second verse.

If we were to repeat the same information in the second verse that was in the first verse—"I've realized that it's over"—the song would be monumentally boring. Yet that is exactly what millions of songs have in common. The song-writers rephrase the same idea in successive verses, thinking that wording it from a different angle is enough to move a song forward. This is absolutely erroneous. Make sure each verse has a further point of view on the overall story, not just a restatement of the situation presented in the opening verse.

One way to deal with the second verse would be to look back to what life was like when the singer was indeed under his spell.

Perhaps one might start the second verse by saying, *I melted every time I saw you at my door / I think I used to live for your kiss.* Saying I used to live for . . . helps us understand the power of the hold he once had over her, how he had mesmerized her, and how she had willingly gone along with it.

By starting the third line of that verse with *You once were . . .* you can start to show the separation happening: *You once were ev'rything that I was living for.* What you say next is really important, as this really ties up the concept before building into the second chorus. So, consider the following line ideas: (1) *I thought that all of love was merely this;* (2) *I thought that what we had was truly bliss;* (3) *I never dreamed we'd lose our way like this;* (4) *I never thought that it would end like this;* (5) *And what we had you know I'll always miss;* or finally, (6) *And what you made me feel is what I'll miss.*

I believe all of these choices would work, but which one works best? Number (1) tells us that the singer judged what love was by the spell she was under. Number (2) tells us that she didn't expect that it was anything less than everything forever. Number (3) says that in a way she blames herself, too, for it being over. Number (4) tells us that she is disappointed that it came down at the end from such a high. Number (5) says that she'll miss the halcyon days of what appeared to be perfect love, under his spell. Finally, number (6) tells us that more than missing him, she will miss how it felt to be in this love relationship. Which premise is most effective to go with the rest of this lyric? It depends on who is writing this song! That's the whole point of this book. We each view the same situation through different eyes. It is your divergent point of view, your unique creative interpretation, that will set your songwriting apart. But we also can all agree that certain ideas are stronger than others. In my opinion, my very first idea was the best one to tell this particular story. By saying *I thought that all of love was merely this,* she is accepting that the relationship had its limitations, but admitting that she failed to see them. Now that the bloom is off the rose, she gets it that this wasn't the end-all relationship after all.

So you think the second verse is done, right? But, no, taking a second look at that second verse, I'm not convinced that it is powerful enough. It doesn't tell what happened, does it. It's too passive. So, let's take another crack at it, remembering how crucial rewriting is to developing the best lyric you can write.

The first line might talk about the spell itself: *As much as I could get of you, I wanted more.* Then I feel we need to say right here and now, what happened, and I'm going to write, *Until I tasted lies in your kiss.* Aha! A reason for her to lose faith, lose her feelings for him. For the third line, *I'd made you ev'rything that I was living for* is active and thus more powerful than *You once were . . .* And for the final line, now that we realize the relationship was all smoke and mirrors, *The fantasy of us is what I'll miss.*

The second build needs to expand on the information about *why* this spell is broken, not just saying *that* it is broken. He led her on, obviously, and we have to question: "Is this person capable of loving anyone else at all?" Writing those two ideas as lyrics, one way of approaching the build would be: *You led me on, you knew I'd want to believe / But I'm seeing things clear, and it's my choice to leave.* A pickup of "'Cause" would be required to segue back into the chorus.

Now that we've got the "facts" out of our system, another way to write this build would be more passionate and less "thinky": *We were on fire, but now the fire has burned out / 'Cause living on lies is not what love is about.* The pickup would change to an "And." So, here's how the final lyrics might read.

I'M OVER BEING UNDER YOUR SPELL

VERSE 1:
I looked at you this morning in the early dawn
Before you'd even opened your eyes
I tried to find the feeling that I knew was gone
And I searched my heart for how a feeling dies

(BUILD):
Maybe it's just cause I once loved you so much
That I can't bear knowing that I don't need your touch

CHORUS:
I'm over being under your spell
I was over the moon, but I fell
My world isn't just about you
And my life will go on without you
I thought I knew you so well—
I was mesmerized by your smile

And it held me for a while
(But) I'm over being under your spell

VERSE 2:   As much as I could get of you, I wanted more
             Until I tasted lies in your kiss
             I'd made you ev'rything that I was living for
             The fantasy of us is what I'll miss

(BUILD):   We were on fire, but now the fire has burned out
             Cause living on lies is not what love is about (And)

CHORUS: **I'm over being under your spell**
             I was over the moon, but I fell
             My world isn't just about you
             And my life will go on without you
             I thought I knew you so well—
             I was mesmerized by your smile
             And it held me for a while
             (But) I'm over being under your spell . . .
             Yes, I'm over being under your spell

THE IMPLICATIONS OF WHAT WE DO IN RELATIONSHIPS

As songwriters, we must keep our antennae up for the implications of what we write. By being vividly aware that seemingly simple incidents of thought, words, and actions are capable of causing such powerful backlashes, we will be in tune with what domino effects they will set off for the characters we've created in our love songs.

Words, thoughts, and actions, once created, all have consequences. Many of us speak without first wondering what the ripple effect of our words might be. Saying something mean or hostile, cruel or insulting, creates a response. We can never take back what

Be mindful, when you're describing the singer's thoughts and plans to act, that you're not just stating situations, but you are creating future implications!

we've said—the damage is already done. Crocodile tears and big apologies cannot erase the stain.

It has been said that "thoughts are things." A partner in a relationship who is thinking mutinous thoughts and creating angry and divisive scenarios in his or her mind is destabilizing the relationship without ever uttering a word. Those thoughts lead to words or actions that might cripple or destroy the relationship.

Actions—be they physical harm to a partner, from slaps to much worse; be they closing off communication channels by turning away and refusing to talk; be they not calling, coming home late without explanation; be they angry or disparaging, disdainful, derisive, or disrespectful looks and behavior—all have consequences, which are frequently irreversible and often fatal to a relationship.

When you write a love song, look at *the implications of the unfolding events* you're describing. Since, unquestionably, each action the singer proposes taking will have a ripple effect on the outcome of events, be mindful, when you're describing the singer's thoughts and plans to act, that you're not just stating situations, but you are creating future implications! For instance, if the singer says, "When you talk about how you love me, it makes me cry," you are implying (a) that the singer is so in love that he or she plans to stay forever; or (b) that the singer doesn't want to be loved by this person any more, and these are tears of regret leading to leaving.

In either instance, the line makes the implication that the singer will be taking action. That means, in the first case, that the next verse might be about how she plans to breathlessly return that love in the future. In the second case, the following verse might be about the apartment she has seen that she's been thinking of taking, or about how she can see dividing up their possessions and their momentos.

My point is, once you understand the implications of what you've set up, you will be better able to form the subsequent verses of your song. Everything that you have your character say to his or her lover creates long-range implications for the health of the relationship.

One obvious example to illustrate this point would be the concept of "cheating." If a partner in a love relationship has a dalliance with another person, then it hurts and dilutes the primary relationship, and then clearly the partner doing this cheating has divided his or her allegiance to the primary intimate partnership. Thus watered down, it becomes no longer a "me and you against the world" relationship, but one that contains a third person's power and energy. The implications of getting your singer into a cheating situation, therefore, are that he or she knows that the primary relationship will be damaged and could be destroyed. That is a powerful element to include in a song about cheating, as remarkably handled in the Randy Travis country smash, "On the Other Hand" *(But on the other hand / There's a golden band)* by Paul Overstreet and Don Schlitz.

Furthermore, the implications of the singer not informing the mate being cuckolded or cheated on are that (a) the mate is being prevented from deciding whether he or she wants to remain in the relationship under the circumstances; (b) the mate doesn't understand why the cheating partner is acting distant and uncaring, and mistakenly suffers from the belief it has to be something he or she has done wrong, which causes personal grief; and (c) the cheating partner is destroying the trust that has been built up between him or her and the mate.

To take yet another angle on the subject, the implications of the singer simply *contemplating* cheating, not even going through with it, just thinking about it, are (a) feelings of dissatisfaction with his or her mate because of the comparisons between the new object of affection—frequently younger or more attractive in some way; (b) it might irrationally lead to emotionally blaming the mate for holding him or her back from "enjoying life"; (c) that a lot of time and energy will be invested in contemplating a fantasy, energy that could be spent indulging in innumerable other more profitable pursuits, such as enjoying the primary relationship.

Thus, when you are plotting the storyline for your song, rather than considering only the moment at hand, it is useful to consider and possibly include the *implications* of how each party to the relationship is going to fare because of it. And if we make it a habit while writing love songs to compare and contrast ourselves with our song characters, considering the long-term implications of our own thoughts, words, and actions, we might keep from making the fatal mistakes that hurt and destroy our own relationships.

There was never a guidebook or answer book written that adequately addressed all of our needs or answered all of our questions about love. The reason is that the answers are only inside of *ourselves.* I've found the only way to fully identify them is to write them down on paper.

USING A SONG TO MANAGE ANGER CONSTRUCTIVELY

We've all learned that where there is smoke there is fire. Sometimes the smoke is the tension that builds inside us after a relationship begins to go sour. It is the unhealthy way in which we suppress our anger that causes us to suffocate our feelings until they finally blow up. And then what we do with them is that we take them out on everyone we know—family, friends, co-workers. We walk around with a sort of nonspecific bad attitude, which poisons our life.

But anger is a wonderful element of the songwriter's toolbox. It spits out:

- **Passion.** This drives a song that is talking about the emotions and feelings and sexual experiences the lovers shared, how right they felt at the time, how betrayed the singer now feels.
- **Righteousness.** The saying "Hell hath no fury like a woman scorned" applies here. It is very difficult for anyone to accept that they have been fooled into thinking a relationship was working and was great. The righteous song expresses such emotions as "how could I have been such a fool as to trust you?" or "I should have seen right through you," and it always says, "I'm better off without you."
- **Fire.** This song chews into the person it's being sung to, without any self-deprecation involved. It's all about affirming the self-worth of the singer. It may even contain humor. Humor is a wonderful way to explode that fireball raging inside of you, and turn it into something productive.
- **Frustration.** Nothing tears a person apart like being frustrated by a callous lover. Getting that push-me-pull-me runaround can make the most sane person miserable. This song talks about such things as "You tell me one thing and then you do another, I don't know what to believe"; or "How can I ever trust you, now I've seen you can be a liar"; or "Don't do me like that—be straight or I'm gone."

An angry song is a way to decipher and elucidate upon the nagging second thoughts, misgivings, and scathing snarls that inhabit your being and have no place to go. It is a release rather like the famed blowhole spout in the rock on the island of Kauai, which builds up pressure from oncoming waves, and then releases a volcano of water erupting high into the air and spraying for hundreds of feet.

Identifying the Source of Anger

Though it should be obvious that one cannot solve a problem until the problem has clearly been identified, many of us skip that step. Identifying the source of our personal emotional pain and suffering isn't always easy. There was never a guidebook or answer book written that adequately addressed all of our needs or answered all of our questions about love. The reason is that the answers are only inside of *ourselves*. I've found the only way to fully identify them is to write them down on paper.

This is what drives songwriting: In our own lives, we cannot change our relationships for the better until we truly know not only *how* things are, but what it is *about* how things are—that is, what underlying issues are hampering our relationships—that charges our emotional state and causes us grief. Songwriters, in other words, use their own experiences of love to motivate their writing. Is it possible to accomplish personal enlightenment and growth by writing love songs? Well, I've been working through my questions about love on paper for the past twenty-five years, and I guess I'm living proof of how well it works! It's a very healthy way to explore relationship issues and find meaningful expression for doubts and grievances.

Let there be a consciousness to the process. As you begin to manage anger through writing love songs, go ahead and rechannel your angry feelings in this truly rewarding and constructive manner. At the end of the day, not only will the angry energy be dissipated, but you will also complete song lyrics you'll be extremely proud to have written. And there's nothing to be angry about in that.

CHAPTER 15

Using Personal Experiences to Stimulate Fresh Ideas

Paradise by the dashboard light.
—MEATLOAF
(Jim Steinman)

Your personal experiences with love can help you to refine and improve your songwriting skills. They can provide you with lots of stimulating resource material, but the songs don't have to be about you. Once you have mastered telling your own stories, the next step is to raid your storehouse of memories for background material to support fictional song ideas.

While I'm sure you have a great deal in your own life that you want to explore in writing, and while your first hundred or so love songs will all be entirely and openly about you and your own relationship experiences, eventually that will change. You will begin to want to preserve the privacy of your own feelings and memories, and will find yourself being drawn more and more to disguising personal stories and home truths. Now that doesn't mean you will not draw on your own adventures for inspiration, or that true items from your life will not pepper and flavor everything you write. It just means you will do it more obscurely.

YOUR MEMORY IS A VAULT OF STORED RESOURCES

Your perspectives on how love works have been shaped largely by your own life and love experiences. Keeping in mind that it is the listener's ears you are always hoping to appeal to, let's explore translating your romantic past into valuable songwriting skills.

Think of your life experiences as a bank account into which you have made millions of deposits every day since you were born. These deposits are nothing less than the details of every experience you've ever had, every brief encounter and every long relationship that has ever touched your world.

Everyone you have met along your path, young and old, has influenced you in some way. Words they have said have stayed in your mind. The ways they appeared, dressed, carried themselves, have made indelible impressions. Even people of wishy-washy character or plainness of appearance have made an impression for their very lackluster nature.

Every time you have watched the clouds part and the sun break through; every time you have gasped at a huge full Harvest moon seemingly hanging on an invisible string like a giant Edam cheese; every time you have encountered a new and remarkable taste; every time you have marveled at a sudden sound—a wind chime, a baby's laugh, Christmas carolers on a snowy street, the crackling and popping of burning wood in a hearth fire—these brief images have all left their indelible impression on your subconscious memory.

You have not *consciously* made these deposits in your experiential "bank account," but the images and thoughts that have constituted your life experience have all been stored and saved. The question is, under what circumstances do people normally retrieve them? People who do not write rarely have the same wherewithal as writers do to draw upon these layers upon layers of saved and stored memories. Though, of course, they call up certain remembered things in conversation, and fragments of memories float to mind as they watch the world go by, it is in the act of writing that we rediscover so much of this stored subconscious material. Without a doubt, artists paint some of these subconscious memories onto their canvases. But I contend that we who write them down, especially in lyrics dealing with love and relationships, are able to draw upon more of them than most.

You do not need to sit down and consciously make lists of your experiences, for although it may seem you've forgotten them, each one is stored there in that immense safe deposit box called your memory. It will remain in storage till one day you lock onto a song idea that provides the key to unlock that forgotten experience, and it will pour out of you onto the page.

Retrieving Ideas from Storage

Actually, it's amazing how those stored images come back to us, jogged by a word, a touch, a sight, and all of a sudden we hear, smell, taste, and visualize something long unremembered from our past. Sometimes it's a vague image that we cannot connect with anything in particular. Frequently it is just a fleeting essence of something—a flash of blue, a waft of scent—and we feel a warmth or a shiver, a visceral response to its return.

We use these images in our lyrics as part of the fabric of the song. They provide the background, the ambience, the color. They allow the listener to see not just a tall woman but a tall *brown* woman *with shiny glistening skin and kohl-rimmed, sparkling eyes.* She's standing not just on a front porch, but on a front porch *on the corner of a street you used to pass on the way to school.* On her feet are not just shoes, but those remembered *red, snakeskin, high-heeled, backless, don't-tell-me-what-I-can-do* shoes.

The image of this woman may stem from a friend of your mother's, a fascinating woman in your neighborhood, an actress on a movie screen. It doesn't matter where the image originated, you see, because now you are going to pull it out of the vault and use it inventively as a place to start visualizing the character in your song.

RECOGNIZING THE LIMITATIONS OF YOUR PERSONAL STORY

Your own love encounters (unless you're like Wilt Chamberlain, who claimed to have been with twenty thousand women) have probably been limited to anything from zero to a couple of hundred experiences. Yet even the most experienced of you have a major limitation, which, surprisingly, is not the number of people you *have* met but the lovers you have *never* met. Those you can only imagine. Ah, did I say that? You can only *imagine* them? Yes, I did. I said it because the best opportunity you have to get beyond your personal limitations is to imagine what you have never personally experienced.

Surely you cannot believe that the world is interested in knowing only about the dynamics and details of *your* relationships? No, listeners are interested in one thing: hearing about themselves! So even if you are writing about your own love experience, you must always remember to engineer your words to be thought-provoking and interesting enough to the listeners for them to immediately find a connection to the story.

YOUR SINGULAR WORLDVIEW

Truly, nobody on the planet can ever hold quite the same perspective on love as you do, based on your own personal journey in that area. You have been touched a certain way, hurt a certain way, and made to feel special a certain way. You have buttons that can be pushed easily because they remind you of events in your past.

Nobody else has ever had the exact same combination of influences and confluences on their life that you have had. I mean, nobody at all. Your angle on love is entirely unique in the history of the world. Isn't that powerful?

But there are thousands of topics that everyone has experienced, that your songs can weigh in on. You just have a unique slant on them. Your view may be uplifting or sad, ironic or angry, or simply a commentary on what's going on in the world. Some subjects, however treated, are more popular for songs than others.

Why are so many songs written, for instance, about good girls loving men who are rotten to them? Because it is such a common phenomenon in society, that's why. Women of all backgrounds, political persuasions, strengths, and weaknesses seem to gravitate at some point in their dating life to men who have "machismo."

Nobody else has ever had the exact same combination of influences and confluences on their life that you have had. I mean, nobody at all. Your angle on love is entirely unique in the history of the world. Isn't that powerful?

What is machismo? The dictionary calls it "an exaggerated sense of masculinity." It plays out as a man acknowledging some sort of indefinable personal power, be it due to his appearance or job description. Macho men frequently wield their power over the women who are attracted to them by being unbending, callous, users, or sexual athletes, which just seems to make them more desirable, for some indescribable reason.

I can't theorize why women are irresistibly drawn to doggedly unreliable, nerve-wrackingly inconsiderate, and boorishly self-serving men. I do know that the harder a woman falls for a louse, the bigger louse he becomes! Macho men manipulate women's emotions like Play-Doh. But I've never met a woman who doesn't think—just like some vainglorious cowgirl riding a wild bronco—that she's up to the task of breaking some bad boy. And, eventually, just when the boy's sure he's invincible, some woman does!

The songs about men crushing women's hearts are not just written by aggrieved women, you should note. A man likely understands the machismo role he or his friends like to play, and he may be just a little bit proud of it (and just a little bit ashamed!). The little bit ashamed part is how he is able to write from a woman's point of view. It allows him to recognize what the man in the song is doing, and to understand how he is manipulating this cat-and-mouse game! Thus, although the writer himself likely never has experienced being on the receiving end of this behavior personally, as a woman has, he is able to write the response rather like a chess player—anticipating and understanding the reasons for the next move of the opponent before he chooses what move he will make to set it up!

In Retrospect

I have mentioned the saying, "Hindsight is 20/20." We all know how we would have handled a situation differently given the benefit of knowing what the consequences of our actions would be. That becomes an incredibly powerful tool for you when you're writing love songs about love lost or pined for. I recently heard a caller confide in a radio psychologist that if she had known what the ramifications of getting a divorce were when she became discontented several years ago, she would never have gone through with it. She related that it has been an endless struggle, hassle, and heartache ever since. And furthermore, she added, none of the men she's met since have been so much better than the one she left. At least with him, she said, she knew what the faults were. She concluded that she should have learned to live with those, and not made them such a big deal. What an interesting piece of information for a songwriter to have at hand when writing about a woman looking back at a relationship she should never have let go. I have alluded to that insight in more than one song I've written since then.

When telling your own story in retrospect, you can tell it accurately, or you can embellish it. I hope I've made it clear that it doesn't matter to anybody in the world if you spice it up, make it more interesting than it was. It will only make it a better love song subject. Also, it's hard to recall pain. Our Creator gave us an amazing ability to forget—not that we had pain, but what that pain felt like. So a lot of what you write about your own past is likely to be a potpourri of truth and invention. You also may have had time to get a more balanced perspective on the other person's point of view and, surprisingly, may need to reinvent the concept of "hurt" for the song.

"IMPROVING" ON THE TRUTH

Let's look at how you, as a songwriter, can embellish the truth—both what you've experienced and what you've observed—to make it more interesting and compelling as song material.

Don't Forget Your Sense of Humor

There is no situation so deep, so dark, so depressing that it does not require a little uplift in a song, whether that uplift is something outright funny, or simply thoughtfully ironic. Humor can induce pathos as well as or better than sad words. It is hard sometimes for people to listen to depressing ideas, but if they have a thread of irony in them, they become wonderful.

Consider the Blackwell-Lee song "I've Got Friends in Low Places," which was such a huge hit for Garth Brooks. The first thing you think is, that concept makes you laugh, right? It's a brilliantly witty title. But it is actually a painfully difficult admission of failure in a relationship. It is in effect saying, "I just couldn't fit into the society that I longed to be part of, I was just not able to live up to your ideal of me, or be part of the upper-crust world you live in. So I'm happier now with my whiskey-drinking cronies who accept me for who I am *not*."

The lyrics to this song could have approached the same subject by saying straight out, "I don't need you with your high and mighty ways." Or they could have gone defensive, "I'm not living for your approval." Instead, they were about how he crashed her party obviously dressed out of place, and the entire premise is that we actually can see him in these lyrics, completely a fish out of water. It's totally visual, and ironically, painfully funny.

Adding Fictional Elements to Your Story

If you're going to draw on a personal experience as the inspiration for a song, you must alter your characters somewhat. Make them older or younger, taller or shorter, more streetwise and savvy, or shyer. Take out some of their bad habits and substitute others of your invention. Fictionalize their behavior, or the reasons for it. Make it more compelling, less mundane. Make us care about the characters in a way that we might not care about the people upon whom they are based.

If you think I'm trying to teach you how not to stick to the truth when writing a song, you're right. The truth is interesting, but a *fictionalized* truth can be even more so. You'll be surprised at what a wonderful storyteller you can become when you add elements of your own invention to it, and redefine what "is" is!

Have It Your Way

Whatever you write about, you must reveal a story with the flair of your own unique talent. Remember, these songs don't have to be your own personal stories to be run through the bias of your own viewpoint and your own take on things.

Whether you are telling your own stories or those of others, you have to describe things honestly, and if you're attempting to describe them by trying to think like somebody else, you don't want it to come out sounding false. If

THE ART OF WRITING LOVE SONGS

you are writing about an unfamiliar character, put some time and effort into "becoming" that character. There is a saying, "Walk a mile in my shoes," which means, if you want to know why I am how I am, try living my life for a while, and you'll soon "get" it. For a songwriter, it's part research and part immersion. See that you don't wade in contextual waters that are way too deep, because you will drown your talents and ambitions in a disappointing mire of ineffectiveness. Make sure that you stay with subject matter and characters that are comfortably within your grasp so that your words and ideas can flow, and you will own the recipe for becoming a fine storyteller.

CHAPTER 16
♥
Whose Point of View Is This?

Don't it make my brown eyes blue.
—CRYSTAL GAYLE
(Richard Leigh)

It's time now to discover how to write from the point of view of the opposite sex, as it is critical for a songwriter to be able to see both sides of a story. As a surprising adjunct, there will be far less miscommunication in your own relationships once you have "eaten the apple" of knowledge, whereby you can see a situation through your partner's eyes. It is enlightening, to say the least, to come to an understanding of why he or she thinks thoughts and takes positions you personally find incomprehensible.

It never ceases to amaze me how differently my husband and I see things that almost any girlfriend and I would view in the same way. Men seem to be attracted to contending with overall issues, while women are inexorably drawn to examining minutiae. The yen of men and women to understand each other is older than time, and yet it is one of the perversities of nature that we are on many levels indecipherable to one another.

There may be some who believe the differences have nothing to do with the sex of an individual, but are all about role-playing. I have certainly heard from friends in gay households that similar roles play out between the two partners, and similar misunderstandings and power struggles occur as within typical male-female relationships.

Whatever the reasons, the male and female players in relationships certainly approach relationship issues from different angles, and it is our job as songwriters to reflect those differences in our songs. Men are rarely as communicative on the subject of love as women are. It's not part of their make-up. A woman can gush on about love to her female friends, sharing advice, discussing in detail "he said and I said" conversations from her relationship, confessing the true nature of her sexuality, admitting sensual fantasies, and worrying endlessly about whether she is romantically loved by the one to whom she is giving all the love and emotion in her body and soul.

A man, however, might talk about the woman he is involved with in terms of her intellect, her figure, her capability in her job, how much she turns him on (or doesn't), where he is taking her for dinner or vacation, and her charming qualities and talents.

A woman writing from a male perspective must keep in mind that men not only have trouble with expressing their love to the person they love, but suffer from also finding it extremely difficult to even discuss it with friends. So, this love feeling, with all of its accompanying twists and turns, is trapped inside of a man like a butterfly in a net. Thus, in writing a love song for a man to sing, a woman must become adept at using her naturally expressive language more succinctly, refraining from flowery words and overly detailed microscopic evaluations of a situation. Her lyrics must retain the male dignity, strength, and solemnity of purpose. That doesn't mean staying away from expressing feelings. It's more about being precise and cutting through the fluff to get to those feelings. Don't write what you'd like or prefer him to say unless you can imagine these words issuing from a man's consciousness.

Conversely, a man writing lyrics for a woman to sing must consider her intense commitment to the relationship, her desire to analyze it and find a way to make it right. He must go against any personal instincts on his part to cut to the core of the matter without the finessing, the questioning, the dissecting, the sharing that is a woman's way of expressing herself. Furthermore, whereas a man's lyrics tend to portray men as laughing on the outside but crying on the inside, a woman is either crying or laughing—both inside and outside.

HOW WOMEN THINK

You might say it's outrageous that I would have the effrontery to say to you that women think a particular way, but I contend that they do.

- ♥ Would a man be late for a party because he didn't like his makeup and washed it all off and started over again?
- ♥ Would a man avoid going to an event because he thought he looked too fat in his outfit?
- ♥ Would a man think he was being treated like chattel if a woman preceded him down the street and left him walking behind?
- ♥ Would a man book a flight in the afternoon instead of the morning in order to work in a nail appointment?

- ❤ Would a man burst into tears because a woman didn't compliment him on his new outfit?
- ❤ Would a man refuse to go to bed with a woman because she didn't compliment him on the meal he cooked her?

I'm telling you, men and women do think differently! Brushing up on how they each see love is a helpful exercise to any songwriter.

Women's thought processes have a lot to do with how they have been brought up, what magazines and books they read, how they have been educated, what they earn, who their friends are, what their religious grounding is, how puritan they are, or how free-spirited. When you create a woman's point of view in a song, also factor in her sexual drive; her tendencies toward standoffishness or coquettishness; her neediness for love; her amount of self-confidence; the degree of hurt that she has suffered from family, friends, lovers, and employers; and, of course, that all-important factor, her appearance—which has a lot of bearing on how she'd feel about herself.

When a man is writing a lyric for a woman to sing, he needs to go to the inside secret core of that woman, shut his eyes, and begin to think the thoughts that particular woman thinks, or it comes out sounding not like a real woman's words, but like the wishful thinking of what a man longs for a woman to say and think. You don't, after all, want your female listeners to roll their eyes and say, *Oh puh-lease! Who wrote that?!*

Apropos of that, I remember once listening to an R&B song that said *I just want to be your la-dy.* I thought about it for a while, and I decided it had to have been written by a guy, as no woman would say that! It is totally a guy thing to say. It is a guy expressing that a woman wants to be subservient to him. What woman in the twenty-first century is looking for a man to be subservient to? Women want to be partners, equals to their men. Men: Check out the lyrics you put in a female singer's mouth with a woman friend. Bounce them off of her and see if they sound real!

It is so important to write your songs from a realistic mindset, saying things that real women would say, and reflecting what real women think. Which is not to say that all women think the same thoughts, or that six women sitting at a table will all react identically to the same question.

For instance, let's consider what happens when a woman is trying to decide whether to spend the night with a new man. For simplicity's sake, let's name our six fictional women Stacey, Tara, Candy, Lori, MaryAnne, and LaVerne. Let's eavesdrop on their conversation.

STACEY:	I have this six-date rule. I do not go to bed with anyone for six dates, no matter what.
TARA:	Six dates! That's really a long time. I mean, if it feels right, why not go for it the first night?
CANDY:	The first night! First that boy'd better get himself an AIDS test, and spend some money on me! He's got to earn the right.
LORI:	I've done it both ways, and you know what, it never works to have sex early on. I think next time I'm going to look for someone who wants to wait till we're married.
MARYANNE:	What if you wait all that time, and then it's awful, you're not compatible, and you're already married!
LAVERNE:	I don't make any rules about it. I just know when it's right; it can be early on, or it can be months down the line. I follow my instincts, as long as I get the sense this man's the real deal.

So, what do we have? Six different points of view, but all very womanly. Can you imagine six men having the same conversation, about when it's "right" to go to bed with a woman? As they would say in England, Not bloody likely! It wouldn't even be a topic that would come up! But it does come up for women, so when you want to write a song from a woman's point of view, understand which woman's voice you're using, and which attitudes are authentic to her.

Elements of attitudes women want to project in songs can include:

- Being respected for who she is or what she thinks
- Being loved for being sexy
- Being loved for all her other attributes, apart from sexiness
- Being appreciated for her contributions to her man's life and happiness
- Being appreciated as a friend
- Being independent—being able to stand on her own two feet, while still loving her man
- Saying goodbye to a relationship and being strong about it
- That she is the best woman this guy will ever find in this life
- That this guy won't be sorry if he gives her love a chance
- That she won't stand for any nonsense
- That she loves him in spite of his faults
- That she'll stand by him because she loves him
- That she's looking for the man who's the answer to her prayers

- That she's there for him, whatever it takes
- That she wants to be loved like a woman needs to be loved

Two women both in new dating relationships might spend their entire lunch hour with each talking about her new man. In the process of discussing his hair, eyes, mouth, physical stature, and rating him sexually, they'll also discuss what was said in a recent conversation and take it apart word by word to analyze—"what did he mean by that??" Each can let off steam talking to her girlfriend about it. Interestingly, a woman having these discussions with a friend is not betraying her man, she is simply searching for clues as to who the man is, and she finds that the feedback offered by this healthy discourse with a friend is both encouraging and enlightening.

Her issues might seem silly to a man, but women understand each other's issues very well. Particularly because men can be so unforthcoming about expressing their inner selves until a long time into the relationship, women resort to their friends' advice and opinions. Thus, many third-person songs, written from a woman's perspective about the man she loves, seem to be sung to her invisible girlfriend.

A woman feels vulnerable in love situations where she has given her body or her heart, and so a great deal of what she might sing about in love songs is questioning a guy's intentions. Conversely, in a secure relationship, she'll exult in singing about how solid this love is.

All of which leads me to this: When you write a woman's point of view in a song, show her vulnerability and her inquisitiveness, her curiosity about what's going on in the relationship. Show her openness to discovery, and show her anger at betrayal. Show her as real flesh and blood, full of feelings and raw emotions, not just as a sex object. Let her come to life in the song, not be a stick figure. The truth is, there may be generic things women talk and think about, but there is no such thing as a generic woman!

HOW MEN THINK

Since I am not a man, I would be pelted with rotten tomatoes by all my red-blooded male readers if I were to presume to tell you I know conclusively how men think. But when I write a love song from a man's point of view, I'd better be convincing! So, I have made a career of observing men both from within my relationships with them and from the outside. Men in varying stages of romance and marriage have also asked my advice on love about a kazillion times. And while I never stop learning, I think I've absorbed enough for my considered opinions to be worth sharing with you.

Notice that a man's background—particularly socioeconomic and religious—greatly influences his thought processes and behavior. How he was treated by the women in his family, how he saw them behave toward themselves and the rest of the world, goes a long way toward giving him his basic examples upon which to base his conclusions about who women are. Among my observations:

- Men in dating situations don't want women to presume too much too soon and will run if pushed.
- Men equate a woman being a great listener with being a great date.
- Men are uncomfortable if they believe they are being analyzed by a woman.
- A man will frequently apologize to a woman even when he doesn't know what he's done wrong, just to keep the peace.
- Most men are scared that if they commit to one woman, they might:
  - Miss out on someone better.
  - Feel chained down and get depressed.
  - Lose their identity and freedom.
  - Get bored sexually.
- Other men are searching for true love because:
  - They want someone to be a mother for their children.
  - They're tired of running around and feeling as if they're "drifting."
  - They've seen it work in a friend's life, and it suddenly seems attractive.
- Most men get that it is deadly to criticize a woman's outfit, hair, or makeup just before she goes out. Better to compliment and soothe her, to soften her up for love. (He doesn't have to be Einstein to calculate that if he wants his partner to be sexually willing, he'd better not make her mad about *anything* for several hours prior.)
- The average man always spouts out the answers to all of a woman's problems and situations, and doesn't understand why she doesn't follow his obviously flawless advice to the letter. (She didn't want a quick fix or a lecture, just a warm and friendly ear off of which to bounce her thoughts and feelings.)

When you're writing songs from men's points of view, remember that men do not discuss relationships as intimately with other men as women do with their women friends. If they are hurt, they tend to hold it inside, and if they are angry, they tend to look for reasons and blame outside of themselves.

When expressing a man's feelings in lyrics, look for the deeper insights into what is motivating them. Don't go to obvious and shallow places with them, or they will sound trite. Understand the complexities of their relationships with women, their vulnerability because they have a limited understanding not of *what* women think but of *why* they think the way they do.

Earlier, we eavesdropped on six women having a private chat. Now it's the men's turn. If six men (let's call them Joe, Jack, Richard, Link, Lou, and Justin) were sitting in a group and one of them asked how to break up with his girlfriend, each of them would surely come up with an equally straightforward approach:

JOE: Just stop calling her, she'll get the idea sooner or later.

JACK: Yes, but then she'll call until she pins you down, man. I say better to spell it out. Call her up and tell her it's over, and if she cries, just listen, and say I'm sorry a lot of times, and then say goodbye.

RICHARD: That's cold! I say take her out to dinner, and take her hand across the table, and tell her you have something to say . . .

LINK: What if she flips the table over on you! Hey, I say just start dating someone else, and when she finds out, *she'll* break up with *you*, brother.

LOU: That's pretty chicken. I say just do it when you're out together. You *know* she's gonna say something that makes you crazy sometime that night, just get into an argument about it, and let nature take it's course. I mean, let her cook her own goose—break up with her over something that's really happening at the moment.

JUSTIN: Hey, how's this: Tell her why you're done with her—maybe she'll fix it, and maybe you don't have to break up after all!

Don't stereotype *all* men. As illustrated in the above "chat," there are as many views as there are men, so when writing a man's lyrics allow each male character to have unique definition. Nevertheless, you may find these concepts useful for men to sing about:

❤ Let's try it and see where it leads us.
❤ I never thought I'd feel this way, but I do.

- Show me what I'm missing.
- Tomorrow will take care of itself; love me tonight.
- You're the one I want to spend the rest of my life with.
- I gave you everything—how could you leave me?
- You're everything I've been looking for.
- I'm the man who can give you what you need.

Since people are not single-minded stereotypes who all behave the same way in every situation, when you put an opinion in someone's mouth in a love song, visualize who this person is. Make sure you feel connected to his opinion, have thought it through thoroughly, and can make a case for it. Stay consistent to your storyline throughout the song, and keep it real.

♥

CHAPTER 17

Originality of Language

Oh-oh, I'm falling in love again!
—JIMMIE RODGERS
(Luigi Creatore/Al Hoffman/Dick Manning/Hugo Peretti)

As you embark upon your grand flirtation with the language, what will ultimately set you apart as a songwriter is your originality. The inventive twists you can put on plain language are what will mark your work not only as unique, but also as something worth a listener's time. And speaking of time, don't rush, don't hurry, and allow your mind all the time you need to connect with those fabulous creative notions.

FINDING A WONDERFUL TITLE

I always begin a song with a title. It is a road map to the idea I'm writing. I choose my titles with care, and always offer my composer-collaborators several choices of titles, so that we can find the one that best expresses the idea we want to write about.

Since a title will usually appear several times in your love song, it is essential to pick one that you can build your story around, something that lends itself to the storytelling process itself. It needs to be the answer to the questions you might set up in the verse, or the natural explanation for the information set up in the verses. In theater writing, it is the lyrical reason for bursting out into song rather than saying something in dialogue.

To choose a title for your love song, clear your mind and let a dozen or two possibilities in a row come through you onto a blank piece of paper, without worrying if they're any good or not. Let this process be a stream of consciousness, and simply write down whatever comes up for you, even though some of them might seem stupid or inappropriate. Some might even be hilarious or obscene: it doesn't matter, 'cause in the end, all you need is one—the right one.

Title or Great Line?

Here's a great tip: You should take a second and third look at your list of titles, as very often you will find among them some wonderful ideas to be included in your lyric! Not all "title" ideas will convey the overview of the story you wish to tell, which is why you don't end up choosing them as the title for your song. Some of them, though not strong enough to be titles, are important ideas that do belong within the story, however, and are valuable to revisit as lines in your verses!

Hoarding Song Titles

Always keep a pad and pen handy, whether you are driving down the street, in a movie, at your work desk, or waiting in the doctor's office. You never know when you'll eavesdrop on a great line coming out of the mouth of some unexpected person.

Great title ideas are like gold to songwriters. Hoard them, save them, store them, worship them in secret, and then flaunt them in your brilliant songs. In the mouth of the person who said the words, they might be just a passing phrase, but as a songwriter you can add dimension, dynamics, divine interpretations.

Keep a list in a separate "titles" notebook or on your computer. Speak ideas for titles into a sound recorder—get one of the new digital models; they're great, as you can record loads of thoughts on them, flick between them, and erase the ones you're done with while retaining the ones you want to keep.

Titles are everywhere—on the news, in magazines, in advertising slogans. They are in your and others' conversations, and in the dialogue of movies and TV shows. There are even titles and wonderful song concepts hidden in novels. I read a great deal of fiction, from contemporary murder mysteries to the essential classics, from historical fiction to science fiction. I find reading novels a wonderful escape from work and stress; there is nothing like a journey into the imagination. Thus, I am always searching for a terrific story well told. Within those stories are countless snippets of thoughts and snapshots of relationships.

Great ideas abound all around you, and they can be yours for a song, if you just observe and listen!

Marrying a Title with a Lyric

Once you have decided on a title for your love song, it is a good idea to out-line--either in your mind or on paper—the relationship story you want to tell, and to discuss it with your collaborator if you have one. Decide where it is you are going with this story and how to best pay off the intent of the title. If there is sadness, we'd better know why by the end of the song. If it is ebullient excitation, we the listeners need to be caught up in it.

> If your lyric nails the ideas innate in your title, you have done your job. A title and lyric are a marriage of a concept and its execution.

If your lyric nails the ideas innate in your title, you have done your job. A title and lyric are a marriage of a con-cept and its execution.

In a song called "If Ever a Love There Was"—which Todd Cerney and I wrote in an inspired rush, at the piano in my songwriter office at Rondor Music, for Aretha Franklin, The Four Tops, and Kenny G—my lyric, which all began with this title, is about remembering a bit-tersweet love affair. For my setting, I chose a chance meeting after many years between former lovers. In my first verse, I set up the meeting and the tenderness of seeing each other again. The second verse describes the woman's reaction, how she almost feels faint at this unexpected sight of the one she loved and lost. She describes how they embraced "Just a little bit too long," and felt a resurgence of the old feelings. Verse 3 talks about her familiar perfume, and the memories it brings up for him. It leads her to say that *Love is a mem'ry like a picture, / And it never seems to fade / And I still believe . . . / All the promises we made.*

The chorus recalls that if ever a love there was . . . that was it! The lyric ends ambiguously, with the listener wondering if they might just get back together. Here it is:

IF EVER A LOVE THERE WAS

HE: I saw your face as I hurried past the cafe, and the rain
Fell like long lost tears
As it trickled down the window pane
And in a moment all the years were simply washed away
'Cause when our eyes met,

SHE:	When our eyes met
HE:	There was nothing left to say
SHE:	I caught my breath . . . I fell out of touch with time, 'cause it was you With a part of me I'd forgotten that I ever knew I stood to greet you and you held me Just a little bit too long Oh we've come so far
HE:	We've come so far
SHE:	But the feeling's still so strong
CHORUS: *BOTH:*	**If ever a love there was** **If ever two stars were crossed** **If ever a dream was lost,** **Then it was yours and mine** **If ever a touch was right** **Or a future looked bright** **If ever a love there was . . .**
HE:	That same perfume carries such a lot of memories of a time When we dreamed sweet dreams, Never knowing they'd be left behind
SHE:	Love is a mem'ry like a picture, And it never seems to fade And I still believe
HE: *BOTH:*	And I still believe All the promises we made
CHORUS: *BOTH:*	**If ever a love there was** **If ever two stars were crossed** **If ever a dream was lost,** **Then it was yours and mine** **If ever a touch was right** **Or a future looked bright** **If ever a love there was . . .** **That was the time.**

© Lyrics/Pamela Phillips Oland; Music/Todd Cerney

THE ART OF WRITING LOVE SONGS

The Power of Words to Express Emotions

The ancients used pictographs—literally, pictorial representations of words and ideas—as their only written language. Every pictograph was a graphic rendering of what the writer had in mind. Mostly, they drew these on the rock walls of caves. When pictographic symbols became standardized within a culture, they began to be narrowed down to represent a particular word or a sound instead of just an image or concept. The phonographic alphabet was born, wherein a character or symbol was used to represent a sound. Today, a word stands for an image in a similar way, though a more intricate one. Colors, for instance, are fairly standardized representations: royal blue, jet black, snow white, sunshine yellow, all mean the same thing to whoever is trying to conjure them up.

Feelings, however, have different shades of meaning according to the speaker or the listener. "I love you," for instance, can be interpreted a thousand different ways. Though you can't predict how a listener will interpret your words, always keep in mind that your words are creating mental pictures for them, and amazingly, each of them will see those mental pictures differently!

Use colorful and interesting words to describe and express anger, frustration, sorrow, humiliation, regret, astonishment, worry, admiration, worship, wanting, loss, and revenge. Incorporate "singing pictographs." For instance, is the anger a "temper tantrum" or "fury?" Is the sorrow "devastation" or "bittersweet"? Is the loss a "letting go" or a "tugging pain"? Words indicate shades of meaning in ways that the ancients' pictographs never could. Be sure to use your thesaurus to help you decide on the shade of meaning you wish to convey, so that you can get it exactly right.

Songs of Advice

Very few people appreciate unsolicited advice—have you ever noticed that? Nobody wants to be told what to think or what to do. It's just a plain fact of life that human beings are, by and large, extremely stubborn. Just ask door-to-door religious proselytizers what a hard sell it is to try to preach their good advice.

Given that fact, I have a piece of advice for you: *Don't preach!* If nobody likes to be given unsolicited advice, why are you writing that song to tell perfect strangers how to live their lives? The only song I can think of which was truly successful in that vein was The Youngbloods' "Get Together," by Chet

Powers. It was an anthem in the 1960s, during the "hippie" years—a song telling everyone to love each other "right now."

Other than that song, the only sort of advice songs that have hit their mark and become successful are songs from the 1940s, such as the two Harold Arlen songs "Accentuate the Positive" and "Get Happy!" and Dorothy Fields' "Sunny Side of the Street."

There is the odd exception, such as a song like Graham Nash's "Teach Your Children," which is so pleasing in every way that nobody pays attention to the fact that it is preaching an idea. Also, please note that Burt Bacharach and Hal David's song "What the World Needs Now Is Love" is not preaching, it is simply artfully stating its message as a fact. There is a real difference between the two approaches.

The point I'm trying to make here is, find another way to say it if you want to preach. If you want to talk about everybody needing to express love by stopping world hunger, or you want to say that everybody should go out and make a difference in the world by being loving, then by all means write it. Just consider that rather than putting it in the context of "you should," you might make it a personal statement about how "I" (the singer) am attempting to do this thing myself. On this point, there is no better example than Seidah Garrett and Glen Ballard's song about starting to make a difference with the "Man in the Mirror," which they wrote for Michael Jackson. That song perfectly illustrates how it's more effective to keep large preachy ideas personal and express how they feel to the singer as the "doer," rather than trying to tell others what they need to do.

Moving Forward as a Songwriter

All I have to do is dream.
—EVERLY BROTHERS
(Boudleaux Bryant)

I've provided a myriad of tips and tools to smooth your path of self-expression as you go forth as a songwriter. You will also want to know about some of the technical aspects of getting into the songwriting business. Here are just a few issues I'm sure you'll need to deal with.

FINDING A COLLABORATOR

Whether you are looking for a composer or a co-writer of words and music for your love songs, you want to be on the lookout for dedicated songwriting collaborators who have a natural gift. They may be as close as your dentist's son, or your friend's brother, or you might meet them standing in line at Wal-Mart.

Collaborator-locator Web sites, such as my own "Collab-Central" at *www.pamoland.com/collabors.htm* (where I've provided a central place to post your name, e-mail address, and what sort of songwriting collaboration you are seeking), are all over the Internet with great new ways to connect. These Internet sites make it possible—using e-mail attachments of lyrics and MP3s to upload and send music—to have long-distance collaborations that were never before so feasible.

Songwriter support and creative groups abound around the country and may just be in your town or the next town over. Check with your local music stores and coffee house cabarets. Or start a local Songwriter Association yourself and advertise it by word of mouth or by posting signs, or get the editor of your local community newspaper to print an article for you. When it comes to seeking out co-writers, where there's a will, there's a way.

Songwriting conferences such as those sponsored by the Northern California Songwriters Association (NCSA) and the Nashville Songwriters Association International (NSAI) are excellent ways to spend a few days hanging out with other songwriters and exchanging ideas and, hopefully, contact information. Also, if you're looking for feedback, these groups also invite the cream of writers, producers, music publishers, and a myriad of other music industry professionals, to teach, critique, and participate in informative panel discussions.

How Collaborations Work

There are thousands of composers of music in this world. Some are professionals and earn their living by writing music for songs, movies, TV, commercial advertising, theater, and other uses, such as Internet Web sites.

I imagine that more than 90 percent of them have thoughts of writing hit radio songs, and so exercise their "songwriting chops" as often as is feasible.

Since aptitude with music is no assurance of coincident abilities involving clever use of language, I would further imagine that most of them need help with their lyrics.

Lyricists can work with composers in three different ways:

1. **Writing to Music.** Some composers like to write music first and want every note to remain the way they hear it, without the alteration of so much as a half note being turned into two quarter notes. This means that the lyricist must be strictly disciplined in approaching the music, making it come to life while retaining the integrity of the melody. Other composers are wide open to changes.

2. **Writing Music to Lyrics.** Some composers like to write to lyrics, and you as the lyricist get to dictate the shape of the song before music is ever written. Unfortunately, a composer writing to lyrics will frequently write music that alters the way the words fall, and you'll have to rewrite to fit the melody that was supposedly written to your lyrics!

3. **Writing Music and Lyrics Together.** Some composers, particularly country songwriters, prefer to sit together in a room with a lyricist and write the song, playing words and music off each other's ideas. The lyricist ends up contributing some melody, and the composer will add some lyrics.

All of these writing styles are learned disciplines. They take a little time to perfect, but once you get the hang of them, you will achieve your own comfort level.

Your results in collaboration will vary from co-writer to co-writer. Some people, let's face it, are easier to work with than others. If you have a negative experience in collaborating, don't try to "flog a dead horse," just move on, chalk it up to experience, don't take it personally, and don't let it interfere with your enjoyment of future collaborations.

COPYRIGHT

You can't copyright a title or an idea, and that's the absolute lowdown on the truth. So have at it, and write anything you want to.

Lots of people use the same titles every day. All you have to do is go to the ASCAP Ace on the Web Database *http://ascap.com/ace/ace.html* and type in a title you're contemplating to see what I mean. I just typed in "I Love You" and turned up 378 results of recorded songs with "I Love You" in the titles. Remember, it is not what you *call* a song, but how well you use the *title* that counts!

The only warning I give you is, make sure you don't actually copy someone else's song, because written work is protected under the copyright laws of the United States, and so are musical compositions of a varying number of bars, depending on how obvious the copy is.

I should also caution you: Use common sense and don't copy established names like "Bad Bad Leroy Brown," a title Jim Croce wrote. Such well-known titles might have some commercial value beyond being a song title, and you might be infringing on the owner's rights.

The Copyright Law (U.S. Code, Title 17) is available for you to study online at *www.copyright.gov.* Copyrighting a song requires a Form PA from the Copyright Office, and blank Form PAs can be printed easily right from the Web site. Click on the words "Form PA," and when it comes up, click "print" on your computer. Simply fill it out, enclose a check, and send it in. It will take several months to receive the confirmation back, but it will be dated as of the date of receipt, which the Copyright Office stamps on it as soon as it arrives.

Copyright Registration for Musical Compositions is covered in depth at the following Web site: *www.loc.gov/copyright/circs/circ50.html.* If you already have or wish to download the free Acrobat Reader program the Web site provides, you will find that the version of the copyright laws in this format is extremely accessible and easy to follow.

Paying Attention to Critiques

I wish I had a dollar for each time I have critiqued a love song lyric, pointing out a glaring problem, and the writer has stubbornly dug in his or her heels and insisted, "I don't agree." Nobody has all the answers; certainly I don't claim to. But you've heard the saying, "where there's smoke, there's fire." If somebody is critiquing what you've written, there may be something to be concerned about, don't you think? Shouldn't a critique raise even the tiniest red flag for you? At least take a second look and try to be objective about your work.

A comment from an A&R person or publisher can be helpful in setting you on the path to rewriting to make your love song more commercially viable.

A comment from your mother, as annoying as it may be to have her in any way suggest that your work isn't perfect, might be a clue to a flaw in your song that you'd missed or were unable to see. In Psalm 8.2 of the Old Testament, there is a phrase that begins, "Out of the mouths of babes and sucklings . . . " To paraphrase: Pay attention to what you hear from all sources; even those you do not expect to have insightful knowledge might proffer great wisdom.

In my first book, *The Art of Writing Great Lyrics,* I went into extensive detail about using good judgment as to what comments and critiques you give credence to, but don't be a "know-it-all," either. Don't close your ears too quickly to input you don't like hearing. I recently received a note in a fortune cookie that reminded me, "Wise men can learn more from fools than fools can ever learn from wise men."

Making a Demo of Your Finished Songs

Many small demo-recording studios are in people's homes or garages, and their prices are reasonable. If you do not know where to look, you might find small studios advertising in *Music Connection Magazine, Recording Magazine,* or other music industry publications.

You could also go online to a good Internet search engine, particularly *www.google.com,* which seems to have an edge on music industry Web sites, and type in "song demo producer." You will come up with many names, complete with samples of their work, and their credits. You will be able to sing a rough demo for them into a cassette, and send it along with your lyrics. For a reasonable fee, they will send you back a professional-sounding demo of your song that you can play for your own pleasure—and, perhaps, try pitching to recording artists and record companies.

Be sure to clearly tell the producer of your demo what genre you are working in, the exact tempo you wish, and the type of singer you need. Be specific as to a male or female singer, and the age range of singer you want. Ask to hear CD or MP3 samples of the suggested vocalists beforehand. Discuss the instrumentation that will be used, and whether the track will be entirely synthesized or there will be "live" musicians on the recording session. Discuss the song style you have in mind. And if you have a particular song you'd like to emulate, give the producer a copy to listen to, so he or she will have something to go on. Or if your voice is professional quality and is appropriate for the genre, by all means, sing it yourself. Whoever is singing, make sure their pitch is perfected on your demo's mix. This can frequently be done electronically.

Find out all costs up front, and don't give away any part of your writer or publisher shares of songs to the demo producers just for producing the demos. Furthermore, never pay to have your song published—a publisher should pay *you!* If a music publisher is arranging to have a demo made of your song, sign your single-song publishing agreement in advance of the demo session. Make sure you understand what rights you are signing away. BMG has a useful Q&A Web site at *www.bmgmusicsearch.com/us/qanda/qanda.asp* for songwriters to learn some basics about music publishing. There are also several books on the "business" end of the music business, including the excellent tutorial, *The Craft and Business of Songwriting,* written by my knowledgeable friend John Braheny.

The Thrill of Hearing the Results
Hearing your love song sung on a demo is one of the great thrills of life. It all started with the germ of an idea, perhaps based on a personal experience. And then you honed the idea, found a great title for it, tapped into a remarkable well of inspiration within yourself, and worked hard to write a wonderful and inspired song. You then either wrote your own melody to it, or went to great effort to find the right collaborator. And now . . . now, the crowning glory: you actually hear your love song recorded, and you sigh with delight.

CHAPTER 19

Developing Your Art

I'll have to say I love you in a song.
—JIM CROCE
(Jim Croce)

My writer-director colleague Devorah Cutler-Rubenstein says, "Art is to describe beauty, to create and elicit emotions so that we can celebrate life's possibilities." May I say, I hope you never miss a celebration.

If, in order to fulfill your artistic vision, you wish to break a rule of song-writing, by all means do so. But always know what the rule is you're breaking, and do it artistically, with full intent and purpose.

Now that you've been enlightened about understanding love in order to write songs about it, you can move forward and develop your artistry, really finding your own unique voice in the world of songwriting.

KUDOS TO SOME GREAT LOVE SONGS

You know great romantic love songs when you hear them. Why? Because they haunt your senses and make you want to hear them again and again and again! When I began writing songs, it was every songwriter's dream and aspiration to write "standards" of the highest caliber, such as these wonderful songs recorded by the following artists: Dinah Washington's "What a Difference a Day Makes," Sarah Vaughn's "Broken-Hearted Melody," Johnny Mathis's "Chances Are," Peggy Lee's "I Got It Bad and That Ain't Good," Dick Haymes's "You'll Never Know," Barbra Streisand's "The Way We Were," Julie London's "Cry Me a River," Brenda Lee's "Break It to Me Gently," Sammy Davis, Jr.'s "Love Me or Leave Me," any of the 550 artists who recorded Hoagie Carmichael and Mitchell Parrish's "Stardust," Jacques Brel's "Ne Me Quitte Pas," Barry Manilow's "Weekend in New England," Carole King's "So Far Away," The Flamingos' "I Only Have Eyes for You," Elton John's "Your Song," Roy Orbison's "Crying," Patsy Cline's "Crazy," The Beatles'

"Yesterday," Edith Piaf's "La Vie en Rose," The Skyliners' "Since I Don't Have You," Nat "King" Cole's "When I Fall in Love," The Righteous Brothers' "You've Lost That Loving Feeling," The Platters' "Smoke Gets in Your Eyes," Buddy Holly and The Crickets' "True Love Ways," The Carpenters' "Close to You," Frank Sinatra's "The Tender Trap," Judy Garland's "The Man That Got Away," and Lenny Welch's "Since I Fell for You."

I wish there were room here to list a hundred more such songs deserving of the highest praise and emulation by all of us who aspire to follow in the footsteps of the great songwriters who gave the world all of these magical songs as the soundtrack of our lives.

Great love songs come in all genres, and if the next generation of vocal stars brings us song stylists who walk in the artistic footprints of some of those greats I've just mentioned, I for one won't complain!

FAMOUS SONGS AS REFERENCE POINTS

You can be extremely original and still have famous songs to refer back to in your head. No songwriter uses the language in the identical way that someone else does, so be comfortable in the knowledge that you will not, short of outright thievery of lines, really be copying anything.

Sometimes one song will inspire another. You might listen, for instance, to the classic "It Had to Be You," which is a song about finding the perfect love and knowing nobody else will do. Your mind might take that concept and turn it around on its ear into a song called "Why Can't It Be Me?" Be inventive!

Always be aware of other love songs that have been written by great songwriters over the decades. Never feel superior to other songwriters, for if you do, your work will most likely prove you wrong. You can learn by studying the talented output of the best songwriters in the world. Let the great songwriters of the past make you a better songwriter for the future. Avail yourself of the incredible overview of music that comes to you free over the airwaves on every radio. Since a lot of music has never been reissued on CD, enjoy it on records. For mere pennies, buy the great oldies on vinyl at the local used record store, thrift shop, or online auction, such as on *www.ebay.com*.

> Let the great songwriters of the past make you a better songwriter for the future.

Used record players are available frequently at garage sales, thrift shops, or in local free-advertising papers; and new ones can be inexpensively purchased online at Restoration Hardware, or at such online sites as *www.dealtime.com*, where at this writing, I saw forty-two different models advertised!

Your growth as a writer of love songs will happen faster if you are willing to learn from the trials, and subsequent accomplishments, of others who have been there before you. Remember, in art school, some of the best painters in the world learn to become "originals" by painstakingly learning to copy the old masters first. It is only after they have mastered established techniques that they truly can become great innovators.

Writers Write—Others Just *Talk* about Writing

I encourage any and all of you to simply *Write! Write! Write!*

Write anytime and anyplace.

Write a few words or fill a page. And whatever you're writing—be it lyrics, poetry, greeting cards, books, novels, or ditties for the company newsletter—just write as often as you can, as it is an extraordinary form of self-expression.

And here's an unexpected bonus: No matter what you write, the act itself of writing regularly will allow you to become a far more powerful and compelling thinker, speaker, and, oh yes, songwriter. And that's something to sing about!

WRITING OTHER KINDS OF LOVE SONGS

Since most popular songs are about romantic couple-love, I've devoted this book to studying that genre. Should you wish to write a love song to a parent, a friend, or a child, however, the rules still apply.

- ♥ Understand the nature of the relationship between the person singing the song and the one being sung to or about.

- Have a reason for writing this song—a specific concept for an aspect of this love relationship that is worthy of singing a song about.
- Dig deep for original thoughts and visuals.
- Let the ideas be universal enough for others listening to relate to.
- Use the verses to set up your storyline, and your choruses to pay off the concept and hook idea.
- Make your language interesting, concise, and thoughtful, and use evocative images.
- Make sure your listeners can figure out who this is being sung to, what it's all about, and why this song begs to be written.

When possible, let the song's message work on two different levels.[1]

Generally speaking, these songs are very personal and rarely get recorded by anybody but the artist who has written them. As a rule, hit records are usually love songs about romantic love. Such songs as the charming "Butterfly Kisses" sung about a father's love for a young daughter, and the wonderful "For Once in My Life," the Stevie Wonder standard that Ron Miller wrote the morning his newborn baby came into the world, are notable exceptions.

Love Songs to God
Gospel songs are actually love songs written to God, and they follow the same rules as other love songs:

- They are sung in the first person—"from me to You"—or in the third person—"He."
- They express a personal relationship, a connection with the Deity.
- They tell what the singer is willing to invest to get closer to and know God better.
- They talk about what the singer needs from God.
- They discuss the problems the singer has with believing in the relationship.
- They ask for answers as to what to do to keep the relationship strong.

---

[1] An excellent example of a song on two levels is "I Don't Know How to Love Him" from the musical *Jesus Christ Superstar*, which had a hit pop recording by Helen Reddy. The lyric by Tim Rice was so artfully written that those who didn't know it was a song about love of God thought it was a romantic love song.

- ♥ They offer praise as to what is great about God.
- ♥ They speak of the singer and God as a team—for instance, "I'm stronger now I've got You," or "I can make it because I know You're there for me."

If you are writing a religious love song, make sure you have a particular point you want to make, and develop it fully. A laundry list of exaltations is not as strong as an original idea with substance, leading into a "hooky" title.

THE JOYS OF KARAOKE TRACKS

Frequently, you will have a lyric idea and no immediate melody ideas to accompany it. If you are solely a lyricist, you may have no musical collaborator in sight at the moment. What should you do? In order for all the verses to scan the same as each other, and in order to give form and structure to your song, you make up a "dummy" melody in your head, a temporary melody that can be discarded when you find your composer. The point is, you don't have to start with a co-writer composer in order to write a great love lyric. You simply have to have a melody on which to base it. And that's where karaoke tracks come in. You can buy most of your favorite songs, and many lesser-known ones, at the karaoke store. Or there are tons of karaoke tracks you can download online.

What is a karaoke track? It is the bed, the underlying music track that accompanies a hit song. The thing is, it doesn't have the vocal on it, just the accompaniment. Therefore, you can use it as a basis for a new love song, and nobody will ever know what melody you wrote your lyric to unless you tell them.

When you later hand your lyrics to a composer, the composer will be able to find a workable shape underlying your lyric. That will make it easy to write music to. Not knowing which melody you used as a template for your words, the composer will be free to be inventive.

EXERCISE 11

An A-to-Z Checklist for Love Songs

Each time you complete a song, take a moment and review it against this helpful checklist:

A. Is there a compelling reason for this song to be sung?   ❏

B. Is the gist of the love story being told here clearly
    understandable?   ❏

C. Is the singer's point of view well-defined? ❑

D. Can the listener connect to the point of view of the person being sung to or about? ❑

E. Is the lyric age appropriate for the target audience? ❑

F. Is the lyric written in the language of the target audience? ❑

G. Are the plot points of this scenario (past, present, and future) clear? ❑

H. Is the lyric telling one single aspect of the love story or trying to tell several substories? ❑

I. Is the emotion you wanted to write about clearly expressed? ❑

J. Are the characters well thought out and defined? ❑

K. Is this the best angle you could find on this title? ❑

L. Does the concept inherent in the title "pay off" in your lyrics so that it drives home your point in a compelling way? ❑

M. If this is a personal love story, does it have a universal appeal? ❑

N. Does the story grow, or is the same idea simply paraphrased in subsequent verses? ❑

O. Is the singer's character someone the listener will root for? ❑

P. Have you stayed away from archaic words and phrases? ❑

Q. Do all your lines use words in the natural order of speech? ❑

R. Does the first line make the listener want to hear more? ❑

S. Have you made the best use of language you possibly can? ❑

T. Is your love story believable and real? ❑

U. If you intended the characters to end up together or apart, did they? ❑

V. Is this song clearly about love for the short term? Or a forever love? ❑

W. Have you fallen into trite or overused phrases or expressions? ❑

X. Can a listener tell who will bend to make the relationship work, and how? ❑

Y. Did you accidentally use key chorus words in the verses? ❑

Z. Is your story resolved—neatly tied up at the end? ❑

THE ART OF WRITING LOVE SONGS

Epilogue

Every new art and skill that you learn as you sail the rivers of life adds a new dimension to you as a human being. Like an ancient tree that is measured by its multiple layers that wrap around its core, you are measured by the way your degree of knowledge and understanding grows with every passing year. The more you know, the more you are.

Since there is nothing more profoundly rewarding in most of our lives than having and sharing a successful love relationship, it is worth a king's ransom to learn what love is all about, and, by learning, to be able to put this knowledge to practical use.

I would like to think that you have, through this study of writing love songs, acquired a new clarity and awareness of love. If you have, it will pervade every aspect of your life, including your relationship with your present or future significant other. The more songs you write about love, the more illuminated you will become on the subject. Love is something you've always known about, after all. You've felt it, thought about it, fantasized about it, discussed it, read about it in books, lived it, and seen it portrayed in movies and television. Now that you have recognized within yourself the desire to express your own experiences of and observations about love, on paper, you need never be one of those repressed individuals who bottles up feelings and never utilizes them productively.

My life's motto is this: If not now, then when? Allow yourself the right to write an entirely self-pleasuring idea on paper every single day. That means don't forget to savor *this* moment because you're too caught up planning *future* moments! Remember, once this moment is gone, neither gold nor silver, hopes nor prayers, can ever bring it back to live over again.

Thank you for allowing me to open these doors in your creative mind, heart, and soul. Writing love songs is for me an amazing road to happiness and personal fulfillment. May it be the same for you.

Many lyrics in this volume were printed with permission from the following sources:

"Before I Stop Loving You," Music/Jeremy Lubbock, Lyrics/Pamela Phillips Oland, © Plaything Music obo Rosongs (BMI); Pam-O-Land Music (ASCAP). All rights reserved. Used by permission.

"How Do We Say Goodbye," from the motion picture *Love Can Be Murder*, Words by Pamela Phillips Oland, Music by Steven Bramson. © 1992 Movida Music (ASCAP), Worldwide rights for Movida Music administered by Cherry Lane Music Publishing Company, Inc., International Copyright Secured. All Rights Reserved.

"If Ever a Love There Was," Lyrics/Pamela Phillips Oland, Music/Todd Cerney, © 1988 Pamalybo Music/Irving Music, Inc. (BMI); WB Music Corp. (ASCAP). All rights reserved. Used by permission.

"I'm Not Him," Lyrics and Music/Pamela Phillips Oland, Andy Vargas, Shirlee Elliot; © Pam-O-Land Music, Andy Vargas Music (ASCAP). Used By Permission. All rights reserved.

"In The Light," Lyrics/Pamela Phillips Oland, Music/Ben Schultz; © Pam-O-Land Music (ASCAP), I Nose Music (BMI). Used by permission. All rights reserved.

"Monday Morning Quarterback," Lyrics by Pamela Phillips Oland, Music by Pamela Phillips Oland and Don Costa; © Sergeant Music Co. (ASCAP).

All rights reserved. Used by permission. WARNER BROS. PUBLICATIONS U.S. INC., Miami, FL 33014.

"Nothing Feels Like Love," Lyrics/ Pamela Phillips Oland, Music/Larry Prentiss; © Pamalybo Music/Irving Music, Inc. (BMI), Melaimee Music (ASCAP). All rights reserved. Used by permission.

"On the Other Hand," by Don Schlitz and Paul Overstreet, Scarlet Moon Music, Screen Gems/EMI Music (BMI), Universal-MCA Music Publishing, Inc., a Division of Universal Studios, Inc., on behalf of itself and Don Schlitz Music (ASCAP). All rights reserved. International Copyright Secured. Used by permission.

"Thanks for Nothing," Words and Music by Angela Kaset and Pamela Phillips Oland; © Purple Sun Music (SESAC), and Pam-O-Land Music (ASCAP). All rights reserved. Used by permission.

"Signs of Your Leaving," Lyrics/Pamela Phillips Oland, Music/Dana Walden © Pamalybo Music/Irving Music, Skinny Girl Music and Her Little Fat Guy Publishing, Yak Yak Music (BMI). All rights reserved. Used by permission.

"Squeeze Box," Written by Peter Townshend; © Songs of Windswept Pacific (BMI) o/b/o Eel Pie Publishing Ltd. and Towser Tunes, Inc. All Rights administered by Windswept. All Rights Reserved. Used By Permission.

Index

THE ART OF WRITING LOVE SONGS

BOOKS FROM ALLWORTH PRESS

The Art of Writing Great Lyrics by *Pamela Phillips Oland* (paperback 6 × 9, 272 pages, $18.95)

How to Pitch and Promote Your Songs, Third Edition, by *Fred Koller* (paperback, 6 × 9, 208 pages, $19.95)

The Quotable Musician: From Bach to Tupac by *Sheila E. Anderson* (hardcover, 7 1/2 × 7 1/2, 224 pages, $19.95)

Gigging: A Practical Guide for Musicians by *Patricia Shih* (paperback, 6 × 9, 256 pages, $19.95)

The Songwriter's and Musician's Guide to Nashville, Revised Edition by *Sherry Bond* (paperback, 6 × 9, 256 pages, $18.95)

Managing Artists in Pop Music: What Every Artist and Musician Must Know by *Mitch Weiss and Perri Gaffney* (paperback, 6 × 9, 240 pages, $19.95)

Making and Marketing Music: The Musician's Guide to Financing, Distributing, and Promoting Albums by *Jodi Summers* (paperback, 6 × 9, 240 pages, $18.95)

Profiting from Your Music and Sound Project Studio by *Jeffrey P. Fisher* (paperback, 6 × 9, 288 pages, $18.95)

Moving Up in the Music Business by *Jodi Summers* (paperback, 6 × 9, 224 pages, $18.95)

Creative Careers in Music by *Josquin des Pres and Mark Landsman* (paperback, 6 × 9, 224 pages, $18.95)

Making It in the Music Business: The Business and Legal Guide for Songwriters and Performers, Revised Edition *by Lee Wilson* (paperback, 6 × 9, 288 pages, $18.95)

Rock Star 101: A Rock Star's Guide to Survival and Success in the Music Business by *Marc Ferrari* (paperback, 5 1/2 × 8 1/2, 176 pages, 14.95)

Booking and Tour Management for the Performing Arts, Revised Edition *by Rena Shagan* (paperback, 6 × 9, 288 pages, $19.95)

Career Solutions for Creative People by *Dr. Ronda Ormont* (paperback, 320 pages, 6 × 9, $19.95)

Please write to request our free catalog. To order by credit card, call 1-800-491-2808 or send a check or money order to Allworth Press, 10 East 23rd Street, Suite 510, New York, NY 10010. Include $5 0for shipping and handling for the first book ordered and $1 for each additional book. Ten dollars plus $1 for each additional book if ordering from Canada. New York State residents must add sales tax.

To see our complete catalog on the World Wide Web, or to order online, you can find us at *www.allworth.com.*